Corporate Social Responsibility

The Dynamic Organization Series

Digests of contemporary articles
by business experts worldwide
compiled from ABI/INFORM®
the leading business database.

This book is Smyth sewn and printed on acid-free paper to meet library standards.

Cover and book design by Terri Wright

Library of Congress Cataloging in Publication Data

Main entry under title:

Corporate social responsibility.

    (The Dynamic organization series)
    Includes indexes.
    1. Industry—Social aspects.   2. Corporations—
Social aspects.   I. Ontiveros, Suzanne R. II. Series.
HF60.C693   1986   658.4'08   86-3416
ISBN 0-87436-469-8 (alk. paper)

10 9 8 7 6 5 4 3 2 1

ABC-Clio, Inc.
2040 Alameda Padre Serra, Box 4397
Santa Barbara, California 93140-4397

Clio Press Ltd.
55 St. Thomas Street
Oxford OX1, 1JG, England

Manufactured in the United States of America

Corporate Social

Responsibility

Contemporary Viewpoints

Suzanne Robitaille Ontiveros, Editor

Foreword by
JOAN L. BAVARIA
President, Franklin Research and
Development Corporation

ABC-CLIO

Santa Barbara, California
Oxford, England

Contents ━━━━━━━━━━━━━━━━━━━━━━━━━━━━━━━

Foreword

"CORPORATE SOCIAL RESPONSIBILITY" is a term that has emerged over the past two decades to describe a growing interaction between corporations and their "stakeholders." Stakeholders include the shareholder owners, employees, customers or clients, and the community within which the corporation conducts business. The dialogue and negotiations that transpire between the corporation and the stakeholders span a wide variety of issues, but basically the interaction focuses on the role, positive and negative, that business plays in the lives of all of us. The people within corporations are being held accountable for policies that are socially damaging and are being encouraged to develop new ways to accommodate emerging social needs.

The corporation as the first line of defense against lawsuit for the management and/or the shareholders of economic institutions is a relatively new phenomenon. Corporations came about in the late nineteenth century and have been evolving and growing since into multi-billion dollar organizations. Originally, the owners, or shareholders, of corporations were entrepreneurs and managers close to their products, their employees, and their community. Around mid-century in this country corporations became "public," in that pieces, or shares of them, were sold with the idea that these institutions were permanent, and that to own shares was a legitimate investment as distinct from speculation.

Over the past few decades, public and corporate pensions as shareholders have grown in importance. By 1990, these pensions are expected to "own" the majority of American corporations through their common stock. Pensions, and even individuals, as shareholders are usually rather passive "owners." They are certainly not involved in the day-to-day management of their companies. Sometimes, as their professional money managers strive toward higher financial returns in a competitive world, stock of corporations changes hands several times a day. Who happens to "own" these companies at annual meeting time is quite unimportant. Since most shareholders look to their ownership position to give them a certain return on their dollar and not to give them pride of involvement, accomplishment, or achievement in the community, the issues around the management of these corporations is left to hired hands. Frequently these hired hands are professional managers trained at the major business schools who are unfamiliar with the basic business of the corporation. Their one-dimensional expertise lies in areas such as "return on equity" or acquisition management rather than how to be a better corporate citizen.

So at the same time that corporations have evolved as infinitely powerful multi-national entities, those at the helm of these economic vessels are more and more often professional managers educated for economic, not social results. Yet few can dispute the impact that corporations have on society. They are often the single employer in a town or county. As economic forces, they can make or break whole regions as they employ or lay off. They provide the environment in which their workers live most of their waking hours. Corporations have emerged as a political influence with large political campaign contributions. As cash-rich organizations in the eighties, their support of the American educational system, and occasional manipulation of it, is becoming the largest single source of income to universities. As corporations grow, they often possess the resources to bully smaller or start-up companies in their industry into bankruptcy or acquisition. As the world shrinks, the power of their dollars to purchase mind-bending media time increases. Their decisions with regard to safety affect lives...especially as man develops more and more ways to affect his environment dramatically, and in very large scale. Modern man doesn't fully understand the power of much that he has created. The corporation is one of the least understood of our inventions.

A partial solution to the conflicts between corporations and stakeholders seems to be evolving spontaneously on a grass roots level. The shareholders of the corporations—the churches, public unions, individuals, and to a lesser extent independent foundations—have begun to use their power to negotiate solutions to human and social problems. The problems these shareholders address range from issues such as fair labor policies, product choices and manufacturing policies, citizenship issues, gifting policies, and many others. Shareholders collectively introduce proxy motions to influence corporate management in their social policies, and many of these proxy motions are negotiated to everyone's satisfaction before actual entry on the ballot. Groups of shareholders "divest" or sell the securities of corporations whose policies or products seem to permanently diverge from their own beliefs or goals. Other shareholder tactics include active communication with corporate managements, occasional demonstrations as protest, and media work to bring issues into the public forum. Thus a voluntary, grass roots public movement has grown to begin to balance the power of corporate America and to insure that corporate policies, as they impact human destinies, will be debated by those who feel that impact. That public effort has become known as Socially Responsible Investing. The cooperative reaction of more responsible corporations thus is called "corporate social responsibility."

The vast majority of corporations remain stuck in yesterday's ways, with their primary goal being their own economic dominance or survival and growth. In this competitive system, survival alone seems difficult enough to achieve for some managers. More enlightened corporate managements, however, now produce "social policy" reports for shareholders to critique. Some of them pride themselves on finding solutions before a problem emerges in the public forum. The social responsibility movement has just begun, and the needs that it addresses are compelling and permanent.

— JOAN L. BAVARIA
President, Franklin Research and
Development Corporation

Introduction _____

IN RESPONSE TO THE DEMAND for a convenient source of current information in the rapidly changing world of business and management practice, ABC-CLIO joined with Data Courier in publishing its Contemporary Viewpoints titles. Designed to provide business persons, students, and scholars with quick access to business thought of the 1980s, the informative summaries of significant articles from a wide range of journals and trade publications enable business persons, students, and scholars to gain a knowledge of topics of current interest. **Corporate Social Responsibility: Contemporary Viewpoints** is the latest title in the Dynamic Organization series.

The source for the titles in the series is the leading business database, Data Courier's ABI/INFORM®. ABI/INFORM was designed for business professionals who need timely information but are unable to scan the hundreds of news magazines, journals, and trade publications that are important to them. To build this database, abstractors, who are experts in law, employee benefits, business-government relations, data processing, finance, and other business fields, condense the international business literature into 200-word article summaries.

For this book, the more than 300,000 records in the database were searched for appropriate articles. From the resulting list the editors selected over 500 articles, published from 1980 to the present, especially relevant to the topic of Corporate Social Responsibility and arranged them in chapters for easy browsing. A detailed subject index gives quick access to specific concepts, and an author index leads the reader to the variety of writers represented.

At the request of librarians and other information professionals, the editors have included a list of the database index terms (descriptors) following each article summary. These terms may be used as a guide for online searches for related articles or those appearing after the publication of this book.

How to Order Articles

The full text of most articles cited here (all articles identified as "Avail ABI") is available through Data Courier's fast, convenient photocopy service. Call their Article Delivery Service Department toll-free at 800/626-0307 (Canada), Monday through Friday from 9 a.m. to 5 p.m. or write to: Article Delivery Service, Data Courier Inc, 620 S. Fifth Street, Louisville, KY 40202. Enclose a photocopy of the citation from this book or full order information including accession number, title, author, and journal title, date, and page numbers.

Full-text articles are available from Data Courier at the following rates (subject to change) and can be charged to American Express, MasterCard, or VISA:

Deposit account customers — $6.75
All other customers — $8.25
Add $2.00 per article for shipment outside the United States and Canada.

A few of the articles (identified by the abbreviations following the word Avail) must be ordered direct from the publisher. A key to the abbreviations and publisher addresses are listed below. Prices vary with publisher.

AEE	Association for Evolutionary Economics University of Nebraska, College of Business Administration Department of Economics Lincoln, NE 68588
Asia	Asia Research Pte. Ltd. P.O. Box 91 Alexandra Post Office Singapore 9115 Singapore
Business	Business Lawyer American Bar Association 1155 E. 60th Street Chicago, IL 60637
Chief	Chief Executive Magazine, Inc. 645 Fifth Avenue New York, NY 10022
Harvard	Harvard Law Review Association Gannett House Cambridge, MA 02138
Haworth	Haworth Press 28 E. 22 Street New York, NY 10010
Institutional	Institutional Invester 488 Madison Avenue New York, NY 10022
MC	Marketing Communications 475 Park Avenue South New York, NY 10016
MCB	MCB Publications, Ltd. 200 Keighley Road Bradford, W. Yorkshire BD9 4JG England

Michigan	Michigan Law Review Hutchins Hall Ann Arbor, MI 48109
NAP	North American Publishing 401 N. Broad St. Philadelphia, PA 19108
Panel	Panel Publishers 14 Plaza Rd. Greenvale, NY 11548
Pensions	Pensions & Investment Age 740 Rush St. Chicago, IL 60611
Public	Public Utilities Reports, Inc. 1828 L Street, N.W., Suite 500 Washington, DC 20036
UCLA	UCLA Law Review University of California School of Law Los Angeles, CA 90024

ABI/INFORM, the Business Database

Data Courier Inc., a Courier-Journal and Louisville Times Co. subsidiary, is the leader in providing online business information worldwide. To produce the ABI/INFORM database, their editors index business articles appearing in more than 700 magazines and journals, and professionals in a number of business fields summarize the articles. For any topic of interest in the field virtually every significant periodical article is included in the database.

ABI/INFORM is available online through the following timesharing systems:

Bibliographic Retrieval Services (BRS)
BRS After Dark
Data-Star
ITT Dialcom, Inc.
DIALOG Information Services, Inc.
DIALOG's Knowledge Index
European Space Agency Information Retrieval Service (ESA-QUEST)
Innerline
Systems Development Corporation Search Service (ORBIT)
VU/TEXT
Human Resource Information Network (HRIN)

Data Courier provides a wide range of customer support services. Information specialists trained in online searching are available each working day toll-free at 800/626-2823 from 9 a.m. to 5 p.m. (Eastern time) to answer

questions about ABI/INFORM and the firm's other products. Training specialists travel worldwide to teach groups of new and experienced searchers time-
efficient and cost-saving search techniques. For more information contact:

DATA COURIER INC
620 South Fifth Street
Louisville, KY 40202-2297

Sample Entry

Title

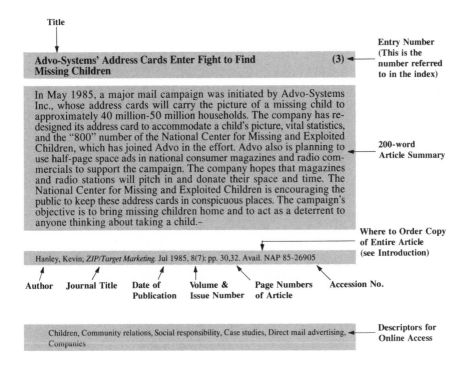

Entry Number
(This is the
number referred
to in the index)

Advo-Systems' Address Cards Enter Fight to Find Missing Children (3)

In May 1985, a major mail campaign was initiated by Advo-Systems Inc., whose address cards will carry the picture of a missing child to approximately 40 million-50 million households. The company has re-designed its address card to accommodate a child's picture, vital statistics, and the "800" number of the National Center for Missing and Exploited Children, which has joined Advo in the effort. Advo also is planning to use half-page space ads in national consumer magazines and radio com-mercials to support the campaign. The company hopes that magazines and radio stations will pitch in and donate their space and time. The National Center for Missing and Exploited Children is encouraging the public to keep these address cards in conspicuous places. The campaign's objective is to bring missing children home and to act as a deterrent to anyone thinking about taking a child.–

200-word
Article Summary

Where to Order Copy
of Entire Article
(see Introduction)

Hanley, Kevin; *ZIP/Target Marketing.* Jul 1985, 8(7): pp. 30,32. Avail. NAP 85-26905

Author   Journal Title   Date of Publication   Volume & Issue Number   Page Numbers of Article   Accession No.

Children, Community relations, Social responsibility, Case studies, Direct mail advertising, Companies

Descriptors for
Online Access

1

General

Accountable for What? Executives Push Changes in   **(1)**
Foreign Corrupt Practices Act
At a recent conference in Boca Raton, Fla. of the Institute of Internal Auditors and the National Association of Corporate Directors, C. Barry Schaefer brought up the touchy issue of the lawyer-client relationship with management. There were a variety of opinions on whether in-house legal counsel should report possible fraud or other wrongdoing involving management to the audit committee of the board of directors. Schaefer suggested that the audit committee and management might want to obtain independent counsel. There was agreement that the Foreign Corrupt Practices Act is complicating matters for audit committees, other corporate directors, internal and independent auditors, and management. One speaker suggested that the move toward greater corporate accountability could compel the Federal government to reform its own administration. Francine Neff, former US treasurer, believes that the public sector should be no less accountable than the private sector. Neff implied that government books were not very well kept and would be difficult to audit. –Scheibla, Shirley Hobbs; *Barron's,* Dec 29, 1980, 60(52): pp. 9-10,14. Avail. ABI 81-02009

     Foreign Corrupt Practices Act 1977-US, Corporate responsibility, Corporate, Accountability, Auditing, Audit committees, Private sector, SEC, Regulations

Administrative Law ... Decision Making ... and Second   **(2)**
Opinions
The comment letter process is as much a part of the regulatory process as the agencies themselves. When federal agencies ask for comment letters on proposed rules and regulations, they may be looking for a number of things, ranging from industry expertise on a particular subject to requests for better ideas than the agency's staff has yet produced. Writing to regulators is a social responsibility, which helps regulators decide how to set policy. The request for comments will appear in the Federal Register, along with a summary of the rule in question. It is estimated that the number of letters received on a particular issue represent only 4% or 5% of the group affected. Letters usually come from trade associations, individual firms, and large

corporations. Members of Congress may write, as well as private citizens. –
Lakin, R. M.; *Bottomline,* Jun 1984, 1(8): pp. 33-36,48. Avail. ABI 84-20554

  Banking industry, Financial institutions, Proposed, Regulations, Public opinion,
  Correspondence, Government agencies, Regulatory agencies, Administrative Procedure
  Act-US, Federal Register-US, Lobbying

Advo-Systems' Address Cards Enter Fight to Find   (3)
Missing Children

In May 1985, a major mail campaign was initiated by Advo-Systems Inc.,
whose address cards will carry the picture of a missing child to approximately
40 million-50 million households. The company has redesigned its address
card to accommodate a child's picture, vital statistics, and the "800" number
of the National Center for Missing and Exploited Children, which has joined
Advo in the effort. Advo also is planning to use half-page space ads in
national consumer magazines and radio commercials to support the
campaign. The company hopes that magazines and radio stations will pitch
in and donate their space and time. The National Center for Missing and
Exploited Children is encouraging the public to keep these address cards in
conspicuous places. The campaign's objective is to bring missing children
home and to act as a deterrent to anyone thinking about taking a child. –
Hanley, Kevin; *ZIP/Target Marketing,* Jul 1985 8(7): pp. 30,32. Avail. NAP 85-26905

  Children, Community relations, Social responsibility, Case studies, Direct mail advertising,
  Companies

The American Corporate Renaissance   (4)

The success of the US economy rests in giving more people at more levels
entrepreneurial benefits. A former American Express senior executive has
proposed that severance pay for personnel laid off during a recession be
treated as "venture capital" rather than as a payoff to individuals. Other
suggestions to promote corporate entrepreneurship include: 1. tax credits for
the development of training programs or internal educational programs
meeting certain standards, 2. self-conscious corporate examination of
purpose and philosophy, 3. a quest for leaders characterized by long-range,
integrative thinking, 4. withholding a portion of an officer's or director's pay
until 5 years after retirement to encourage more careful succession planning
and long range planning, 5. provision of a greater sense of community and
social responsibility, 6. eliminating assumptions of managerial superiority,
male superiority, and white superiority, and 7. encouraging employees who
could function simultaneously in several organizational modes. The potential
for a corporate renaissance would also be enhanced by public financing of
higher education, particularly in the liberal arts. –Kanter, Rosabeth Moss; *Directors
& Boards,* Winter 1984, 8(2): pp. 38-42. Avail. ABI 84-06799

  Corporate management, Corporate planning, Innovations, Management styles, Leadership

Ancient Marketing Practices: The View from Talmudic   (5)
Times

Marketing has often been considered a relatively young field. However,
principles and practices of marketing can be traced back through history. As
a particular example, the philosophy and guidelines for marketing as written

in the Talmud approximately 1,500 years ago are examined. Because the Jewish religion encompasses a total way of life, the compilation of Jewish oral law in the Talmud established ethical practices for business. While the Talmud promoted a very favorable view of business, its principles of fair competition, honesty in business, product quality, and consumer protection were very strict. It is shown that the ancient Talmudic business laws are, in some cases, more conducive to social responsibility than are current business laws and practices. References. −Friedman, Hershey H.; *Jrnl of Public Policy & Marketing*, 1984, 3): pp. 194-204. Avail. ABI 84-33393

Marketing management, Techniques, History

Assessing the Nestle Boycott: Corporate Accountability (6) and Human Rights

In October 1984, the International Nestle Boycott Committee announced the end of a 7-year consumer boycott of Nestle. The boycott was organized because of alleged marketing abuses in the promotion and sale of infant formula products in less developed countries (LDC). In 1981, the World Health Organization (WHO) adopted a code of marketing for infant formula products. Since the adoption of the WHO code, there have been trends in LDCs toward: 1. more price competition, 2. promotion of formula products through the health care system, and 3. a flooding of the market by formula companies. The boycott and the surrounding controversy have had several results: 1. Precedents have been set in the area of corporate accountability. 2. New ground has been opened up in the discussion of human rights and commercial interests. 3. Nestle has created a commission to review allegations of violation of company and WHO code policy. 4. The WHO code provides a way to define and evaluate corporate responsibility in infant formula marketing. Table. References. −Post, James E.; *California Mgmt Review*, Winter 1985, 27(2): pp. 113-131. Avail. ABI 85-11300

Nestle-Switzerland, Boycotts, Corporate responsibility, Human rights, Case studies, WHO, Market strategy, Accountability

Assessment of Attitudes Toward Corporate Social (7) Accountability in Britain

Relatively little rigorous behavioral research has been conducted on managerial attitudes toward corporate social accountability. An empirical study is presented on the attitudes of management in the UK toward corporate social accountability. Corporate concern for social responsibility is assessed for the peak period of such concern - 1974-1979 - by all interested parties. Respondents were 112 high-level managers at some of the largest companies in the UK. Most respondents did not seem to consider the systematic recording and reporting of corporate social responsibility to be an urgent need, nor are they very concerned about the possibility of having to produce or use such information. This explains why companies have not yet developed social accounting systems adequate for the needs of either management or external users. The respondents agreed that firms should include information regarding corporate social performance in their published annual reports, but most felt that this disclosure should not be required. References. —Filios, Vassilios P.; *Jrnl of Business Ethics (Netherlands),* Jun 1985, 4(3): pp. 155-173. Avail. ABI 85-21875

> Social responsibility, UK, Managers, Employee attitude (PER), Accountability, Interest groups

Associations Ask Themselves: Who Are We? Why Do   (8) We Exist?

Because of dramatic changes in the nature of the savings and loan business, a few associations are developing new basic philosophies and review committees to ensure that the philosophies remain living, workable documents. Common areas addressed in association philosophies are: 1. social responsibility, 2. the role of profit, 3. responsibility to employees, 4. the place of new products, 5. the role of government in the savings and loan business, 6. the role of private initiative, and 7. the quality of customer service. After an association has developed a mission statement, it can then develop corporate goals, long-term objectives, and the strategy to achieve those goals and objectives. Mission statements need to be periodically reviewed and updated to provide guidance and direction for future planning. A main goal of this process is to help establish a sense of purpose in the employees' minds and to give customers and community groups a clear idea of the association's role in the community. Although a business philosophy is an ideal which may not be totally achieved, it is important to have one. —Anonymous; *Savings & Loan News,* Jul 1980, 101(7): pp. 56-59. Avail. ABI 80-14985

> Savings & loan associations, Corporate, Strategy, Corporate planning, Policies, Goals, Manycompanies

Associations Between Social Responsibility Disclosure   (9) and Characteristics of Companies

A trend toward increased disclosure of social responsibility accounting information has developed, according to surveys in a number of countries. The reporting of social responsibility information has become more often incorporated into annual reports. Not all companies disclose social responsibility information; those that do have a variety of methods for providing the information. The concern for corporate social responsibility on the part of a company is perceived to be a sign of good management. Six social responsibility areas were considered relevant: 1. environment, 2. energy, 3. human resources, 4. products, 5. community involvement, and 6. other. It has been demonstrated that companies that provided social responsibility information are normally larger in size, have a higher systematic risk, and place stronger emphasis on the long term than do companies that do not disclose this information. Table. References. —Trotman, Ken T. and Bradley, Graham W.; *Accounting, Organizations & Society (UK),* 1981, 6(4): pp. 355-362. Avail. ABI 82-01472

> Social responsibility, Accounting, Information, Disclosure, Surveys, Financial reporting, Annual reports, Studies, Statistical analysis

Associations in Society: Learning To Be a Better Neighbor (10)

Many institutions, including associations, have lost public credibility. Much of the public believes that social institutions are motivated largely by self-interest and that these institutions act in the public good only if they stand to benefit economically. Associations must concern themselves about all of society, not just about those persons who are association members. They can do this by means of social programs which become a bridge of understanding in the community. Before starting such a social program, the association must: 1. Set up a good information and feedback system. 2. Choose an issue logically connected with the association. 3. Persuade the leading members of the association to support the issue. Money to carry out the program may be obtained through a dues add-on program or through foundation funding, but government funding is not recommended because of the many strings attached. The association may offer the use of resources or personnel instead of money. —Rivchun, Sylvia; *Association Mgmt,* May 1980, 32(5): pp. 40-45. Avail. ABI 80-10218

Associations, Association management, Social responsibility, Disclosure, Communication, Public relations

Auto Insurance - The Shared Market (11)

The shared market is the third largest auto insurer nationally, accounting for about 8% of total commercial and private vehicle insurance written premiums. As a last resort insurer, the shared market's population increases as voluntary insurer activity in the competitive market decreases. Although available in every state, most shared market exposures are concentrated in 10 states. According to one study, the reasons for this concentration are: 1. underpriced rates in the competitive market, 2. compulsory insurance statutes, 3. burdensome regulations, and 4. absence of a nonstandard market. Although availability to any licensed agent may contribute to its volume, specialization in shared market insurance has been found to be an insignificant factor in the concentration. Despite many misconceptions about the shared market, it demonstrates the industry's social responsibility by exceeding legal requirements to provide coverage, while absorbing increasingly substantial losses. The shared market operates in each state through one of 3 types of plans; 1. Automobile Insurance Plan (AIP), 2. Joint Underwriting Association (JUA), 3. Reinsurance Facility, and 4. a state fund (operating only in Maryland). Tables. —Marks, Jim; *Jrnl of Insurance,* Jul/Aug 1982, 43): pp. 34-39. Avail. ABI 82-19353

Automobile insurance, Shared, Markets, Insurance coverage, Losses, Business conditions, Insurance industry

Big Business Day and Federal Corporate Chartering (12)

The goal of Big Business Day (April 17, 1980) was to focus attention on abuses of corporate power by large corporations. The main concern of Big Business Day was the Federal legislation entitled "The Corporate Democracy Act." This Act would require a restructuring of the board of directors. In addition, directors would be prohibited from serving as directors for more than 2 companies at one time. The most radical provision, however, would be that a federal corporate chartering system would replace the present state-granted charters for largest corporations. Even though federal corporate chartering has been proposed in the past, there are several practical problems, such as: 1. federal incorporation versus federal licenses, 2. substantive provision of the law, 3. politicalization of the corporation, and 4. the economic effects. Recommendations for federal corporate chartering include: 1. a thorough analysis of the corporation's commitment to social responsibility by the executive, director, or corporation itself, and 2. an independent study set up by Congress to examine the need for federal chartering. References. –Bona, Thomas M.; *Review of Business,* Fall 1980, pp. 15-17. Avail. ABI 81-01453

Federal, Corporate, Charters, Proposed, Federal legislation, Implications

Big Business vs Big Government - A New Social Contract?   (13)

The US economy is characterized by the conflicting of 2 political philosophies of liberal corporate social responsibility and "big government" regulation versus conservative supply-side policies and a laissez-faire approach to "big business." The conflict between the 2 ideologies of liberalism and conservatism may be resolved to produce an economic system that increases both social welfare and entrepreneurial freedom. Research studies on a "Return on Resources Model" suggest a 3rd perspective, called the "social contract," that reconciles both perspectives to create a more powerful synthesis. The social contract could produce a "decentralization strategy" in which control of the economy would shift from government to a self-regulating, more productive private sector. Speculations on these possibilities and suggestions for fostering this "New Capitalism" are offered. Tables. References. –Halal, William E.; *Long Range Planning (UK),* Aug 1984, 17(4): pp. 30-37. Avail. ABI 84-32913

Corporate responsibility, Social responsibility, Economic policy, Big business, Government, Cooperation, Strategic, Planning

Blacks Hit Racial Roadblocks Climbing Up the Corporate Ladder   (14)

The situation of the black individual in corporate America and society has moved from one of overt exclusion to that of covert subrogation. The greatest problem is that black managers are not even aware of what covert roadblocks exist or of the remedies to pursue. As a race, blacks use their money to purchase high-risk opportunities, such as franchises and start-ups; they fail to enter areas that are really unrestricted territory. This occurs because blacks have been systematically excluded from the information chain. While an investment of $300,000-$500,000 can buy a franchise, that same investment put into proven leveraged financing techniques could acquire a company of $1 million-$3million in sales volume with less risk, a management group in place, and an opportunity to expand on a business segment that is already growing. While many contend that college and university training is the way to expand economic horizons, such areas as paralegal careers and electronics require only 2 years of specialized training but reap high financial rewards. Weak or nonexistent information streams prevent this counseling from reaching young blacks. —Grant, Charles T.; *Business & Society Review,* Winter 1985, (52): pp. 56-59. Avail. ABI 85-12761

Blacks, Racial discrimination, Career advancement, Management development, Barriers, Social responsibility

Blowing the Whistle on Corporate Misconduct   (15)

A small, but growing, number of employees of all corporate levels and persuasions throughout the world are reporting apparent company misconduct. Employee "whistleblowing" costs the firm not only any fines it may incur but also can undo a carefully developed public relations program. The result for the whistleblower is usually adverse including almost certain firing and difficulty in finding new employment. A number of companies learned that the best defense is an in-house mechanism for employees to relieve their concerns. Companies with internal mechanisms for disclosure of misconduct, such as the Singer Company, find that employees use the company mechanism instead of going outside the company to the media or the civil authorities. Usage of the internal mechanism allows the employees to discharge their duties to the company and gives the company a chance to prepare a defense. Cases. —Clutterbuck, David; *International Mgmt (UK),* Jan 1980, 35(1): pp. 14-18. Avail. ABI 80-03838

Social responsibility, Manypeople, Manycompanies, Corporate responsibility, Employee problems, Internal controls

Budgeting Social Responsibility of Affiliates in Latin   (16)
America

Multinational affiliates in developing countries experience problems in dealing with social responsibility. While social problems have been handled in the past in a rather haphazard manner, in more recent years, social responsibility has come to be viewed as an integral and necessary part of business activities, and thus is provided for in the overall corporate financial planning and control process. Before social planning is undertaken, company social objectives must be determined. The overriding long-term objective seems to be to impress the host government. The problem is to determine which regular operations and additional activities will make the best impression. Returns on expenditures involved in these activities must be taken into consideration. After objectives and specific activities are established, plans for operations are factored into the budget. Controls must be exercised over social responsibility activities, and these controls are made possible through evaluation of results. Social activity disclosure to target groups will provide the feedback necessary for adequate control. References. —Whitt, John D.; *Managerial Planning,* May/Jun 1983, 31(6): pp. 32-34. Avail. ABI 83-15557

Multinational corporations, Latin America, Foreign subsidiaries, Social responsibility, Budgeting, Corporate responsibility

Burger Wars   (17)

Although McDonald's, Burger King, and Wendy's spent $457 million on television advertising buys in 1984, public relations is becoming a more important element in the battle for public awareness. Public relations can help the companies distinguish themselves in local, minority, and national markets. McDonald's, with its huge advertising and public relations budget, has more than a dozen public relations programs, including support for the Ronald McDonald Houses for parents of terminally ill children. McDonald's also sponsors several sports and music teams and competitions. Wendy's and Burger King have used public relations to spin off their competitive advertising. Wendy's "Where's the Beef?" campaign was helped by heavy public relations to promote spokesperson Clara Peller on network TV. Burger King created a media tour surrounding its comparative ads and resulting lawsuits filed by McDonald's and Wendy's. On the community level, McDonald's continues its focus on sports and music, Burger King sponsors educational assistance programs, and Wendy's supports the fight against childhood diseases. All three also make a public relations effort to reach minority consumers. –Blake, Rick; *Public Relations Jrnl,* Sep 1985, 41(9): pp. 22-25. Avail. ABI 85-30002

Fast food industry, Market shares, Public relations, Competition, Sponsors, Promotions (ADV), Social responsibility, Publicity

Business and Social Challenge   (18)

The evolving relationship between business and society has gone through turbulent times since 1960. Conflicts arose in the early 60s as various elements of society voiced their grievances. The rebellion was born of desperation. The 70s brought partial resolution of these problems. Resolutions of past inequalities have become institutionalized in solutions that have created new rights and entitlements without imposing reciprocal obligations on the recipients. The tragedy has been the failure of the corporate community and the social activists to work as partners in solving social problems. We have come to realize that big government can be just as insensitive to individual needs as big business sometimes is. There is some questioning of the viability of solutions offered by social activists. The conflict in the 80s is between 2 types of inequity. The corporation must become an active agent for social change. Effective participation demands a coherent political position. Business people cannot participate effectively in the political process until they can present themselves as part of their society, and present the roles their products and services play as part of the culture. –Sethi, S. Prakash; *Public Relations Jrnl,* Sep 1981, 37(9): pp. 30-31,34. Avail. ABI 81-23440

Business, Social policy, Political power, Social responsibility, Social change

Business and the Media/Part 1: An Uneasy Balance   (19)

The relationship between business and the news media was examined during a panel discussion at the recent Financial Executives Institute conference on Current Financial Issues. Paul Kolton, chairman of the Financial Accounting Standards Advisory Council moderated the discussion of panel members Dan Dorfman, Richard F. Janssen, and Robert T. Metz (all business reporters), and John J. Quindlen of Du Pont. Problems discussed centered on freedom of the press versus corporate responsibility. Media and business have many major differences of opinion. Problems seen with the press included inexperienced reporters, tight deadlines, and complicated subjects. Journalists report perceived violations of public trust by companies;

executives feel they know what is best for their companies and should not be criticized by outsiders. There is widespread belief that the press sensationalizes bad news and ignores the good. Some also believe that press reports tend to become self-fulfilling. Members of the press feel companies could improve the situation by being more available and giving more facts. —Anonymous; *FE: The Magazine for Financial Executives,* Apr 1985, 1(4): pp. 20-27. Avail. ABI 85-18935

Trade publications, Business, Media, Relations, Reporters

Business and the Community (20)
Many Canadians do not believe in "good corporate citizenship" - that a business can be good and profitable at the same time. The belief that it is the nature of business to exploit society has been with us for too long and has been supported by widespread ignorance of the role of benefits in the economy and the realities of private enterprise. It is in the public's interests that the community be informed how, when, and by whom it is being well-served. If mutual trust and cooperation are to be built, business and individual businesspeople must contribute to society by doing their jobs responsibly and well. A company that does its job well is fulfilling its first responsibility to society. Business has a basic role as the efficient and effective generator of the jobs, goods, and services that society wants. Social responsibilities are not the main priority of business, and there is some danger in society treating corporations as if they had unlimited resources. – Taylor, Allan R.; *Vital Speeches,* Dec 15, 1984, 51(5): pp. 154-157. Avail. ABI 85-04131

Corporate responsibility, Social responsibility, Accountability, Canada

Business Ethics and Social Responsibility: The (21)
Responses of Present and Future Managers
To determine whether business students differ from executives in their personal business ethics and social responsibility, a questionnaire study was conducted of 113 manufacturing executives and 349 business students at a major state university in Arizona. Survey measures included Clark's Personal Ethics and Social Responsibility Scale, the Crown-Marlowe Social Desirability Scale, and personal data. While executives scored higher on the personal business ethics scale, they scored only slightly higher on the social responsibility scale, suggesting an important difference between the ethical standards of the 2 groups. Students appeared more accepting of actions that are latently unethical in various situations. No support was found for the hypothesis that students would score higher as a result of their exposure to personal business ethics and social responsibility issues in a particular college course. The conclusion drawn is that colleges of business need to teach business ethics. Tables. References. —Stevens, George F.; *Akron Business & Economic Review,* Fall 1984, 15(3): pp. 6-11. Avail. ABI 84-31461

Ethics, Corporate responsibility, Social responsibility, Accountability, Corporate, Managers, Business, Students, Comparative studies, Statistical analysis

Business, Ethics and the Bottom Line (22)
The issue of business ethics is getting more attention today than ever before, and a growing number of companies are developing codes of ethics and

devising ways to live up to them. Increased attention from the media and the public have forced business to pay more attention to its ethical standards. General rules for business ethics are not hard to develop and may include: 1. Avoid harm to others. 2. Respect others' rights. 3. Keep promises. 4. Help those in need. Every employee in a firm knows what that company's attitude toward ethics is, and each corporate level follows the standards set by the one above. The growing use of computers in business has resulted in new ethical considerations, such as the possibility of altering key formulas in a spreadsheet model to produce a different result. The increasing global thrust of US business also complicates the ethics issue, but ethics can still be put to a direct test if individuals ask themselves whether they would want their family or friends to hear about a particular decision and its ramifications. – Wakin, Edward; *Today's Office*, Feb 1985, 19(9): pp. 22-30. Avail. ABI 85-08410

Ethics, Profitability, Employee attitude (PER), Corporate responsibility

Business Ethics: A Trojan Horse?   (23)

Peter F. Drucker, professor emeritus of management at the Graduate Business School of New York University and Clarke Professor of Social Science and Management at Claremont Graduate School, has long been an advocate of a more humane and responsive capitalism. Drucker maintains that the courses offered in business ethics so focus on the social effects of business decisions that they teach the student how to justify nearly any act if it can be demonstrated that the act will benefit a number of people. These courses provide a set of ethics for those in power that is different from the ordinary demands of ethics applying to them as individuals. It is suggested that Drucker's concern is misplaced. Because of the complexities of the business world, many corporations have found it helpful for managers to take courses on business ethics. However, one must be modest about the influence, positive or negative, of an ethics course on a student. Courses in business ethics are essential, but these courses are no substitute for the development of character traits such as loyalty, sensitivity, justice, compassion, and honesty. References. –Williams, Oliver F.; *California Mgmt Review*, Summer 1982, 24(4): pp. 14-24. Avail. ABI 82-28391

Ethics, Cummins Engine-Columbus Ind, Theory, Case studies, Social responsibility

The Business Manager's Dilemma-III. Identifying the   (24)
Social Responsibilities of Business

The problem of identifying the social responsibilities of business is aggravated by: 1. the fact that public expectations of business are constantly changing, and 2. the respective social roles of business and government are becoming less distinct. It is even more difficult to identify the responsibilities of any given firm. Few social and political guidelines for acceptable social action exist. Management can identify the social responsibilities of the firm through the use of: 1. categorization, 2. internal social audits, 3. forecasting, 4. management reeducation programs, 5. joint conferences, and 6. constituent groups represented by public board members. A preliminary critical examination of presently-held values will enhance the process. Any gains from these endeavors must be shared with key personnel at the company's operating levels. It is important that these personnel share top management's social action values or the promise of enlightened corporate social policy will remain unfulfilled. Chart. References. —Strier, Franklin; *Jrnl of Enterprise Mgmt*, 1980, 2(2): pp. 119-126. Avail. ABI 81-00443

Social responsibility, Corporate responsibility, Corporate, Social policy, Identification, Regulatory agencies

Business Meets Its Social Responsibility (25)

The social responsibility of business is still a much debated topic. Social responsibility has been defined by one expert as the incident when a corporation volunteers to expend its resources to do something not required by law and without immediate economic benefits. Some who argue that business should help in reaching society's goals set 2 conditions: The goals should truly be a demand from society at large; how they are accomplished should not be dictated. It is difficult to quantify successes, but some of the more quantifiable successes involve minority hiring and affirmative-action programs. The pressure to measure the social responsibility of corporations still persists, and the American Institute of Certified Public Accountants has published a study that furnishes general information on social-responsibility reporting, as well as guidelines for developing and implementing data. — Moskal, Brian S.; *Industry Week*, Apr 20, 1981, 209(2): pp. 54-59. Avail. ABI 81-11177

Corporate responsibility, Social responsibility, Manycompanies, Manypeople

The Business of Business is People: Free Enterprise (26) Enhances Life, Liberty and the Pursuit of Happiness

The purpose of business is to provide needed and wanted goods and services to people at a profit. Three essential social arrangements constitute a system whereby millions of people voluntarily cooperate and function together: 1. free-pricing mechanism, 2. competition, and 3. private property. In the market economy, economic activity begins with individuals at any level. Within this system, the ferment for change is a spontaneous activity making for progress and growth. Happiness may be elusive and indefinite, but people in the US have the right, within limits, to define happiness in their own way and set out to pursue it. The fact that individual liberty is a living reality is very much the result of America's free-market economy. In the USSR, economic and political decisions are made and enforced by the Politburo. In the US, economic decisions are made largely by corporate management in accord with market conditions in the hope that these will be implemented voluntarily. —Williams, Harold M.; *Industrial Mgmt*, Mar/Apr 1982, 24(2): pp. 10-12. Avail. ABI 82-19088

Free enterprise, Capitalism, Corporate responsibility

Business Speaks: A Study of the Themes in Speeches by (27) America's Corporate Leaders

A recent analysis was conducted of speeches made by 550 leaders of the largest corporations in the US. The issues that emerged from the analysis consisted of 6 problems perceived by these corporate leaders to be confronting the American business community: 1. government regulation of business, 2. energy, 3. insufficient capital investment, 4. inflation, 5. business's public image, and 6. international business issues. The 3 general strategies proposed for dealing with them were: 1. increased social responsibility, 2. influencing government policy, and 3. economic education for the public.The regulation of business and industry by government was the issue of greatest concern. More than half of all the speeches treated this issue, and there seemed to be a consensus that the cost of regulation was now excessive and that the system now had too much control of private economic activity. There was also a considerable number of speeches devoted to the subject of energy, and the speakers were generally critical of federal energy policy. With capital investment, speakers contended that prospects for improvement are not good as traditional sources of capital continue to erode. Most speeches on inflation placed the majority of the blame on government, and the media and a general loss of confidence were cited as reasons for the present image of business. References. –Myers, Robert J. and Kessler, Martha Stout; *Jrnl of Business Communication,* Spring 1980, 17(3): pp. 5-17. Avail. ABI 80-10020

Public speaking, Speeches, Trends, Studies, Corporate presidents, Directors, Corporate officers

A Businessman's Perspective (28)

The role of the business leader is becoming increasingly complex. In addition to the usual challenges of running a business, business leaders are asked more often to help solve social problems. There are several guidelines for a business leader to follow when becoming involved in a social services program: 1. The effort should be a serious one. 2. There should be a common interest with the corporation. 3. The effort should be action-oriented. 4. The business contribution should make a difference. A successful public/private partnership, where business can play an important role, has 3 key characteristics: 1. effective personal leadership of chief executive officers, 2. businesslike management, and 3. coalitions based on solving problems rather than identifying issues. –Cavanagh, Richard; *Bureaucrat,* Spring 1983, 12(1): pp. 21-22. Avail. ABI 83-13096

Public sector, Private sector, Social responsibility, Chief executive officer, Leadership, Coalitions

Career Development and the Woman Manager-A Social (29) Power Perspective

Women managers currently represent the greatest proportion of entry-level management but hold fewer than 1% of top management positions. Women tend to become entrenched in "velvet ghettos," which include such areas as personnel and public relations, consumer affairs, and corporate social responsibility. Thus, despite the shifts in societal norms concerning sex roles and anti-sex discrimination laws, the stereotype for women remains strong among both men and women. Alternate strategies to the "velvet ghetto" for women aspiring to or holding management positions, include: 1. using perceptions of feminine characteristics to advantage, 2. adopting masculine standards of behavior, and/or 3. seeking entry into informal networks. Each strategy has its distinct advantages and disadvantages. One or any combination of the strategies may or may not work for all women. Choices of career strategy are ultimately made according to an individual's personal goals and to the nature of the organizational setting. What is needed is increased awareness on the part of those making their career choices and those responsible for developing the human resources of their organizations. Chart. —Powell, Gary N.; *Personnel*, May/Jun 1980, 57(3): pp. 22-32. Avail. ABI 80-13281

Women, Managers, Career development planning, Social, Power, Strategy, Career advancement

The Case for Corporate Democracy (30)

The American political agenda of the 1980s should focus on the size and abuses of big business. The key issue of corporate governance reform is who should make the decisions. Should it be executives or a representative board that is open and responsive to the views of a company's many stakeholders? The basic issue of unaccountable corporate power warrants federal legislation for several interrelated reasons: 1. state chartering has failed, 2. corporate illegality is extensive, and 3. the largest corporations are private governments. This spring, the Corporate Democracy Act was introduced into the House. The Act would establish minimum governance standards for the 800 largest US nonfinancial corporations. The goal is self-regulation to give greater access and voice to the corporations' stakeholders. Title I of the Act seeks to restore the influence and independence of the board of directors. Title II is concerned with corporate disclosure in simple fashion. The Act also has provisions for community impact analysis, constitutional rights of employees, and criminal and civil sanctions. —Green, Mark; *Regulation*, May/Jun 1980, 4(3): pp. 20-25. Avail. ABI 80-14919

Proposed, Federal legislation, Corporate, Democracies, Self regulation, Disclosure, Corporate responsibility

The Case for Using "Real People" in Advertising (31)

The ways advertising portrays people affects social attitudes and values. At issue is: 1. the prevalence of selective portrayals, 2. the effectiveness of using only attractive, young, ethnically central people in advertising, and 3. the social responsibility of advertisers. In Canada, older people, unattractive or plain looking people, and visible minorities are seldom or rarely seen in advertising. However, recent ad campaigns by Westin Hotels and Woolco Department Stores have run against the tide by using "real people." Research indicates little reason to stay with the practice of using only young, attractive people in advertisements. Advertisers using appeals not salient to the product may find a reversal of the desired effect. Because of overuse, young and attractive people have become relatively banal in viewers' eyes. References. —Singer, Benjamin D.; *Business Qtrly (Canada)*, Winter 1983, 48(4): pp. 32-37. Avail. ABI 84-10422

Advertising, Commercials, Advertising campaigns, Social research, Canada

A Case Study in Concern (32)

Although other credit unions (CU) practice social responsibility and community action, at Marquette Credit Union (Woonsocket, Rhode Island) it is a way of life and a daily, integral part of operations. Something that benefits the community is always going on at Marquette. The CU's facilities are often opened to public use, and the officers are usually busy with a community project. Much of the community involvement comes from John

Dionne, vice-president of marketing and public relations. In the first 5 months of 1984, Dionne and Marquette have: 1. sponsored a radiothon to raise funds for 2 youths to travel with a national service group, 2. made numerous donations of money, 3. donated trophies to a high school, and 4. offered facilities for free tax advice for the elderly. Dionne is quick to point out that the CU's board and management are strongly committed to social responsibility. The free publicity and word-of-mouth advertising Marquette receives as a result of its social efforts are enormous. —Anonymous; *Credit Union Magazine,* Jul 1984, 50(7): pp. 14,16. Avail. ABI 84-26122

Credit unions, Social responsibility, Community action, Case studies, Donations

Cash Flows That Require Negative Discount Rates   (33)

Students and analysts should know how to handle situations where projects may have negative internal rates of return (IRR), because these projects play a part in practice as well as teaching about capital budgeting. The use of Monte Carlo simulation techniques and the fact that some firms conduct obviously uneconomical problems (such as for reasons of social responsibility) makes familiarity with negative IRR ramifications necessary. A related problem is that regardless of whether IRR is positive or negative, a project's present value analysis may require a negative discount rate. IRR problems are usually solved by referring to present value tables, but these are only good with positive interest rates and for solving IRRs of more than zero. A definitional equation must be used to solve negative IRRs. Further, compounding techniques cannot be used in this situation. Equations. References. —Joy, O. Maurice and Grube, R. Corwin; *Engineering Economist,* Winter 1981, 26(2): pp. 154-158. Avail. ABI 81-07839

Cash flow, Negative, Internal rate of return, Discount rates, Capital budgeting, Projects, Present value

Catholic Bishops Take on Economics   (34)

The social activism of the Roman Catholic Church is demonstrated in several ways. Many segments of the church are members of the Interfaith Center on Corporate Responsibility (ICCR), which coordinates shareholder activism. In addition, Catholic bishops have spoken out on economic issues such as welfare reform, unemployment, and international economic concerns. This increased activism has not been without criticism. Edward L. Hennessy, Jr., head of Allied Corp., has criticized the bishops' economic ethics. As the church lacks an established body of literature and a tradition of economic ethics, individuals trained in theology and economics are needed. The upwardly mobile US Catholics need support and guidance in exercising their new power and influence. Finally, a movement to produce economics ethics similar to the movement which created medical ethics is necessary. —Williams, Oliver F.; *Business & Society Review,* Summer 1985, (54): pp. 21-26. Avail. ABI 85-33833

Religious organizations, Activists, Interest groups, Corporate responsibility, Social responsibility, Ethics

The Changing Role of Corporations in Political Affairs- (35)
Corporate Free Speech

There is an increasing trend toward strong corporate involvement in public affairs. People in the business world must support this trend by making even greater use of economic education programs and political action committees. The corporation, per se, does not influence political affairs, because the corporation is a written charter authorized by a state. It is often against the law for a corporation to contribute money to political leaders. It is the managers of the corporation who must take the responsibility, as individuals, to fulfill their duties to their stockholders and to the public at large. Today's corporate leaders have opportunities to become influential in political affairs to an extent that has not previously existed. Corporate leaders need to extend themselves further by developing more personal contact among employees, business management, the academic community, and political groups, to a point where there are effective communications, interaction, and ongoing relationships. –Corn, Ira G., Jr.; *Vital Speeches,* May 15, 1981, 47(15): pp. 463-468. Avail. ABI 81-13049

  Corporate, Roles, Society, Politics, Corporate responsibility, Political action committees, Growth, Freedom of speech, Economic, Education, Programs

Church Activists in the 1980s: The Conscience of (36)
Corporate America

Since 1970, churches have joined others in the US in advocating that businesses assume social responsibility. Church involvement in shareholder advocacy has been maturing, and this involvement has taught the churches the importance of documented research, as well as how to negotiate effectively. Issues have ranged from South Africa to toxic waste removal. There are many ways in which companies can react to church advocacy: 1. as an opportunity for joint learning and constructive action to solve problems, 2. as an early warning system to pinpoint important new issues, and 3. as an opportunity to demonstrate corporate leadership. There should be no separation between church and business because the church and business communities can and should learn much from each other. –Smith, Timothy H.; *Business & Society Review,* Summer 1985, (54): pp. 15-20. Avail. ABI 85-33832

  Corporate responsibility, Social responsibility, Religious organizations, Activists, Ethics, Advocacy, Interest groups

A Clean, Well-Lighted Place (37)

McFaddin Ventures Inc., with revenues of about $70 million, operates 44 bars, or theme clubs. Despite declining alcohol consumption and growing antidrinking sentiment, McFaddin has been growing rapidly. Lance McFaddin, the firm's founder, supports antidrinking campaigns and says his clubs are mainly in business to provide places for people to meet. The company trains personnel to recognize drunkenness, and it offers to pay for taxi rides for customers who should not drive. A McFaddin training film has been lent as a model to Mothers Against Drunk Driving chapters. McFaddin's clubs offer dance floors, central bars, and quiet areas, and the themes change with fashion. Despite the company's rapid growth, net margins are below 10%, partly because of heavy advertising expenditures. Moreover, the corporate organization is top-heavy because of being structured for centralized marketing, research, purchasing, and accounting. McFaddin is not concerned that antidrinking sentiment will close bars. – Chakravarty, Subrata N.; *Forbes,* Sep 23, 1985, 136(8): pp. 118. Avail. ABI 85-31030

Case studies, Restaurants, Alcohol, Market strategy, Target markets (MKT), Social responsibility, Entrepreneurs

The Clearing Banks and Small Firms (38)

Banks provide at least 2/3 of small firms' funds from institutional sources, yet there has been growing criticism of the role of banks in this financing. The main criticisms are: 1. requirements of "excessive security," which subvert limited liability, 2. banks' tendency to assess firms for their break-up value rather than as going concerns, and 3. an insistence upon relatively low leverage ratios. However, neither critics nor the banks have much fact to support the case. The potential for bank lending to small firms is a profitable opportunity rather than an exercise in corporate social responsibility. Banks' real obstacles to this endeavor are their organization and general attitudes, not the difficulties in devising new lending packages. The size and structure of highly concentrated British clearing banks require a remoteness of central decision-makers from branch managers in the field. The rewards of banks that conquer this problem are considerable. Existing small businesses in the UK have borrowings of about L20 billion from banks. This could be doubled in real terms by 1990. Much bigger changes in the revolution in clearing banks' attitudes to small businesses are necessary. Tables. References. – Bannock, Graham; *Lloyds Bank Review (UK),* Oct 1981, (142): pp. 15-25. Avail. ABI 81-25654

Clearing banks-UK, Small business, UK, Bank loans, Statistical data

Collaborative Capitalism: The Future of American Enterprise (39)

US economic growth has been sustained because of collaborative capitalism, i.e., the balance between capitalism and democracy, between the public and private sectors, and between power and free enterprise. The continuation of collaborative capitalism depends upon identifying the mutually beneficial relationships between the private and public sectors. The major relationships in collaborative capitalism are those between: 1. industry and the ecology, 2. management and labor, 3. businesses and businesses, and 4. government and business. Each of these relationships must be made more collaborative and synergistic to overcome barriers to economic expansion. Other important contributors to collaborative capitalism include: 1. voluntarism, 2. lobbying, 3. corporate social responsibility, 4. urban revitalization, and 5. innovation. Balanced efforts between the private and public sectors should be focused toward developing an holistic framework for dealing with the social, political, and economic difficulties involved in revitalizing the economy. References. –Mescon, Michael H.; Mescon, Timothy S.; and Pearson, John N.; *Business,* Jan/Feb/Mar 1984, 34(1): pp. 57-61. Avail. ABI 84-19712

Capitalism, Economic theory, Labor relations, Business, Government, Relations

The Common Venture Enterprise: A Western Answer to   (40)
the Japanese Art of Management?

Because Japanese success in business enterprises is in part due to cultural and spiritual values, the Olga Co. drew on principles from Judeo-Christian teachings to provide clear guidelines for a new style of corporate life. The guiding principles were: 1. the dignity of all people, 2. the trusteeship of life and resources, 3. leadership through service, 4. the concerned community, and 5. the right of the producer to a share of the production. The common venture enterprise is a new corporate model which emphasizes and facilitates consensus instead of promulgating the traditional confrontation between labor and management. Components of the common venture include a highly intensive profit-sharing plan, ownership-sharing, and a commitment to permanent employment. Olga has enjoyed growth, annual new sales records and new aftertax profits records, and only rare permanent layoffs. Graph. —Erteszek, Jan J.; *New Mgmt*, 1983, 1(2): pp. 4-10. Avail. ABI 83-29035

Corporate, Culture, Values, Corporate responsibility, Clothing industry, Case studies, Personnel policies, Profit sharing, Management styles

Communicating Your Social Role   (41)

Traditionally, a corporation's economic mission and its social role have been seen as separate issues. Enlightened executives today see the 2 issues as intertwined. A corporation can enhance its economic mission if it also pursues other objectives: 1. maximizing the company's positive impact on customers, employees, and communities, and 2. participating in solving pressing social problems. Improvement in internal corporate communications is recommended, including face-to-face dialogue with employees and encouraging employees to make suggestions to an accessible management. External communications can be made more effective by following 6 guidelines: 1. keeping a long-range view, 2. opening communications, 3. promoting confidence-inspiring spokespersons, 4. using advocacy ads with caution, 5. avoiding social responsibility reports, and 6. becoming directly involved in community problem-solving. —Johnston, David C-H; *Public Relations Jrnl*, Dec 1981, 37(12): pp. 18-19. Avail. ABI 82-03391

Internal public relations, Public relations, Communications, Social responsibility

Companies That Hide Behind the Sullivan Principles   (42)

The Sullivan Principles are 6 guidelines for companies with subsidiaries or affiliates operating in the Republic of South Africa. Investors wishing to make socially responsible decisions sometimes make decisions based on whether a company is a signatory of the Sullivan Principles. The issue is more complex than merely signing an agreement, however. Of approximately 280 US corporations doing business in South Africa, 160 have not signed the Principles or have signed and then later withdrawn support. Among the reasons for not signing include: 1. a small operation (fewer than 10 employees), 2. burdensome reporting requirements, and 3. costs of operating the compliance program. People who want to avoid supporting apartheid with their investment dollars should look beyond whether a company is a Sullivan signatory. Actually, many companies that are not signatories have better race-relations records than some that are. Table. —Slater, Robert Bruce; *Business & Society Review,* Spring 1984, (49): pp. 15-18. Avail. ABI 84-18803

Social responsibility, Apartheid, South Africa, Investments

The Conflict Between Business and the Church (43)

Church involvement in issues of business institutions has been fairly widespread and has affected all types of businesses. Church bodies wield significant social, political, and economic power. However, the role of the organized church as an adversary, or even an active participant, in an attempt to change or influence long-range goals and operational policies of private corporations holds implications for society in terms of: 1. institutional legitimacy, 2. accountability, 3. relevance, and 4. effectiveness. In response, corporations tend to avoid matters of public discontent until such matters reach crisis stages. Recently, however, some corporations have developed more positive and constructive responses to social issues. Business-church conflicts arise not out of the need for change, but over its nature and direction and the process by which it is effected. For the corporation to become a positive agent for change, it must become more active in the political process by offering choices that are rooted in people's needs rather than corporate convenience. —Sethi, S. Prakash; *Business & Society Review,* Winter 1980-81, (36): pp. 23-29. Avail. ABI 81-07567

Religious organizations, Conflict, Business, Social responsibility, Corporate responsibility

Contradictions (44)

A doctrine that is widely accepted regarding business in Capitalist societies involves the contradiction that pursuing business self-interest will benefit society as a whole. However, support for the doctrine may be waning, as evidenced by situations in which businesses are publicly attacked and held accountable for the detrimental social consequences of their wealth-maximizing activities. Most managers do not operate from a business ideology which explicitly recognizes the dual imperative to both maximize business and social interests. Improved public relations, enhanced monitoring of external environments, and increased corporate philanthropy are not sufficient to meet the challenges of protecting self-interest and ensuring corporate responsibility. A sense of corporate integrity is required for business to reconcile its contradictory imperatives. Corporate integrity must spring from the integrity of corporate leaders, who establish and communicate the values of their organizations to all internal and external stakeholders, and must focus on honesty and cooperation in stakeholder negotiations. References. —MacMillan, Keith; *Jrnl of General Mgmt (UK),* Spring 1984, 9(3): pp. 3-17. Avail. ABI 84-18133

Social responsibility, Public relations, Corporate image, Ethics

Contributing Factors (45)

By reversing the trend toward more government responsibility for social-welfare programs, the Reagan Administration has placed a new emphasis on the private sector. Reagan expects business to take fresh initiatives to deal voluntarily with society's problems. Congress has matched his expectations by raising business tax deductions for charitable contributions to 10% of taxable income. The private sector has responded positively; however, the private-sector approach to solving social problems is doomed to failure. For every federal dollar cut from poor people's programs, business donated only one cent in 1981. Moreover, budget cuts have left less money for the nonprofit agencies that deliver government-funded services. Thus, it is ridiculous to expect the corporate sector to fill the gap left by government withdrawal. Moreover, the bulk of corporate donations do not find their way into programs serving the people hurt most by the budget cuts. —Jacob, John E.; *Cornell Executive,* Spring 1983, 9(2): pp. 25-27. Avail. ABI 83-28403

Private sector, Social policy, Donations, Welfare, Social services, Social responsibility, Affirmative action

The Contributions of Religious Traditions to Business Ethics (46)

Judeo-Christian concepts have contributed to business ethics throughout history, and their contribution today is evident in some primary areas involving the concepts of social responsibility, the living wage, stewardship, and subsidiarity (participation). One of the greatest challenges will be to apply the concept of living wage to the theory of comparable worth. Also, a new concept of stewardship opens up new avenues for justifying changes in the role of corporations in society. A serious concern for the future is relating organized religion to contemporary managers and executives, who find little value in religion's contributions to social adhesiveness or to development of ethical and moral principles. Today's "young careerists" are compared to the "organization men" revealed in a 1955 study. If many young careerists are agnostics, organized religion must reach them to broaden their horizons and encourage higher motives. New ways must be found to frame traditional religious concepts and principles. References. – McMahon, Thomas F.; *Jrnl of Business Ethics (Netherlands),* Aug 1985, 4(4): pp. 341-349. Avail. ABI 85-32310

Business, Ethics, Social responsibility, Career advancement, Attitude surveys, Trends, Social, Justice, Religion, Influence

Controlling Costs in the 80's (47)

As the economy enters the 1980s, double-inflation is prevalent and will continue to be a factor for the foreseeable future. However, unlike in the past, the insurance industry is better prepared to cope with the impact of inflation. Prevention is being stressed to control cost pressures, and more effective claim administration is being supplemented by expanded reliance on computers. At the same time, new techniques of cash flow management are being used. The insurance industry has also taken active roles in supporting legislative proposals to halt excessive cost increases in some lines of the business. There are also programs to reduce arson and to lower costs in workers compensation and the health care field. These tactics as well as others demonstrate to the public that the insurance industry shares its concern over rising costs. No industry can operate without public support, and the insurance industry must continue to develop communications

programs to inform the public of its social responsibility. —Budd, Edward H.;
Insurance Marketing, Apr 1980, 81(4): pp. 28. Avail. ABI 80-09509

 Insurance industry, Costs, Insurance rates, Communication, Cost control

Controlling Giant Corporations: Myths and Realities   (48)

The interrelationship between respected, quality scholarship on the subject
of large corporations and what is actually happening in the world of politics,
law, and business is discussed. The Modern Corporation and Private
Property (1932), written largely by Adolf A. Berle with the assistance of
Gardiner Means, was the classic beginning of serious scholarship on the
question of the administration, governance, and behavior of large
corporations. Berle adopted traditional legal and political models, not
economic ones, to criticize the behavior of corporations. Central to his notion
of corporations was the famous observation of "the separation of ownership
and control". He examined the control of shareholders over management.
Berle's The 20th Century Capitalist Revolution raised the question of
corporate social responsibility. Scholarly defense of the corporate system
followed. Anthony Downs, in his book An Economic Theory of Democracy
(1955), introduced the economic theory of voting concept. In 1972,
economists Armen Alchian and Harold Demsetz examined when an
entrepreneur would use a command system and when he would rely on
market forces to coordinate production. More recently, thinking about
corporations has been dominated by the growing sense of how strongly
markets and different sets of property rights constrain behavior and the
"efficient market" concept. These ideas persuasively argue that
shareholders, contrary to Berle's beliefs, do exert influence on management.
—Manne, Henry G.; *Vital Speeches,* Sep 1, 1981, 47(22): pp. 690-694. Avail. ABI 81-21942

 Big business, Boards of directors, Controls, Ownership, Stockholders, Management

The Corporate Democracy Act-A Renaissance or Death   (49)
Knell for the Corporate World?

Recognizing that existing external controls over large business corporations
cannot prevent "anti-social" behavior, some groups are pushing companies
to assume a role of corporate social responsibility. To this end, "The
Corporate Democracy Act of 1980" was put before the US House of
Representatives. This bill sets up minimal standards of conduct to be
inforced through the initiative of the injured party. Thus, corporate behavior
would regulate itself through the "natural interplay" of contending parties
under a new regime of legal rights and duties. The role of the board of
directors and shareholders would change as the responsibilities of the
corporation were augmented. The nature of the corporation would also
change. The changes proposed by this law need to be thought through
carefully because the reverberations will be extensive. References. —
Millspaugh, Peter E.; *Corporation Law Review,* Fall 1981, 4(4): pp. 291-306. Avail. ABI 81-22922

 Proposed, Federal legislation, Corporate, Law, Corporate responsibility, Boards of directors,
 Stockholders, Roles, Disclosure, Annual reports, Employees, Rights

Corporate Ethics and Corporate Governance: A Critique (50) of the ALI Statement on Corporate Governance Section 2.01(b)

The American Law Institute (ALI) has released a tentative draft concerning corporate law entitled, Principles of Corporate Governance and Structure: Restatement and Recommendations. It states that the object of the business corporation is to conduct business activities with a view to corporate profit and shareholder gain. The exceptions to the above are: 1. Section 2.01(a) requires that the corporation obey the law regardless of economic cost. 2. Section 2.01(b) permits the corporation to make decisions based on ethical principles generally recognized as relevant to the conduct of business even if this will not enhance profits. 3. Section 2.01(c) allows the corporation to make reasonable donations to charities. Section 2.01(b) should not be adopted because it: 1. is unnecessary, 2. wastes judicial resources, 3. motivates incorrect ethical behavior, and 4. expands discretion of the officials of dissolving corporations. References. —Pritchett, M. J., III; *California Law Review*, May 1983, 71(3): pp. 994-1011. Avail. ABI 83-16606

Ethics, Corporate responsibility, Corporate officers, Maximizing profits, ALI, Principles, Standards

Corporate Power and Public Issues (51)

The autonomy of corporate decision making in Canada is coming under increased pressure from violent and nonviolent special-interest groups. A recent Conference Board survey indicates that many executives in the industrialized world feel such pressure. Moreover, many of these pressure groups are funded by government, public, private, and corporate donations. Business is confused about its role, and such factors as media involvement in public issues and the consumerist movement have created a society that demands a "new contract with business." The political process may not help alert business to impending public issues, and managers may feel inadequate in the role of social scientist. When a firm decides to reshape its relationship with the outside world, it must review the lessons already learned by others, including the inadvisability of an ad hoc approach to managing outside pressure. Pro-active management of socio-political trends involves such changes as development of an external relations policy and an environmental auditing system. —Graham-Dwyer, Peter; *Canadian Manager (Canada)*, Dec 1983, 8(4): pp. 8-10. Avail. ABI 84-04713

Corporate responsibility, Decision making, Public opinion, Public relations

Corporate Reputation Counts (52)

A company's reputation rests on how well its public rates it in the following areas: product or service quality, leadership, research and development, modernity, size, service, social responsibility, perceived competence, and warmth or style. How the public sees the company, feels about the company, and talks about it determines corporate reputation, which is a very important asset in the pursuit of corporate objectives. A reputation is important in recruiting, in internal morale, and in the marketplace. Management must shape a reputation that is a true reflection of the company. It is essential to communicate the essence, of the company to the public in ways they understand. It is only possible to communicate with impact when corporate reputation is known. Such knowledge can be gained through research, and following research, communications objectives must be set. A communications program should be developed that is affordable and maintainable. —Brouillard, Joseph; *Advertising Age,* Nov 14, 1983, 54(48): pp. M-46. Avail. ABI 83-32955

Public relations, Consumer relations, Corporate image

Corporate Responsibility - Reconciling Economic and Social Goals   (53)

Corporations are increasingly being called upon to support community programs that have suffered cutbacks in federal spending. However, this increased social responsibility comes at a time when corporations have suffered constrained resources due to economic recession, requiring them to develop innovative ways to combine economic and social goals. Case studies are presented to illustrate how social responsibility can contribute to corporate economic well-being, including: 1. Kellogg's successful promotion of a property tax reduction for local businesses, based on an agreement that tax savings would be contributed to community development, 2. Control Data Corp.'s commitment to and profitable development of inner city plants, 3. Pittsburgh Brewing Co.'s fund raising/sales campaigns to support food programs for laid-off steelworkers, 4. American Express Co.'s support of arts programs through donations of proceeds from services, and 5. Du Pont's successful accident prevention program. Charts. References. —Chrisman, James J. and Carroll, Archie B.; *Sloan Mgmt Review,* Winter 1984, 25(2): pp. 59-65. Avail. ABI 84-15289

Corporate responsibility, Social responsibility, Economic conditions, Case studies

Corporate Response to Social Actions   (54)

Social actions are sometimes taken against business, and managers at all levels must learn to recognize and deal with them. Since such protests can cost a firm time, money, and public image, when emotions take control, managers must seek creative strategies that produce win-win situations. A social-action model is presented which defines motivating factors, the roles of the participants, targets, channels of influence, and the strategies of social action. This information provides management with the outlines of its own responsive strategy. In the case cited, the defensive action of political advocacy has to be supplemented by a proactive strategy of providing tangible consumer benefits, to be sold via effective communications. Resulting recommendations for managers include: 1. understanding the social problem triggering the social action, 2. clearly defining change agents in the social action, 3. responding effectively to the role played by the media in social action, 4. guarding against overreaction to the leadership style of change agents, and 5. exploring strategies leading to creative solutions. Diagram. References. —Fleming, John E.; *Business,* Jan-Mar 1982, 32(1): pp. 10-14. Avail. ABI 82-05499

Social issues, Corporate, Responses, Models, Social responsibility, Organizational change

Corporate Services for the Community (55)

Because of federal budget cutbacks and the "new federalism", business will be increasingly called upon to provide some of the social services which were formerly provided by the government. US Bancorp, holding company of the US National Bank of Oregon, has long recognized that the economic health of US National Bank of Oregon-its subsidiaries, owners, customers, and employees-is directly related to the social health of the communities in which the bank operates. US National Bank believes it has a responsibility to utilize its resources for the economic and social improvement of Oregon. By positively using this influence, US National Bank has been able to help reduce or eliminate some of the unemployment, poverty, and physical deterioration in Oregon's communities. For more than a decade, US National Bank's community affairs department has focused on equal job opportunities, low-income housing, education, and small and minority business enterprises. The department administers a number of programs, including: Opportunity Loan, employment, community involvement, corporate social services contributions, activist strategy and negotiations, and corporate community and internal liaison. –Worley, Nola M.; *ABA Banking Jrnl,* May 1982, 74(5): pp. 58-61. Avail. ABI 82-12828

US Bancorp-Portland Ore, Case studies, Banking industry, Bank marketing, Public relations, Social responsibility, Corporate responsibility

Corporate Social Responsibility-A Philosophical Appraisal (56)

Social responsibility considerations are not a goal of the firm, but operate as a constraint on the business. It can be argued that the firm which takes social responsibility considerations into account only when there is outside pressure to do so, is not truly a socially responsible organization but one which is looking after its own interests. The socially responsible organization is one which realizes that its decisions affect the welfare of other people and takes the time to find out how and to what extent they will be affected. With the recognition that a business organization is part of a wider society, its activities must be judged against the standard implicit in the wider society. Although in legal terms, the responsibility for corporate decisions may be attributed to a legal fiction called the "corporate person"; in moral terms, the responsibility for corporate decisions rests on the individual members of the corporation. –Atkinson, Christine and Atkinson, Adrian; *Jrnl of Enterprise Mgmt,* 1980, 2(2): pp. 131-135. Avail. ABI 81-00445

Corporate responsibility, Social responsibility, Individual, Responsibilities, Allocations

Corporate Social Responsibility: Will Industry Respond (57) to Cutbacks in Social Program Funding?

The question has been raised as to whether corporate industry will respond to cutbacks in social program funding by the federal government. Corporate social responsibility (CSR) involves the conduct of a business so that it is economically profitable, law abiding, ethical, and socially supportive. To be socially responsive, profitability and obedience to the law are foremost conditions to discussing the company's ethics and the extent to which it supports the society in which it exists with contributions of money, time, and talent. CSR is composed of economic, legal, ethical, and voluntary elements. Business will not and should not respond in a manner sufficient to fill the void created by federal cutbacks in funding of social programs. Business has not been inactive, however; there are a number of examples of private sector initiatives that are responsive to social needs in communities today. The recent pressures on business will provide initiative to examine more closely its capacity to serve society constructively, in ways that address both economic and social agendas. —Carroll, Archie B.; *Vital Speeches,* Jul 15, 1983, 49(19): pp. 604-608. Avail. ABI 83-21517

Social responsibility, Corporate responsibility, Social policy, Social issues

Corporate Social Responsibility and Financial   (58) Performance

Whether or not the relationship between a firm's corporate social responsibility (CSR) and its financial performance exists is obviously an important issue for corporate management, since only upon determining this can the question of causation be addressed. This research extends prior empirical research in 3 areas. Certain factors left out of previous studies are explicitly controlled for by the use of improved financial performance measures and additional variables. Logit analysis is also employed. The sample is enhanced by the use of a large industry-specific control group and 2 test intervals. This expanded analysis shows that the key correlate with CSR is asset age and that the omission of this variable in previous studies may have resulted in spurious positive correlations between CSR and financial performance. However, even with this variable included, a weak positive correlation still exists. Tables. Equations. References. —Cochran, Philip L. and Wood, Robert A.; *Academy of Mgmt Jrnl,* Mar 1984, 27(1): pp. 42-56. Avail. ABI 84-11379

Social responsibility, Corporate responsibility, Financial ratios, Studies, Statistical analysis, Statistical methods

Corporate Social Responsibility in the Reagan Era and   (59) Beyond

The debate on the role of business in society has generated a list of social issues and problems that may be viewed as a proper focus for socially responsible business actions. Some of these issues involve: 1. environmental pollution, 2. consumer abuses, 3. threats to the safety and health of employees, and 4. questionable or abusive practices by multinational corporations. After nearly 3 decades of scholarly debate and trial-and-error experimentation by business, an effort is made to determine the current status of corporate social responsibility. It is suggested that no significant gains in corporate social performance can be expected during the Reagan era. Mandated social performance standards have been relaxed. It is impossible for voluntary private initiatives to match social needs. One means of moving beyond present levels of corporate social responsiveness is to form social partnerships or coalitions of business, government, labor unions, universities, and various community groups. Such coalitions might be able to address social needs that are beyond the economic and technological reach of corporations acting alone. References. —Frederick, William C.; *California Mgmt Review,* Spring 1983, 25(3): pp. 145-157. Avail. ABI 83-14843

Social responsibility, Donations, Deregulation, Social services, Cooperation, Coalitions

Corporate Social Responsibility Revisited, Redefined (60)

Interest in corporate social responsibility as a form of self-control that includes normative constraint, altruistic incentives, and moral motivation has increased because of recent criticism of the business community. The question of corporate social responsibility can be divided into 2 related areas: 1. whether business should adopt the concept of corporate responsibility, and 2. how it should be implemented if it is adopted. This concept is based on the supposition that corporations owe a voluntarily accepted and broad obligation to societal groups other than their own shareholders. The implementation of the theory involves placing new emphasis on management decisions which will have to be evaluated in light of their social impact. Some companies may implement social study groups or use outside consultants or institution of special purpose directors to formulate social policy. Even with these changes, it is often difficult to define improved corporate behavior and will continue to be until society has more specific goals in mind. Tables. References. —Jones, Thomas M.; *California Mgmt Review,* Spring 1980, 22(3): pp. 59-67. Avail. ABI 80-16901

Corporate responsibility, Social responsibility, Foreign investment, Social policy, Decision making, Organizational behavior

Corporate Social Responsibility (61)

Corporate social responsibility has long been an issue in the US. Evidence indicates that corporate social responsibility does not adversely affect economic performance. However, Reagan's cutbacks in social programs, the recent economic downturn, and international competition have all contributed to corporations' recent lack of social involvement. A survey was conducted of 291 executives from firms with major facilities in South Carolina during the summer of 1984. The results indicated that corporate social responsibility was not a major goal of most firms. The survey also found that: 1. the respondents believed social involvement should be pursued as long as profitability is not overlooked, 2. positions on social responsibility have become more liberal, 3. social responsibility had been defined and discussed in the past year by the majority of respondents, 4. social responsibility ranked as the 6th most important goal, 5. social responsibility expenditures varied with corporate profits, and 6. public image was an important determinant in social involvement. Major concerns were seeking matches between corporate competencies and social needs and implementing involvement policies. References. —Logan, John E.; Logan, Sandra P.; and Mille, Jean M. Edouard; *Business & Economic Review,* Jan 1985, 31(2): pp. 25-27. Avail. ABI 85-19652

Corporate responsibility, Social responsibility, Surveys, Corporate objectives

Corporate Social Responsibility Revisited (62)

Bankers are abandoning their old image of trying to be all things to all people in their communities and redefining their roles as corporate good

citizens. In the new era of concentration on quality of life, it is evident that corporate social responsibility and the bottom line are closely related. A good program of corporate social responsibility requires commitment from all levels within a bank. Manufacturers National Corp. (Detroit, Michigan) has put its public commitment to its many communities clearly in writing. Pressure for banks to deal with social issues will continue to intensify. The Community Reinvestment Act (CRA) actually mandates a role for corporate citizenship within the community in which a bank operates. Banks should develop CRA programs to establish their identities as good citizens. These programs might include seminars to educate the public about available credit and financial counseling services offered. Newspapers can serve as an excellent vehicle for informing the public about pertinent issues. Among the changes fostering corporate social responsiveness in the future will be: 1. less regulation, 2. business listening more to consumers, 3. a growing partnership between the private sector and the community, and 4. greater accountability.
—Schneider, Brenda L.; *United States Banker,* Apr 1982, 93(4): pp. 55-57. Avail. ABI 82-10871

   Banks, Corporate responsibility, Social responsibility, Community Reinvestment Act 1977-
   US, Public relations

The Corporation Haters   (63)

In a recent Yankelovich survey to determine whether business strikes a fair balance between profits and the public interest, only 19% gave an affirmative answer, compared with 70% a decade ago. The common theme of most anti-corporate coalitions is that in the capitalist economic system, profits and social responsibility do not mix. The center of the current anti-corporate campaign may be the National Council of Churches. The gap between radical Christian and Marxist thinking expounded by the Council and that of individual congregations has been widening without much attention. Yet there are still powerful warnings against seeking salvation through radical social and economic change. Church activists often present business-related issues as morally clear-cut and simple, when they actually may be quite complex. The infant-formula issue is an example of how the process can work. Everyone agrees that breast-feeding is the best and cheapest nutrition for babies, but feeding patterns have become intertwined with social change. The large food and pharmaceutical companies have been accused of enticing Third World mothers on formula by giving free samples to doctors and hospitals. The Swiss food giant, Nestle S.A., has become the selected villain, despite the absence of reliable data. The most frightening implication of the formula movement is the support it has gained among government functionaries. —Nickel, Herman; *Fortune,* Jun 16, 1980, 101(12): pp. 126-136. Avail. ABI 80-12351

   Anti, Big business, Movement, Social responsibility, Corporate responsibility, Marketing

CRA and the Loan Officer   (64)

The Community Reinvestment Act (CRA) states that regulated financial institutions have a continuing and affirmative obligation to meet the credit needs of their communities, consistent with their safe and sound operation. Financial regulators will consider the bank's record in meeting these needs, including low- and moderate-income neighborhoods, when evaluating applications for a deposit facility. CRA stresses effective communication, such as formal call programs, visits to key community leaders, or participation in community forums, and asks for programs to make the community aware of credit services. Documentation of CRA efforts is crucial, as is the participation of commercial loan officers. Such officers can foster cooperation between local government and financial institutions through familiarity with Federal government programs and by cooperating with local officials to better understand community needs. —Innis, Janet W.; *Jrnl of Commercial Bank Lending,* Oct 1980, 63(2): pp. 16-22. Avail. ABI 80-21650

Community Reinvestment Act 1977-US, Banks, Social responsibility, Community, Commercial credit, Bank loans, Affirmative action

Criminal Liability of Corporate Officers for Strict (65) Liability Offenses-a Comment on Dotterweich and Park

Only 2 cases involving the criminal liability of corporate executives for strict liability offenses committed by the executives' corporations have been decided by the US Supreme Court; United States v. Dotterweich (1943) and United States v. Park (1975). Dotterweich was largely superseded by Park, and recent opinions applying Park are appearing in the Ninth Circuit. An overview of Dotterweich and Park shows how the Supreme Court has failed to develop a doctrinal modification of strict liability for corporate officers. Park is somewhat more advanced in its apparent requirement for some showing of culpability. The Park case also allowed a shift in the burden of going forward, which is a variation on placing the burden of proof of due care on the defendant. An improved method, modifying the strict liability approach, would be to adopt a "corporate responsibility" or "standard of care" approach-one that would definitely hold that the responsible executive had knowledge of or control over the violation alleged. While adequate conditions of health and cleanliness are important in our society, a corporate standard of care must not be so high as to impose unfair criminal liability on an individual. References. —Abrams, Norman; *UCLA Law Review,* Feb 1981, 28(3): pp. 463-477. Avail. UCLA 82-00821

Criminal law, Corporate officers, Liability, Supreme Court decisions-US, Court decisions, Corporate responsibility

The Criminal Liability of Corporations and Other (66) Groups: A Comparative View

Recently, economic or white-collar crime has attracted much attention in the US and Europe. An attempt is made here to survey the status of corporate and group liability in Europe and in the common-law countries, and to study the alternative techniques of control devised in different legal systems. Three positions concerning corporate liability may be identified: 1. systems of full corporate criminal liability, such as those in the UK and the US, 2. systems that recognize only partial corporate criminal liability, for example Denmark, Belgium, and France, and 3. systems which do not allow such liability at all or permit it only under the guise of administrative offenses. Italy and Germany are examples of the restrictive view of corporate liability. It is concluded that there is a sufficient similarity among the basic ideas for each system to learn from the other. References. —Leigh, L. H.; *Michigan Law Review,* Jun 1982, 80(7): pp. 1508-1528. Avail. Michigan 82-28432

Corporate, Liability, White collar crime, Corporate responsibility, Manycountries

Critical Issues Confronting Managers in the '80s   (67)

Predictors almost always err as they assume that basic human nature changes as rapidly as technology and they always underestimate intervening variables. While some issues, such as the energy crisis, minorities in organizations, women's liberation, business ethics, etc., are very real, they are often not considered as they are already well identified and are the subject of much exploration. Management issues in the 1980s are likely to include: 1. US work force motivation, 2. quality control and workmanship, 3. individual responsibility vs. social responsibility, 4. shielding of top decision-makers from unpleasant but vital data, 5. limited resource management, and 6. business-government relationship. Although some of the issues are not trainable, increasingly, training personnel may be forced to view their jobs as inextricably related to societal and world problems. Training personnel must guard against claims and predictions of training breakthroughs. While each such claim may contain some truth, none is likely to have over 3% validity. —This, Leslie E.; *Training & Development Jrnl,* Jan 1980, 34(1): pp. 14-17. Avail. ABI 80-02530

Training, Problems, Business conditions, Management, Social issues, Predictions

CUs Thrive When Their Communities Thrive   (68)

"Social responsibility" is a concept that covers the obligation that credit unions (CU) have to their members, employees, communities, and society as a whole. Social responsibility can range from aiding disaster victims to adopting a code of ethics to govern operations. Social responsibility involves playing a constructive and active role in improving the community and its environment and making sure that products and services fulfill their promises and are beneficial to consumers and society. CUs are ideal vehicles through which social responsibility can be practiced. However, a recent survey of 1,000 CU managers indicates that many credit unions are not actively involved with consumer and community affairs. Many confine their contribution to relatively small monetary donations to various charities or community groups. Social responsibility is good business. The most important benefit of community involvement is the positive image it generates among the public. —Anonymous; *Credit Union Magazine,* Jul 1984, 50(7): pp. 10-12. Avail. ABI 84-26121

Credit unions, Social responsibility, Surveys, Community action

Dangerous Territory: The Societal Marketing Concept   (69)
Revisited

The concept of "societal marketing," or the view that a marketer should act in accordance with the public interest just because it is the right thing to do, is objectional on philosophical and pragmatic grounds. A marketer can not be certain that a given action will produce a net benefit to society. Marketers who attempt to act in the public interest arbitrarily usurp a public policymaking role they were not elected or designated to perform.

Pragmatically, marketers have no particular competence for determining what is in the public interest. When marketers base their actions on their perceptions of public interest instead of on customer satisfaction, they lessen product-related satisfaction and raise the costs of their products. Marketers should act to satisfy customers until the public defines its interest through regulation and forces marketers to conform. Charts. References. —Gaski, John F.; *Business Horizons,* Jul/Aug 1985, 28(4): pp. 42-47. Avail. ABI 85-26521

Marketing, Social responsibility, Public interest

Data in Search of a Theory: A Critical Examination of   (70) the Relationships Among Social Performance, Social Disclosure, and Economic Performance of U.S. Firms

Numerous empirical studies of corporate social responsibility published during the last decade have focused on the relationships among corporate social performance, social disclosure, and economic performance. These studies approach the topic with a variety of methods, using varying samples and focusing on different time periods. The findings have been inconsistent, so no clear tendencies can be detected. The primary reasons for these inconsistencies are: 1. a lack in theory, 2. inappropriate definition of key terms, and 3. deficiencies in the empirical databases currently available. In order to achieve more convincing and consistent results, 2 steps are necessary: 1. a strategic framework, and 2. methodological improvements. The current findings concerning the relationships among social performance, social disclosure, and economic performance can at this time best be characterized as empirical data in search of an adequate theory. Tables. References. —Ullmann, Arieh A.; *Academy of Mgmt Review,* Jul 1985, 10(3): pp. 540-557. Avail. ABI 85-28467

Corporate responsibility, Social responsibility, Social, Disclosure, Performance, Models, Studies, Organizational behavior

Defining Corporate Social Responsibility: A Three-   (71) Group Survey

The term "corporate social responsibility" is frequently used by government officials, business practitioners, researchers in business, and students in collegiate schools of business. Because of the increased usage of this term, there has been a proliferation of meanings and definitions of the term. Lack of agreement on any definition has hindered the work and communication processes of those who must be concerned with this aspect of business. A research project was conducted to explore the attitude toward socially responsible behavior expressed by students, researchers, and persons in the business world. The research was designed to determine attitudes toward various concepts or definitions of corporate social responsibility by the 3 groups and to determine whether a consensus opinion could be obtained by a panel whose members are drawn from each of these groups. Panels of individuals, representative of each group, were surveyed. It was discovered that while the groups could not agree on the definition of the most preferred statements regarding corporate responsibility, they could agree on the least acceptable definition. Additional research, conducted along the same lines as this project, could perhaps achieve greater refinement of a definition. Tables. References. —Ford, Robert and McLaughlin, Frank; *Review of Business & Economic Research,* Fall 1981, 17(1): pp. 72-77. Avail. ABI 82-08841

Corporate responsibility, Social responsibility, Attitudes, Studies

The Desperate Plight of the Underclass (72)

The Reagan Administration has encouraged the private sector to assume a greater role in meeting the needs of unemployed and impoverished Americans; the role of government in this project was not specified. Employment is only part of the solution, as the poor have become disenfranchised and isolated from the mainstream of US culture. A holistic approach to community building is required. Neighborhood organizations, funds channeling organizations, private industry councils, semigovernmental development organizations, and direct corporate interventions offer potential for community integration. Business stands to gain by participating in these efforts. However, businesses must not underestimate the difficulty of the task and the level of corporate commitment which is required. A realistic perspective of the community must be established. Business must cooperate with other organizations and actively influence government policy for community development. References. —Lodge, George Cabot and Glass, William R.; *Harvard Business Review,* Jul/Aug 1982, 60(4): pp. 60-71. Avail. ABI 82-19208

Corporate responsibility, Social responsibility, Poverty, Welfare, Manycompanies, Government, Policy

Developing Corporate Policies for Innovation: A Program of Action (73)

Today's private enterprise is characterized by a lack of new products and service innovations. Innovations yield increases in productivity which allow for a higher standard of living, subdue inflation, and create jobs. Large companies have failed to be more innovative and this is partly a function of the growing low-risk culture. The current emphasis is on immediate payoffs from marginal improvement in existing offerings, and also from lower labor costs via mechanization and automation. Development of new products and services is stifled in this environment. Innovation can help restore productivity to reasonable levels. An effective program is needed to address major unmet needs that represent vast markets for the future, such as lower cost sources of energy, lower cost and more effective health care and education, urban revitalization, and rural development. Big business needs to provide the leadership necessary to address these unmet needs. A major part of this initiative must come from corporate top management in the form of policies that encourage innovation. Appendix. —Norris, William C.; *Long Range Planning (UK),* Aug 1981, 14(4): pp. 34-42. Avail. ABI 81-20997

Innovations, Product development, Policy, Corporate responsibility, Big business, Leadership, Case studies, Control Data-Minneapolis

Developing Effective Minority Purchasing Programs (74)

Minority purchasing programs are becoming an increasingly prominent part of corporations' total purchasing activities due to stricter legislation, more forceful emphasis by the executive branch, and the growth of national and regional Minority Supplier Development Councils. Firms may consider the following reasons to have such a program: 1. Public Law 95-507 requires such programs in firms conducting business with the federal government, 2. fulfillment of social responsibility, 3. increased employment opportunity for minorities, and 4. enhanced efforts to sell to the minority communities. A survey of major US manufacturers indicates that large corporations had higher levels of minority purchasing activity. Program emphasis changed with experience. Successful assistance techniques to develop minority vendors are highly related to minority purchasing activity. Payment of a price differential was not a standard policy. Tables. Graphs. References. – Giunipero, Larry C.; *Sloan Mgmt Review,* Winter 1981, 22(2): pp. 33-42. Avail. ABI 81-08637

Minorities, Business ownership, Suppliers, Purchasing, Programs, Federal legislation, Social responsibility, Planning, Implementations

Dinosaurs Did Not Survive (75)

The corporation, like the dinosaur, is dependent upon its environment. Thus, to avoid problems, corporations must create internal structures and policies to allow survival in their legal, political, and social environment. Surveys show that the business community is held in low esteem despite public interest advertising. Companies need to install adaptive mechanisms in order to achieve ongoing social validation and legitimacy. Developing such an adaptive capability involves: 1. making an environmental analysis of the social/political forces affecting the corporation, 2. identifying the core constituencies of a corporation, 3. identifying the actions of the firm affecting the constituents, and 4. developing a voluntary disclosure code. The corporate organizational structure to implement this self-adaptation process requires: 1. boards of directors' overview, 2. senior management coordination, and 3. the establishment of a corporate social policy department under a top level executive. References. –Langton, James F. and Lewin, Arie Y.; *Enterprise,* Winter 1982, 1(2): pp. 14-19. Avail. ABI 83-05868

Public relations, Corporate image, Corporate responsibility

Directorship: A Year in the Life (76)

The first woman was elected to the board of directors of ONEOK Inc. (Tulsa, Oklahoma), a diversified energy firm, as a result of a decision by Chairman of the Board and past chief executive officer, Charles Ingram. Ingram's aim was to match the new director's knowledge and interests with that of a newly established ONEOK department - corporate responsibility. The reasons many boards do not have more women members may be because the management ranks for women are still thin. Formerly, most women chosen for board membership had wealth and social position. However, this basis for selection seems to be changing, as women can provide the same professionalism as men. Furthermore, women are exposed to a different dimension of life that can be beneficial to boards. Another changing element is that more women are assuming responsibility for both their business and their private lives. –Newson, Douglas Ann; *Directors & Boards,* Summer 1983, 7(4): pp. 37-42. Avail. ABI 83-24463

Boards of directors, Directors, Women, Personal, Profiles, Case studies

Discovering the 65 + Consumer (77)

So far visible marketing efforts directed at consumers 65 and older have been lacking. However, more attention may be paid to this age group as many industries realize they can benefit from a new perspective on this market segment. There are 2 reasons to expect target marketing of goods and services to "seniors": 1. Seniors have dramatically high and increasing purchasing power. 2. Business is being pressured to contribute to a better image for older Americans. Seniors are becoming an increasingly attractive market because: 1. They are a large and fast-growing segment of the population. 2. They have purchasing power beyond their income, having the highest per-capita assets of any age group. 3. Previous assumptions that older people do not identify with their age segment are being challenged. An examination of the senior market and the societal arguments for explicit marketing attention to seniors can help managers appraise the profitability and social responsibility of such effort and increase the effectiveness of a targeting attempt. References. –Gelb, Betsy D.; *Business Horizons,* May/June 1982, 25(3): pp. 42-46. Avail. ABI 82-14227

Target markets (MKT), Older people, Market potential, Market segments, Profiles

Dissident Shareholders Start Shouting at the SEC (78)

While stockholders won more votes than ever for controversial resolutions at annual meetings in 1984, new Securities & Exchange Commission (SEC) rules on proxies have taken some of the strength out of antimanagement positions. The Interfaith Center on Corporate Responsibility is suing in federal court to force the SEC to liberalize its proxy rules. The suit has attracted the attention of other dissident groups and has reactivated the debate over making it easier for shareholder activists to get issues placed on corporate ballots. According to Paul M. Neuhauser of the University of Iowa, current rules undermine the basic concept of corporate democracy. Debate centers on the costs of bringing such activist issues to a vote and the question of whether many such issues are indeed viable questions for such a forum. Both social issues and actual business questions are the subject of current shareholder wars with which the SEC must deal. –Glaberson, William B.; *Business Week,* Dec 10, 1984, (2872)(Industrial/Technology Edition): pp. 80-81. Avail. ABI 85-00137

SEC, SEC proxy rules, Stockholders, Social responsibility

Doing Well While Doing Good (79)

Corporate leaders remain leery of the idea that the private sector should take more responsibility for meeting social needs. If there is to be a fundamental restructuring of the relationship between the public and private sectors, business executives first must be assured that they will not be expected to pay the future costs of social services in the US. Executives continue to fear that, as govenment social programs are cut back, corporations will be pressured to increase their charitable contributions beyond levels they consider responsible or prudent. However, corporate involvement in social concerns is an investment into the society in which the corporation does business. Social programs need not be viewed as charity or lost money; it is in the company's best interest to keep the social climate from deteriorating.

Implementing the new public philosophy may take years of refining and reassessing existing legislation and programs. —Baroody, William J., Jr.; *Cornell Executive*, Spring 1983, 9(2): pp. 28-30. Avail. ABI 83-28404

Private sector, Social services, Social responsibility, Donations, Economic aid, Economic policy

"Don't Rain on My Parade" (80)

Emphasis on self-development, self-improvement, and self-fulfillment are the changing social values that began in the 1960s and flourished in the 1970s. Technology and growth have been replaced by environment, health, and safety as national priorities. People feel that they should be guaranteed social, political, and economic arenas to have everything they want in life. Business institutions have lost public confidence due to widespread cynicism and distrust that business is socially responsible only when no self-interest conflict is involved. Practitioners need to monitor and interpret the role people expect of the institutions if there is to be any hope of reconciliation between business and public. To identify specific entitlements and go further than general public opinion surveys, the Public Relations Society of America's (PRSA) Emerging Issues Committee undertook a study structured to elicit responses not commonly available to public relations professionals. The survey was conducted in conjunction with Opinion Research Corp. (ORC). The questionnaires were sent to approximately 8, 500 members of the PRSA with 4,284 responding, and the ORC audience was based on a national sample of 2,054 individuals in households in the US. Respondents were asked to rank 18 categorized items in order of importance. The survey illustrates differences in what the public wants and what it feels it has now. Tables. —Dardenne, Peg; *Public Relations Jrnl,* Mar 1980, 36(3): pp. 39-40,45-49. Avail. ABI 80-08255

Job attitudes, Employee attitude (PER), Motivation, Social change, Corporate responsibility, Corporate image, Public opinion, Public relations, Surveys

Down Home Reflections of Corning Glass (81)

Corning Glass Works appears to have the same concerns about its image as other major US corporations, but the company spends twice the American industrial average, as percentage of sales, on research and development. The firm has no continuous corporate image advertising program. However since 1952, the Corning Glass Works Foundation, principally funded by Corning Glass Works, has paid more than $37.5 million in grants to communities where Corning employees work and live, to higher education, and especially to innovative programs searching for initial project support. Corning Glass is involved in the restoration of Corning, New York, which began after the flood devastation of 1972. Other projects have included: 1. the Corning Museum of Glass, 2. the 3 Rivers Development Foundation, and 3. the restoration of the Hawkes Building. From 1971 to 1976, the Corning Glass Works Foundation has furnished about $2.9 million of the preservation of its local community. —Thomas, Pat Gray; *Advertising Age,* Jan 24, 1983, 54(4): pp. M-40. Avail. ABI 83-04677

Glass & glassware industry, Corning Glass Works-Corning NY, Case studies, Social responsibility, Community relations, Corporate image

The Dual Career Family: A Modern Dilemma (82)

As the number of dual career families increases, the number of potential problems for all supervisors also increases. Corporate personnel officers, corporate managers, counselors, and placement directors need to deal effectively with the results of this societal shift. In many cases, a woman's career is as important as a man's, both in terms of commitment and contribution to the family's net income. It is in the best interests of society to sustain a cohesive family relationship. Corporations have a moral obligation to strengthen family stability. Management needs to strive for policies that are more open-ended and flexible. The "business as usual" attitude in the corporate community works against a young dual career couple opting to have children. This situation could result in the eventual depletion of the genepool. Corporations should creatively and realistically revamp their human resource and manpower programs to alleviate pressures on dual career couples and to provide people the chance for a rewarding career and home life. —Gurtin, Lee; *Managing,* 1980, (2): pp. 31,35-36. Avail. ABI 81-14880

Dual career couples, Corporate responsibility, Social change, Family, Careers, Marriage, Children, Problems

The Dynamics of Corporate Accountability (83)

There is increasing public scrutiny of the corporate sector, especially of the process used to fashion corporate policies and behavior. Most proposals to modify the corporate process to assure corporate accountability intend to improve the internal governing processes, but some seem to suggest and legitimize concepts such as corporate democracy. Effective corporate accountability, however, cannot be based on a single factor such as the identity of individual directors. It must depend on due regard for the environment where it grows. There can be severe negative consequences from changing a system without understanding all the ramifications of actions. Effective corporate management must take risks to ensure profitability, but many managers today avoid risks to "play it safe." The board structure is not the sole determinant of independence. Governmental regulation in the area of corporate accountability needs to be carefully considered to avoid undue harm to the corporation. —Williams, Harold M.; *Los Angeles Business & Economics,* Fall 1980, 5(4): pp. 29-31. Avail. ABI 80-20729

Corporate, Accountability, Corporate responsibility, Social responsibility

Effect of Sponsor Advocacy on Message Perception and Attitude Change (84)

Trustworthiness is considered a significant factor in advocacy; however, the degree of perceived trust may be a function of the extent to which the advocate is seen to have a vested interest in the outcome of persuasion. To test this hypothesis, a film on the nuclear waste problem was shown to a college class. Before the film began, students' opinions on the danger of nuclear waste were assessed. Subjects were randomly exposed to experimental manipulations including: 1. film sponsorship credited to an anti-nuclear group, 2. sponsorship by a neutral organization, 3. sponsorship by a pro-nuclear organization, and 4. no sponsorship indicated. Findings include: 1. Pro-nuclear sponsorship increased the film's credibility. 2. Any type of sponsorship increased its emotional impact. 3. Regardless of sponsor, the film had a significant effect on opinion change. 4. The direction of sponsor advocacy was not significantly related to opinion change. Charts. Tables. References. –Cook, Robert W. and Joseph, W. Benoy; *Jrnl of the Academy of Marketing Science,* Winter/Spring 1982, 10(1) ,2: pp. 140-153. Avail. ABI 82-15792

Advocacy, Institutional advertising, Social responsibility, Nuclear energy, Public opinion, Credibility

An Empirical Examination of the Relationship Between (85) Corporate Social Responsibility and Profitability

A review of research on the relationship between corporate social responsibility and profitability reveals that most studies have suffered from: 1. lack of methodological rigor, 2. ineffective measurement instruments, or 3. ideological bias. In the present study, a rigorous, forced-choice measure of social responsibility was developed based on Carroll's (1979) 4-component model. Carroll's model, incorporated in 20 sets of statements, measured: 1. economic responsibility to be productive and profitable, 2. legal responsibility to pursue profitability within the limits of law, 3. ethical responsibility to uphold social values, and 4. discretionary or philanthropic responsibility. The instrument was administered to chief executives from a large sample of firms. Data on corporate returns on assets over a one-year and 5-year period were included. Scores for the economic and ethical components were found to exhibit a strong inverse relationship. No significant positive or negative relationship between social responsibility and either short- or long-term profitability was found. Tables. References. – Aupperle, Kenneth E.; Carroll, Archie B.; and Hatfield, John D.; *Academy of Mgmt Jrnl,* Jun 1985, 28(2): pp. 446-463. Avail. ABI 85-24840

Social responsibility, Profitability, Standards, Corporate responsibility, Corporate profits, Studies

Enlightened Self-Interest Pays Off (86)

The concept of social investment was first used in the insurance industry in the late 1960s, when urban unrest and rioting were widespread. Associations in the insurance industry have come to realize that helping society makes business sense because members benefit from a better society and a better public image. Social investments are business propositions which are made on consideration of investment return and risk. A large association can readily mobilize its vast resources and membership to deal with difficult problems facing the public. Smaller associations can serve the community by using their members' resources and expertise to develop public service programs. In order to be responsive to their members' needs, some associations find that public service is a necessity, rather than an option. – Vickery, Hugh B., III; *Association Mgmt,* Oct 1983, 35(10): pp. 69-73. Avail. ABI 83-27968

Associations, Social responsibility, Community relations, Case studies, Association management

The Enterprise's Role in Society　　　　　　　　(87)

One concept of the relationship between the business enterprise and society views the corporation as wholly passive, pulled along by social forces, while the other views the enterprise as a powerful and independent entity, shaping individuals and social forces by manipulating material resources. However, neither concept is valid; the current relationships between enterprise and society are still undergoing change. Neither the character of the enterprise nor that of society is static, and each corporation interfaces with society in different ways. Over time, society has reacted to the enterprise and has amply demonstrated its superiority. The enterprise is a unique entity with distinct social responsibilities and a collective conscience, and its social legitimacy depends on its ability to provide society with its material needs. In relation to social matters, when the enterprise acts with a view to maintaining its long-term viability, its actions tend to reflect the social outlook of the nation in general, thus providing testimony to an interdependent relationship between corporate behavior and social values. Corporations, government, and individuals act together to bring about social change. —Neufeld, Edward P.; *Canadian Banker & ICB Review (Canada),* Apr 1983, 90(2): pp. 56-59. Avail. ABI 83-13824

　Corporate, Social, Roles, Corporate responsibility, Social responsibility, Effects, Corporate image

Entrapment or Opportunity: Structuring a Corporate　　(88) Response to International Codes of Conduct

In the last half of the 1970's there was a widespread movement toward international codes of conduct for multinational corporations (MNCs). Only a few business observers have closely evaluated the political, intergovernmental meaning of these code exercises or positioned themselves for active participation in follow-up implementation. This failure could seriously affect the ability of the MNCs in this decade to represent their positions in a public, political bargaining process between competing interests, where international codes of conduct will provide generalized and important ground rules for corporate behavior. The first step in structuring a positive corporate role toward voluntary MNC codes is an awareness that these codes are a process rather than a product. Corporations need to position and prepare themselves to engage in a public bargaining process with a variety of interest groups. Corporations must address themselves to a much broader range of issues, at an earlier stage, which involves self-evaluation and policy assessment exercise. —Kline, John M.; *Columbia Jrnl of World Business,* Summer 1980, 15(2): pp. 6-13. Avail. ABI 81-03625

　Multinational corporations, Corporate responsibility, Standards, Voluntary, International, UN, OECD, ILO

Escape from the Management Island　　　　　　　　(89)

According to Peter Parker, new head of the British Institute of Management, only a new realism in management will prevent the UK and its industry from being stranded far from international competitiveness. He warns that managers must publicize their own successes to combat the adverse treatment they often receive in the press. The touchstone of the new realism he describes is a fusion between business and social objectives. Leadership is a key element in what he believes to be the optimal approach to management. People in all walks of life are seeking leadership and are willing to respond to it. This attitude implies a return to the traditional values wherein people look for more in leadership than just compliance with regulations or response to economic pressures. Managers must reconcile the imperative of efficiency with that of social responsibility, and leadership must respond to standards set by the working people themselves. –Spooner, Peter; *Chief Executive (UK)*, Feb 1985, pp. 12-14. Avail. ABI 85-14623

Management, Trends, Managers, Roles, Profitability, Chief executive officer, Personal, Profiles, Leadership, UK

The Ethical Premise for Social Activism (90)

Deepening involvement of US churches in corporate-social responsibility issues has created conflict and misunderstanding. Some have questioned whether church ideology is hostile to business. The Nestle boycott is illustrative of the problems that can arise between the church and business communities. The more negative or coercive the actions taken by a church, the more disciplined and accountable a church must be. A church must be especially clearheaded when it undertakes pressure tactics. While there are times when the relations of church and business must be adversarial, it should be remembered that the people confronted as adversaries are not enemies. –Wogaman, J. Philip; *Business & Society Review,* Summer 1985, (54): pp. 30-36. Avail. ABI 85-33835

Religious organizations, Corporate responsibility, Social responsibility, Activists, Ethics

Ethics in Business: Problem Identification and Potential (91) Solutions

Today's public demands that businesses become more ethically and socially responsible. Corporations must guide their employees in ethical decisions. Three ways of doing this are: 1. Be committed to using a corporate code of ethics. 2. Set personal examples in management. 3. Educate the employees as to ethical theory. The business community must also make the public aware of their ethical codes of conduct. They can do this through favorable media coverage and, again, through education. References. –Hayes, Thomas J.; *Hospital Materiel Mgmt Qtrly,* May 1983, 4(4): pp. 35-42. Avail. ABI 83-13472

Ethics, Social responsibility, Problems, Conflicts, Roles

Ethics: MIS/DP's New Challenge (92)

Persons dealing with data and information face a dilemma when it comes to the rights and responsibilities of individuals. According to a panel of professionals from civil-rights, data processing (DP), and information management communities, ethics is knowing right from wrong or a personal code. One of the foremost issues of ethical behavior is privacy of records, especially medical records, according to panel members. According to Bruce Spiro of Defense Communications Agency, many major organizations do not recognize the privacy problem. The Data Processing Management Association and Association for Computing Machinery have formal standards in such areas as competence and professionalism. Areas where ethics are a major concern include vendor relationships and copying of

(93) CORPORATE SOCIAL RESPONSIBILITY

software. —Whieldon, David; *Computer Decisions,* Oct 1984, 16(13): pp. 92-110. Avail. ABI 85-00023

Corporate responsibility, Data processing, Information management, MIS (MAN), Management, Ethics, Codes, Manypeople

European Managers' Views on Social Responsibility (93)

The social responsibility of businesses is becoming a part of the corporate framework for many of the large US corporations. However, chief executive officers have issued relatively infrequent public statements on the issue. During 1979 and 1980, interviews were conducted with top managers of several large West German and Italian corporations to determine their views on the social responsibility of business. The ideas of these European executives on social responsibility were soon found not to be imitative of US notions, although their attitudes and opinions were similar in substance and in terminology. The issues brought up by these European managers included: 1. employment, especially the prevention of layoffs, 2. the quality of output, 3. safety concerns, of the product and the work environment, 4. the quality of the work environment, 5. environmental concerns, and 6. the underdeveloped nations of the world. The tentative conclusions from this study include: 1. Most European managers see a close connection between product quality and the quality of workers' environment. 2. Most European managers see their firms as a part of an elaborate network of interdependence, connecting the community, the nation, the Common Market, and the nations of the world. 3. Most European managers demonstrate an attitude of "mixed capitalism" in setting their work standards. References. —Wilson, Erika G.; *Business Forum,* Winter 1982, 7(1): pp. 26-28. Avail. ABI 82-09524

Social responsibility, Europe, Managers, Executives, Opinions, Attitudes

The Evaluative Relevance of Social Data (94)

Managers selected from 9 large firms in diverse industries were used to determine factors which influence managers' perceptions of the relevance of social data to business activity. Social information is defined as that which affects accountability relationships that require expectation, communication, and obligation. The objective of social information is to establish and to maintain accountability relationships between business corporations and various segments of society. Data obtained from the questionnaire indicate that both the ability of a message source to impose sanctions against a firm and the firm's "financial health" influence perceptions. An association exists between managers' attitudes about the social role of business and perceptions of the relevance of social messages to business activity. Attitudes are associated more strongly with perceptions for some individuals than for others. Charts. Tables. Appendix. References. —Williams, Paul F.; *Accounting Review,* Jan 1980, 55(1): pp. 62-77. Avail. ABI 80-03995

Social accounting, Social responsibility, Accountability, Social, Information, Attitudes, Perceptions, Management, Evaluation, Variance analysis, Cluster analysis, Correlation analysis, Studies

38

Excellence in Management Awards: Profile of a Winner (95)

As a means of recognizing that corporate leaders must get involved in societal and governmental activities, the Excellence in Management Award was established 5 years ago by Industry Week. The award is given to chief executive officers (CEO) for their special efforts: 1. in getting involved in defending the free enterprise system, 2. in reaching new levels of community service, 3. in working to improve relations between government and business, and 4. in breaking new ground in management/employee relationships. The 1981 recipients are: 1. Thomas C. Graham, CEO of Jones & Laughlin Steel Corporation, for implementing and maintaining sound labor-management relations which resulted in a significant improvement in productivity and profits, 2. E. Mandell de Windt, CEO of Eaton Corporation, for reflecting a sense of corporate responsibility to the community by providing to Cleveland, Ohio, a citizen leadership that improved the management of the city, 3. Raymond Shamie, president of Metal Bellows Corporation for the establishment, nationwide, of multi-faceted employee education programs for conveying knowledge of the free enterprise system's economics, and 4. Reginald H. Jones, CEO of General Electric Company, for improving understanding in the relationship of government and business by establishing Business Roundtable, a lobby of 200 CEOs who personally involve themselves in interfacing with the government on matters that affect corporate affairs. −Anonymous; *Industry Week,* Oct 19, 1981, 211(2): pp. 51-63. Avail. ABI 81-25383

Chief executive officer, Personal, Profiles, Manypeople, Manycompanies, Eaton-Cleveland, General Electric-Fairfield Conn

Excellence in Management Awards: Dr. Edwin A. Gee (96)

International Paper Co. (IP) has developed an 11-part public interest advertising series called "The Power of the Printed Word." It addresses the reading and writing deficiencies of Americans and is designed to reach 50 million young people. The company has spent some $5 million on the campaign, and has received some 8 million requests for reprints, along with critical acclaim. Edwin A. Gee, chairman and chief executive of IP, is very proud of the program. Gee has been involved in public activities since the early 1970s and has steadily increased his community involvement. He has also helped plan the company's new outdoor plaza, a facility which benefits both employees and the community. Gee is very concerned about safety at his company, and injuries have been greatly reduced since he has been at IP. Gee also feels corporations should increase their charitable donations. − Anonymous; *Industry Week,* Oct 18, 1982, 215(2): pp. 42-43. Avail. ABI 82-27391

International Paper-New York, Case studies, Chief executive officer, Personal, Profiles, Corporate responsibility, Social responsibility

Fading Images at Eastman Kodak (97)

Eastman Kodak (Rochester, New York) continues to dominate the community as an employer and a major political influence. Almost 20% of the jobs in Rochester come directly from Kodak, while many others are indirectly dependent on the camera and film producer. Kodak's image as an employer has improved a great deal over the last 20 years, but the company has faced other problems in terms of international competition and new products that have not done as well as expected. Kodak is completely nonunion, and has stayed that way because of competitive pay and benefits and extraordinary job security. The Kodak workforce has a good record in terms of productivity, turnover and absenteeism. However, Kodak's image in the community fell some in 1983 with personnel layoffs, leading the community to believe that the company was no longer the pioneer it once was. Kodak is now generally viewed as a conservative, bureaucratic company that may not be able to attract the top-level talent it needs to reposition itself. –Paul, Karen; *Business & Society Review,* Winter 1984, (48): pp. 54-59. Avail. ABI 84-08189

Eastman Kodak-Rochester NY, Social responsibility, Personnel policies, Corporate image, Case studies

"Fair" Support by Employees Spurs Hospital UW Drive (98)

The development office of the Portland (Oregon) Adventist Medical Center undertook the task of coordinating the United Way (UW) campaign for hospital employees. The effort started before the actual campaign in a meeting with the director of the UW and the formation of a grass-roots committee of 9 hospital employees. The campaign started with an "agency fair" in which various organizations receiving UW funds set up booths at the hospital to explain to employees what they did and how contributions were being used. UW public relations personnel helped to obtain media coverage for the fair, which became the focal point of the entire campaign. Other employee-oriented activities and speakers encouraged employee involvement by specifying community conditions that needed UW assistance, and community leaders wrote to employees urging contributions. Solicitors visited agencies receiving UW support, and hospital administrators demonstrated total commitment to the UW campaign, thus setting a good example. –Hallock, Duane D.; *Fund Raising Mgmt,* Sep 1983, 14(7): pp. 22-25. Avail. ABI 83-24412

Employee, Donations, Charitable foundations, Fund raising, Campaigns, Case studies, Social responsibility

Forging a Public Affairs Apparatus for Business (99)

Rafael D. Pagan, chairman of Pagan International (Pi), a new public affairs and issue management firm located in Washington, DC, suggests that it has been difficult to oppose codes regulating multinationals because of the accident at Union Carbide India Ltd.'s (Bhopal, India) pesticide plant. It is time for companies to look beyond their own spheres of influence to broader public policy issues. Pi has been formed around a nucleus of executives who devised and implemented the strategy that helped end the boycott of Nestle products related to marketing problems with that company's infant formula. The staff includes specialists with varied backgrounds in such areas as science and health, media relations, and political strategies. The company has responded to industry's discovery of the need for a public affairs apparatus by working with action organizations and offering strategic advice on a continual basis or per occasion. —Block, Paula M.; Bradford, Hazel; and Pilarski, Laura; *Chemical Week,* Jun 19, 1985, 136(25): pp. 42,44. Avail. ABI 85-22743

Public policy, Public relations, Boycotts, Corporate responsibility

The Four Faces of Social Responsibility (100)

Social responsibility is unavoidably a matter of degree and interpretation. Forces outside of the business can find a product socially unacceptable, even when the company has undertaken an extensive impact analysis. A precise evaluation of what is socially responsible is difficult to establish. Peter Drucker has presented a useful way to distinguish between behaviors in organizations. The first involves what an organization does to society, while the other has to do with what an organization can do for society. This suggests that organizations can be evaluated on various combinations of legality and responsibility that can characterize its performance. These combinations are the 4 faces of social responsibility: 1. illegal/irresponsible, 2. illegal/responsible, 3. irresponsible/legal, and 4. legal/responsible. Each is subject to criticism. There are 3 fundamental principles which an organization should consider in choosing a strategy for social responsibility: 1. knowingly doing no harm, 2. organizational accountability, and 3. double standard. Table. References. —Dalton, Dan R. and Cosier, Richard A.; *Business Horizons,* May/June 1982, 25(3): pp. 19-27. Avail. ABI 82-14224

Corporate responsibility, Social responsibility, Legal, Illegal, Organizational behavior, Strategy

Free Enterprise in a Free Society (101)

The future of the free enterprise system will be shaped by the public's perception of whether corporations are accountable to rational, objective decision makers acting according to publicly acceptable norms. Two traditional answers concerning accountability apply to: 1. the discipline of the marketplace and its destruction of those who irrationally wield corporate power, and 2. the board of directors acting as the watchdog of management power. Neither of these arguments is supported by the facts. More effective and stronger boards can be formed by increasing outside representation, re-examining the role of the corporate chief executive officer (CEO) as chairperson, and considering responsibilities and the best approach to tasks; independent committees can also play a role. Top management must set the moral tone and must personally see that the staff stays on course. The board must consider all social aspects of its actions and devote time, commitment, and talent if the free enterprise system is not to be eroded. References. — Williams, Harold M.; *California Mgmt Review,* Winter 1980, 23(2): pp. 29-34. Avail. ABI 81-04663

Corporate, Accountability, Boards of directors, Roles, Corporate responsibility, Corporate management

Free Market vs. Social Responsibility: Decision Time at (102) the CED

The Committee for Economic Development (CED), a group of 200 top-level business executives who project business concerns and try to find solutions to them, changed its stand on the issue of corporate social responsibility from

1971 to 1979. In 1971, its policy statement advocated that business take a broader human view of its rule. CED favored a business-government relationship that would jointly work to solve pressing social problems. In 1979, as economic problems became more critical, the CED's view changed and favored free market solutions, emphasized economic rather than social values, and opposed government regulation as a solution to social problems. The 1971 policy statement was written during a period of great social turbulence when business was under attack on many fronts. The 1979 statement may represent mainly a change in personnel rather than in philosophy, as only 36.7% of the '71 members on the Research and Policy Committee remained on the '79 committee. However, business cannot expect the free market system approach to single-handedly solve social and economic problems. Rather, business must continue to work through the political process and formulate public policy. References. —Frederick, William C.; *California Mgmt Review,* Spring 1981, 23(3): pp. 20-28. Avail. ABI 81-19649

Social responsibility, Corporate responsibility, Public policy, Economic development, Committees, Market economies, Changes

The FTC's Advertising Substantiation Program (103)

The Federal Trade Commission's (FTC) advertising substantiation program is a regulatory mechanism which impacts many marketers' decision making. The original idea to require substantiation of advertising claims resulted from the activities of the Center for the Study of Responsive Law which asked that different firms document their advertising claims based on unspecified tests or clinical studies. One of the most far reaching notions of substantiation was the FTC's indication that advertisers should be obligated to substantiate advertising claims before they are made. The Commission's opinion was that it is unfair and illegal to advertise an affirmative claim for a product without having "a reasonable basis" for making such a claim. This new concept was of major importance to the advertising industry because it reversed the position that the regulatory agency was required to prove that claims made in advertising were deceptive or unfair.Documentation necessary to substantiate claims ranging from safety to beautification include: 1. competent scientific tests, 2. independent laboratory tests, 3. competent and reliable scientific tests or the opinion of experts, and 4. competent scientific engineering data. Firms must deal with the regulatory requirement. Any strategy should include a system for disseminating information pertinent to the program and its requirements throughout the organization and the use of consumer surveys for gathering data. Tables. References. —Cohen, Dorothy; *Jrnl of Marketing,* Winter 1980, 44(1): pp. 26-35. Avail. ABI 80-06877

FTC, Advertisements, Advertising, Regulations, Advertising restrictions, Claims, Corporate responsibility, Truth in advertising, Puffery, False advertising, Penalties, Supreme Court decisions-US

A Gamble Insurers Can't Afford (104)

The high cost to the insurance industry of compulsive gambling is in the areas of personal property floaters, 3-D policies, and surety contracts. The frauds perpetrated on the industry are the result of the sociopathology of compulsive gambling. The compulsive gambler causes problems for self and family in areas ranging from theft to being beaten by loan sharks. The compulsive gambler is involved in alcoholism, in many cases, which results in a shorter longevity because of suicide or the consequences of high blood pressure, stroke, and heart disease. Bankruptcy, criminal arrest, or family exclusion are the only things that can attempt to limit a compulsive gambler's habit. Premium-paying insureds and the insurance industry help pay for the losses on personal property floaters, 3-D policies, and surety contracts caused by the compulsive gambler. The signs that can help identify a possible compulsive gambler are: 1. loan defaults, 2. petty cash manipulations, 3. collectors coming to a gambler's place of business, 4. criminal charges, and 5. civil collection suits. When an employer becomes knowledgeable about the gambler's propensities, there are referrals available to assist the gambler in coping with his/her condition. An awareness program and therapy approaches to the problem can help protect a company and its employees against victimization by the compulsive gambler. The insurance industry should consider a program for compulsive gamblers which would be similar to its commendable program on alcoholism. –Lewis, Albert B.; *National Underwriter (Property/Casualty),* Jun 18, 1982, 86(25): pp. 23-24. Avail. ABI 82-16968

Insurance industry, Gambling, Costs, Insurance coverage, Fraud, Social responsibility

General Foods Roasted Over Coffee Buying Policy (105)

General Foods, the 39th-largest industrial corporation in the US, has generally had a good reputation on social responsibility issues. However, several human rights organizations are taking General Foods to task over its purchase of coffee from El Salvador and Guatemala, whose governments collect half of the revenue from coffee sales. Both governments are known for violations of human rights. El Salvador nationalized the marketing of coffee in 1980, and a government agency, INCAFE, became the sole authorized exporter of Salvadoran coffee. By regulating prices, INCAFE has effectively put most small growers out of business. Guatemala obtains its cut of coffee revenue through the highest coffee export tax in Central America. When faced with a stockholder petition in 1983, a General Foods executive stated that it was not the place of a business corporation to make foreign policy decisions, such as cessation of trade with countries violating human rights. –Fiske, Mary Ann; *Business & Society Review,* Spring 1984, (49): pp. 19-21. Avail. ABI 84-18804

General Foods-White Plains NY, Social responsibility, Coffee, Case studies, Food processing industry

Giving and Getting (106)

Efforts to provide more jobs and better education and housing continue to fail because the vast resources of the private sector are not directed at meeting these needs. A fundamental change is required so that the private sector and government will work together. Much has been said about how the private sector should respond to the decreased federal role under the Reagan Administration. The only solution is a joint response by public and private sectors that includes strong profit-driven investment by the private sector. For more than 10 years, Control Data Corp. has been cooperating with many other public and private organizations in successful programs that pertain to major unmet social needs as profitable business opportunities. These social programs include: 1. inner-city plants, 2. computer-based education, 3. Fair Break centers to teach the disadvantaged how to find and keep jobs, 4. Outreach programs to help disadvantaged youths get started in careers, and 5. urban revitalization. –Norris, William C.; *Cornell Executive,* Spring 1983, 9(2): pp. 32-35. Avail. ABI 83-28406

Private sector, Social responsibility, Donations, Corporate responsibility, Computer based, Education, Small business, Venture capital, Urban development, Tax incentives, Control Data-Minneapolis, Case studies

Good Works and Good Business (107)

Early in this century, 2 radically innovative US businessmen initiated major community reforms in their own distinctive styles. Andrew Carnegie, who believed in the social responsibilty of wealth and philanthropy in its purest form, financed the free public library. Julius Rosenwald of Sears, Roebuck and Co., who believed in the social responsibility of business, fathered the county farm agent system and adopted the 4-H Clubs. A third philosophy is proposed by William C. Norris of Control Data Corp. He perceives that the solutions to social problems and satisfaction of social needs are opportunities for profitable business. He is considered an entrepreneur and represents the most needed and effective approach to corporate responsibility today. Business must transform the social needs created by shifts in technology and demography into opportunities to create new capital. The first responsibility of business is to create the capital to finance tomorrow's jobs. –Drucker, Peter F.; *Across the Board,* Oct 1984, 21(10): pp. 12-15,64. Avail. ABI 84-33739

Corporate responsibility, Social responsibility, Labor force, Capital investments

Goodyear Toughs It Out (108)

Goodyear Tire & Rubber Co. (Akron, Ohio), with an investment of $100 million that accounts for almost 2,500 jobs, is one of the largest US-based employers in South Africa. Goodyear's top management are all against apartheid, but they are unanimous in their agreement that Goodyear should not pull out of the country. Robert E. Mercer, Goodyear's chairman, says disinvestment would only hurt blacks and stiffen the government's determination not to amend racist laws. Company officials point out that, long before any pressures were applied, Goodyear was doing what it could to counter apartheid because it thought it was the right thing to do. Goodyear also does not want to leave the country because profits have always been high, and because it could set a precedent by giving into pressure. Goodyear operates in 29 foreign countries, and with overseas operations contributing 33% of its $10.2 billion in revenues in 1984, the company does not want to send a message to other countries that Goodyear "folds its tents" under pressure. Goodyear has been manufacturing in South Africa since 1947. Tables. –Kessler, Felix; *Fortune,* Sep 30, 1985, 112(7): pp. 24-26. Avail. ABI 85-32799

Goodyear Tire & Rubber-Akron Ohio, Case studies, Foreign investment, South Africa, Foreign subsidiaries, Rubber industry, Multinational corporations, Social responsibility

Governing the Large Corporation: More Arguments for   (109)
Public Directors

Under the assumption that more socially desirable corporations would result, placing public directors on the boards of major corporations has been proposed. Although they would be unrelated to their impact on actual corporate decisions, 3 specific benefits would be provided by public directors. Simply because corporate social responsibility is best viewed as a process, process-altering responses are valuable for their own sake, regardless of their assumed impact on outcomes. Furthermore, the legitimacy of conscious corporate involvement in social decision making would be enhanced if the public directors were selected by government. By providing some formal representation for corporate constituents currently without such representation, the public director proposals are a means of partially accommodating democratic principles in the corporate governing process. References. —Jones, Thomas M. and Goldberg, Leonard D.; *Academy of Mgmt Review,* Oct 1982, 7(4): pp. 603-611. Avail. ABI 82-25814

Public, Directors, Social responsibility, Decision making, Public policy, Public interest

Great Expectations   (110)

Expectations that corporations can fill the gap brought about by President Reagan's cuts in social-services spending are unrealistic. There is no way, especially in these times of plunging corporate profits, that the $3 billion contributed by corporations in 1981 could offset any significant part of the $30 billion cut from the federal social-services budget. Corporations can, however, make a substantial difference by contributing time, talent, and materials. Unfortunately, many companies capable of making major social contributions have not done so. Much of the effort has come from those companies that have long been leaders in corporate-responsibility activities. However, corporations have neither the responsibility nor the capability to manage or fund any significant part of the current US social-service delivery system. Government must continue to assume the major part of the responsibility for providing these services. —Colodzin, Robert S.; *Cornell Executive,* Spring 1983, 9(2): pp. 31-32. Avail. ABI 83-28405

Private sector, Social responsibility, Corporate responsibility, Social services, Social policy

Great Places to Work: Levi Strauss & Co.   (111)

Levi Strauss & Co. (San Francisco, California), the world's largest clothing manufacturer, employs 43,000 people worldwide, 30,000 in the US. In 1980, the firm's sales were close to $3 billion. Although Levi Strauss & Co. is now a publicly owned company, direct descendents of Strauss, who founded the company in 1850, still own 47% of all the stock. Stock awards are given to employees after a certain number of years of service, and there are also a stock investment and savings plan, a profit-sharing plan, and a pension plan. In 1982, the company moved to a new headquarters complex. The building features an exercise facility and a Quiet Room. Miniplazas on each floor of the building are furnished with sofas, tables, chairs, and kitchenettes. Levi's has also been extremely generous in its support of the social and cultural needs of the communities where its facilities are located. —Levering, Robert; Moskowitz, Milton; and Katz, Michael; *New Mgmt,* 1984, 2(1): pp. 10-11. Avail. ABI 84-25281

Levi Strauss-San Francisco, Clothing industry, Case studies, Social responsibility, Affirmative action

Handling the Realities of Business: A Perspective of the European Societal Strategy Project (112)

The success and survival of business enterprises have been challenged both by recessionary economic conditions and by public pressure for business to be socially, politically, and environmentally accountable. To combat these challenges, many businesses have either developed media campaigns in support of free enterprise or have instituted social responsibility programs. However, a concerted effort is required for business to constructively handle public pressure. Such an effort, undertaken by academics and industrialists from 9 European nations, is described. The Societal Strategy Project initially identified social needs and demands for the role of business, then determined the freedom of action which business had within these social constraints. Several possible dimensions of business response to public pressure were identified, including the use of: 1. information and planning systems, 2. management development programs, and 3. rewards systems to promote corporate responsibility. References. —Edwards, John P. and Romano, David J.; *Futures (UK),* Aug 1983, 15(4): pp. 264-271. Avail. ABI 83-25824

Europe, Social issues, Corporate, Strategy, Social responsibility

Has Social Responsibility Cleaned Up the Corporate Image? (113)

The public has become increasingly mindful of corporate wrongdoings but pays little attention when business behaves in a socially responsible manner. Despite growing evidence of social responsibility through increased philanthropy, environmental concern, and consumer and public affairs efforts, business is perceived more negatively than it was 15 years ago. Failure to improve corporate image through enhanced social responsibility can be traced to misdirected efforts and ineffective marketing. Brief case studies illustrate successful and unsuccessful efforts at improving corporate image through socially responsible behavior. These cases reveal some guidelines for developing social responsibility programs, including: 1. Focus on problems of high concern to the public. 2. Concentrate efforts in high-impact, high-visibility areas. 3. Exploit marketing skills to promote programs and their results. 4. Avoid excessive participation in areas perceived by the public to reflect corporate self-interest. —Hathaway, James W.; *Business & Society Review,* Fall 1984, (51): pp. 56-59. Avail. ABI 84-37387

Social responsibility, Corporate image, Marketing, Communications, Public relations

Here Comes the Era of the Blended Agenda (114)

In the early 1980s, changes in US social values led to the shaping of a new public policy climate that calls for a pragmatic blending of the social and economic agendas of earlier decades. This blending consists of a renewed commitment to the economic growth typical of the 1950s, combined with an ongoing attention to social concerns typical of the 1960s. The 4 basic characteristics of this new public policy climate are: 1. a tempered American optimism, 2. an emphasis on cost-effectiveness, 3. a renewed emphasis on quality and excellence, and 4. a focus on local government and community concern. Within this new climate, business can gain restored national confidence by a successful response to the dual challenge of meeting economic leadership and social responsibility. The public relations professional should: 1. work with corporate leadership to establish priorities, 2. identify the public policy initiatives compatible to individual corporate objectives, and 3. help to implement these objectives. —Blatherwick, Gerald D.; *Public Relations Qtrly,* Fall 1984, 29(3): pp. 5-9. Avail. ABI 85-06436

Public policy, Changes, Characteristics, Social change, Public relations, Implications, Social responsibility

High Noon for Social Proxy Activists (115)

The Securities & Exchange Commission (SEC) has issued 3 proposals that would fundamentally change the present shareholder resolution process. One would make it more difficult to file such resolutions, and the other 2 would change the rules for filing. Public interest groups and shareholders alike oppose the changes. Shareholders started bringing their social concerns to stockholder meetings in the late 1960s and early 1970s. The number of social-oriented resolutions has increased from less than 6 in 1972 to more than 200 in 1982. SEC Proposal 2 would allow each company to develop its own rules for shareholder access to proxy statements, and Proposal 3 would eliminate all but 2 of the SEC's present 13 grounds for excluding proposals from the proxy statement. The historic trend of the last 40 years, and especially of the last 10, has been toward active shareholder involvement in the confrontation of social issues by corporate management. Shareholder activists believe that their presence has improved both business and society during those years. Most business leaders, however, would like to see them back off. —Lydenberg, Steven; *Business & Society Review,* Summer 1983, (46): pp. 62-66. Avail. ABI 83-22625

SEC proxy rules, Stockholders, Proposals, Participation, Shareholder meetings, Social responsibility

How Do State Commissioners Assess the Corporate (116) Social Performance of Major Insurers?

Corporate social performance has become a major issue in the US. The impact of this interest has been felt in the private insurance industry, where the burden of social responsibility must be borne largely by the leading firms. As interest in social corporate performance increases, the failure of a major insurer to measure up to competition in these terms may result in a market performance decline and adverse relations with regulators. An investigation was conducted to determine how commissioners make assessments of corporate social performance. The results indicated that commissioners rely most heavily on 3 clusters of criteria: 1. market-conduct activity, 2. company reputation and top management philosophy, and 3. financial solvency. Results also showed that commissioners as a group rely much more on the criticism or praise they receive from their peers than on the criticism or praise from federal agencies and officials, the public media, or organized interest groups. Commissioners place the least reliance on the public relations activities of the insurers. Tables. —Miles, Robert H.; *Best's Review (Prop/Casualty),* Nov 1981, 82(7): pp. 32-36,122-127. Avail. ABI 82-00184

Insurers, Insurance companies, Social, Performance, Evaluation, Insurance commissioners, Criteria, Chief executive officer, Surveys, Insurance industry, Studies

How Information Flows Upstream at a Minneapolis Bank   (117)

Four years ago, Northwestern National Bank (Minneapolis, Minnesota), headed by new chief executive officer John Morrison, decided that the bank needed to expand its idea of corporate responsibility while focusing on specific issues. The approach Morrison had in mind would: 1. anticipate social issues, not react to them, 2. focus on the bank's various stakeholders and their competing claims, 3. aim toward policy development, and 4. involve employees from all levels of the bank. A Social Policy Task Force program was formed to involve employees with top management in the formulation of policy on social issues affecting the bank. Since the first task force in 1978, the topics addressed include: 1. the bank's role in revitalizing inner-city neighborhoods, 2. the changing relationship between work and the family, and 3. improving the effectiveness of communication among different levels of employees and between geographic locations. The task force has been very successful at Northwestern, and it can work for other companies who follow some important guidelines. —Wallace, Douglas and Dudrow, Janet; *New Mgmt,* Spring 1983, 1): pp. 26-29. Avail. ABI 83-26710

Northwest Bancorp-Minneapolis, Banking industry, Case studies, Information management, Communication, Social policy

How Information Flows Upstream   (118)

Four years ago, the management of Northwestern National Bank of Minneapolis (now Norwest Bank Minneapolis, NA) charted a new course in its exploration of corporate responsibility issues; it now uses a sophisticated process of long-range formulation and upward communication that really works for top management. Development of the new approach had several objectives: 1. Anticipate social issues, rather than react to them. 2. Focus on the bank's various stakeholders and their competing claims. 3. Aim toward policy development. 4. Involve all levels of bank employees. A Social Policy Task Force was developed to involve employees in formulating policy on social issues affecting the bank. Among the issues addressed were the role of the bank in revitalizing older neighborhoods, individual rights in the corporation, and support for working families. To begin a task-force program on social policy, a company must follow several steps, including obtaining an appropriate topic, and good staff support. The work of the task force must be well planned and the program's goal kept in mind. —Wallace, Douglas and Dudrow, Janet; *Public Relations Jrnl,* Feb 1984, 40(2): pp. 28-31. Avail. ABI 84-12052

Northwest Bancorp-Minneapolis, Case studies, Banking industry, Social policy, Social responsibility

How to Develop a Contingency Plan (119)

Disaster planning should be part of the operation of every data processing (DP) facility. Corporate responsibility for a disaster plan and its effectiveness rests with senior management as part of its overall responsibility for the success or failure of the whole organization. Direct responsibility for the contingency plan rests with the data center operations manager because of his or her involvement with every day operations. If a plan does not exist or the DP manager feels uncomfortable with an existing plan, it is his or her duty to make senior management aware of the need. If needed, the DP manager should hire consultants or external auditors to help present the case to senior management. Although the actual contingency plan will vary from organization to organization, every contingency plan has certain common characteristics: 1. The plan must be properly documented and outline the steps to be followed in the event of a disaster. 2. The plan must be comprehensive enough to bring the stricken data center back into production as rapidly as possible and flexible enough to accommodate changes. 3. Equipment vendor representatives should be listed, and alternate personnel should be taught emergency procedures. Once completed, the plan should be duplicated several times and copies collected into a contingency plan packet. —Murray, John P.; *Information & Records Mgmt,* Jun 1980, 14(6): pp. 38-42. Avail. ABI 80-13957

Data processing, Back up systems, Planning, Contingent, Plans, Guidelines

How to Get Operating Managers to Manage Public (120) Affairs in Foreign Subsidiaries

The management of public affairs in a multinational company (MNC) is a difficult task. It is especially difficult for operating managers, who are facing pressures to produce in traditional business areas, to develop the awareness, sensitivity, and skills necessary for the effective management of relations with groups in the environment. These managers are the ones who make decisions which affect the environment, so it is necessary that they recognize their responsibilities for fostering good relations with groups important to the success of the firm. Management must adopt a conscious policy to institutionalize the public affairs approach into the basic tasks of the operating position. Specific tools and techniques should be developed that will convince the operating manager of the importance of this area and that will encourage him to incorporate these skills into his management repertoire. —Blake, David H.; *Columbia Jrnl of World Business,* Spring 1981, 16(1): pp. 61-67. Avail. ABI 81-20666

Multinational corporations, Host country, Public relations, Foreign subsidiaries, Social policy, Environment, Strategy, Social responsibility

Ideologies and Management Training (121)

Three surveys of ideological preferences were taken among 3 different groups: 1. 1,800 readers of the Harvard Business Review, 2. 2,600 college business students, and 3. a random sample of members of the American Society for Training and Development. The results showed that all 3 groups preferred the traditional and individualistic Ideology One, which advocates the work ethic, self-reliance, individualism, pride in self, self-achievement, free competition, and as little government interference as possible. However, the results also showed that all 3 groups expect or are resigned to the increasing influence of the communication Ideology Two and its dominance by 1985. Ideology Two advocates the necessity of increased central government planning and control, social responsibility for all individuals within society, cooperation as opposed to competition within society, and the good of the community as a whole. Chart. Graphs. –Owens, James; *Training & Development Jrnl,* Mar 1980, 34(3): pp. 66-70. Avail. ABI 80-06455

Management training, Implications, Social change, Values, Surveys, Social responsibility, Self interest

The Implicit Assumptions of Television Research: An   (122) Analysis of the 1982 NIMH Report on Television and Behavior

The report from the National Institute of Mental Health (NIMH) on Television and Behavior stresses that current entertainment programs have generally negative social effects and that other kinds of programming have been identified by researchers that have more positive effects socially. The primary negative claims in the report are that violence on TV causes aggression and that the altered world presented on TV can cause viewers who watch more than the average to see the world as more hostile and frightening than it really is. The NIMH report offers a realistic summary of present knowledge about TV, its effects, and its potential. Most current television research depends heavily on an individual rather than an institutional level of analysis. The model of research used focuses little attention on where possible leverage lies for changes in programming. Reservations about the report also come from an overblown sense of the confidence that can be placed in many past findings. This report, as with most all TV research, has no mechanism for proceeding from the evidence presented to changes in television practice. Charts. Graphs. References. – Cook, Thomas D.; Kendzierski, Deborah A.; and Thomas, Stephen V.; *Public Opinion Qtrly,* Summer 1983, 47(2): pp. 161-201. Avail. ABI 83-18918

Television broadcasting, Programs, Research, Reports, Social responsibility, Children, Violence, Impacts, Statistical analysis

The Importance of Being Important   (123)

According to the British Government, there is a shortage of very important persons (VIPs) in the UK. All chief executives qualify for commercially important person status, but few are prepared to make the extra effort to become VIPs. In the UK, the VIP concept is a remnant of the Victorian era that industry leaders are expected to be philanthropists, patrons of the arts, and law abiding citizens. Attaining the honor of VIP requires time, goodwill and money. VIPs tend to associate with other VIPs at home and abroad. Getting to know the right people is important but so is cultivating the media. Executives who can communicate with the public help their companies and the industry. In becoming a VIP, it is ultimately the individual who creates that image, and his belief in his own worth helps him maintain that status gracefully. —Underwood, Lynn; *Chief Executive (UK),* Dec 1981, pp. 21-23. Avail. ABI 82-06416

UK, Chief executive officer, Corporate officers, Public relations, Social responsibility

Improving Ethical Awareness Through the Business and Society Course (124)

Many business schools offer courses which review the social responsibility of the corporate sector. The objective of these courses is to promote ethical awareness in the business leaders of the future. A study was conducted to determine whether these business courses affect student values. Corporations and society were viewed as social systems mutually dependent upon one another. Certain ethical issues, i.e., business-government relations, product and occupational safety, labor relations, socio-economic and environmental accounting, equal employment and consumerism, were considered in depth. The Defining Issues Test was used to assess change in moral reasoning resulting from completion of the ethics course. Results of the study indicate that the level of moral reasoning is significantly increased in students who take the Business and Society course. The change is significant in both men and women. In conclusion, the moral development of some college students is significantly accelerated through completing a Business and Society course. Tables. References. —Boyd, David P.; *Business & Society,* Winter 1981/Spring 1982, 20(2) /v21n1: pp. 27-31. Avail. ABI 82-26942

Ethics, Students, Studies, Sampling, Curricula

In Minnesota, Business is Part of the Solution (125)

In response to their concern that business was often hindering public/private sector relationships, 11 executives from major corporations in the Minneapolis-St. Paul (Minnesota) area have formed the Minnesota Business Partnership (MBP) with the goal of increasing corporate responsibility and participation in civic affairs. The executives and their staffs analyze and act on such issues as jobs, energy, and taxes. The MBP has become a credible group in the state government's estimation. The MBP is organized around a base of the more powerful corporations' representatives, and is designed to be a small and manageable force able to have maximum clout. The MBP has taken steps to recognize the reality that the large and powerful businesses have an obligation not only to provide goods and services, but, because of their de facto influence upon their communities, to act as a good citizen of those communities. The MBP leaders hope the concept will extend into other states and regions. Tables. Appendix. —Bemis, Judson and Cairns, John A.; *Harvard Business Review,* Jul/Aug 1981, 59(4): pp. 85-93. Avail. ABI 81-18914

Minnesota, Public policy, Corporate responsibility, Manycompanies, Chief executive officer, State government

In Search of a Quick Fix (126)

James O'Toole, the director of the Twenty-Year Forecast Project of the University of Southern California's Graduate School of Business, does not believe that it is possible to run an organization on a set of rules and laws. There are certain characteristics that are practically guaranteed to get a company into trouble, including: 1. diversifying away from areas of established expertise, 2. losing sight of the basics of their business, 3. becoming complacent and failing to learn, and 4. thinking short term. There are certain underlying principles that the great corporations have in common: 1. The companies recognize they have responsibilities to consumers, employees, suppliers, and dealers. 2. They believe there is more than one way to manage. 3. The companies have a stated purpose concerning what they are doing. 4. They are committed to being premier in all aspects of their business. –Mondy, Joe; *Managers Magazine,* May 1985, 60(5): pp. 4-9. Avail. ABI 85-19701

Management styles, Motivation, Corporate planning, Corporate responsibility

The Independent Director-Heavenly City or Potemkin (127) Village?

One of the more frequently proposed suggestions for bringing corporate power under control is the appointment of an independent director to the corporation's board. Such an independent director might oversee corporate social responsibility without imposing the costs of external regulation. The history and performance of such directors is reviewed. Within this context, the independent director would: 1. monitor the company's managerial integrity and efficiency, and 2. monitor its social responsibility. Independent directors have experienced little success to date in policing conflicts of interest and the maximization of shareholder wealth. Thus, the losses incurred from using them as substitutes for regulation might well exceed any gains. Improvement in corporate social responsibility will require institutional reforms within the corporate structure. Methods must be found to bridge the gap between the command structure and control procedures. However, such responsiveness to public needs will not occur absent public guidance and demand. References. –Brudney, Victor; *Harvard Law Review,* Jan 1982, 95(3): pp. 597-659. Avail. Harvard 82-06621

Boards of directors, Independent, Directors, Outside directors, Roles, Social responsibility, Corporate responsibility, Stockholders

India's JRD Tata: Can He Handpick a Successor to (128) Carry on a Corporate Legend?

J. R. D. Tata, the leader of India's giant Tata industrial empire, has selected his nephew Ratan as his successor. This decision has met with controversy. At stake is the most prestigious position in India. The Tata group is composed of 30 autonomous companies, employing some 238,000 people. While the Tata companies have pioneered much of India's heavy and basic industrial development, these companies have also adhered to a philosophy of social responsibility, often at the expense of profits. Newly named successor Ratan is a graduate of Cornell University and for the past 10 years has worked in turning around 2 Tata companies, the National Radio and Electronics Corp. (Nelco) and a 100-year-old textile mill. Some of the controversy over Ratan's being placed in first position of successor to J. R. D. stems from a few expectant and more experienced Tata executives. Ratan tends to be more business-oriented than J. R. D., which could result in a loosening of the Tata humane philosophy. Ratan contends that while continuing the founder's traditions, he would also stress profit motives and management styles that fit today's business environment. —Arbose, Jules and Marshall, Pearl; *International Mgmt (UK),* Feb 1983, 38(2) (European Edition): pp. 24,26. Avail. ABI 83-08453

Corporate management, Industrial, Parent companies, Chief executive officer, Profiles, India

Industrial Compliance with Social Legislation: (129)
Investigations of Decision Rationales

Since the late 1960s, a proliferation of legislation has attempted to insure that business organizations will respond to societal needs. Although the goals are not in question, the means for achieving the goals have created controversy. Ineffective and inefficient legislation and regulation can obscure the advantages of pursuing goals of socially responsible action. The need to study the efficacy and efficiency of social legislation and its compliance systems is obvious. This research presents a model of compliance behavior, as well as a research paradigm for testing the validity of the model in organizational settings. The model attempts to determine whether compliance decisions are founded on normative or calculative criteria and whether the rationales are individual or organizational. Studies employing the model are reviewed. The studies appear to support the validity of the model and the instrumentation around it. Specific implications for compliance with social legislation derived from these studies are discussed and additional areas for further research are suggested. Figure. Table. References. —Greer, Charles R. and Downey, H. Kirk; *Academy of Mgmt Review,* Jul 1982, 7(3): pp. 488-498. Avail. ABI 82-18268

Social, Legislation, Industrial, Compliance, Social goals, Social responsibility, Corporate responsibility

Industrial Sales Management in the 1980s (130)

Industrial sales management will have to adapt in the 1980s to energy and material shortages, increased governmental regulation, and increased pressure for social responsibility. To meet problems of energy shortage, greater use of phone contacts between sales representatives and clients can reduce auto travel time and expense. Increased advertising and sales promotion efforts can help make up for the reduced number of personal contacts. More economical automobiles can be used in cases where travel is essential. In dealing with government regulations, self-regulation is the first step. Upgrading the sophistication of the sales team will help these people to handle the resulting increased burden. Management should encourage continuing education programs, particularly Master of Business Administration (MBA) programs, that focus on the increased presence of government. Increased pressure for social responsibility, i.e., consumerism, requires management to make salespeople aware of ethical problems. Reviewing goal-setting techniques so that impossible-to-reach goals are eliminated, can reduce unethical behavior. Increased pressure from society requires management to make decisions with social implications as an important factor. Table. —Bellizzi, Joseph A. and Murdock, Gene W.; *Industrial Marketing Mgmt,* Oct 1981, 10(4): pp. 299-304. Avail. ABI 81-24824

Industrial, Sales, Management, Industrial markets, Marketing, Predictions, Regulation, Social responsibility, Ethics

An Industry Perspective (131)

Several major insurance companies, including Aetna Life & Casualty and The Prudential, have entered partnerships with other agencies and organizations to commit resources to address social problems. The insurance companies have brought both leadership and company resources to community partnerships. Steps to establish an effective partnership include: 1. establish a purpose, 2. initiate and communicate ideas, 3. establish ways to achieve goals, 4. create a structure, and 5. develop a management plan. Examples of the insurance industry's experience with partnerships to solve social problems include: 1. a $2 billion Urban Investment Program, 2. industry investment dollars to help finance the College Endowment Funding Plan, 3. Prudential's partnership with private financial institutions to save jobs at a General Motors plant, and 4. the Harlem Interfaith Counseling Service's construction of a $4.1 million clinic and care facility. Through such programs, the insurance industry has earned the reputation of a pacesetter in public/private-sector cooperation. −Karson, Stanley G. and Murray, Barry A.; *Bureaucrat,* Spring 1983, 12(1): pp. 23-26. Avail. ABI 83-13097

Leadership, Insurance companies, Social responsibility, Public sector, Private sector, Cooperation, Donations, Community development, Nonprofit organizations

The Institutional Crisis of the Corporate-Welfare State (132)

The current institutional crisis is examined in an effort to show that it is rooted in the holdover of an outdated ideology and culture that results in a profound ideological gap. This argument implies that 19th-century folkways should be abandoned, not the social economic goals of the last 50 years. The structural crisis of the corporate-welfare state merges into the cultural crisis, while the legitimation crisis is entwined with a crisis of character. Both the legitimation crisis and the crisis of character in the corporate-welfare state illustrate the common confusion and ideological obfuscation existing with regard to the good society and the place of the economy within it. The roots of this confusion and ambiguity are found in the nature of the market capitalist social order. Social economics can be instrumental in resolving these crises. References. −Stanfield, J. R.; *International Jrnl of Social Economics (UK),* 1983, 10(6) /7: pp. 45-66. Avail. MCB 84-17191

Private sector, Public sector, Welfare economics, Social policy, State government, Accountability, Social responsibility, Capitalism

Integrating Corporate Social Policy into Strategic (133) Management

It is hypothesized that most conceptualizations of strategic management pay little attention to corporate social policy and its integration into corporate strategy. The 1960s saw the emergence of corporate social responsibility, companies in the 1970s focused on the management of social responsiveness, and in the present decade, firms are struggling with the issue of making social responsibility a part of overall strategic management. A way of thinking about corporate social responsibility is proposed that: 1. integrates it into the concepts of strategic management/corporate strategy, and 2. demonstrates how social policy and goals can be operationalized into organizational practice. It is at the macrolevel (societal, corporate, and business levels of strategy) that a more positive stance is required for dealing with social policy. Corporate executives must include social policy guidelines in strategic plans from which functional policies can be derived, and the burden for achieving social goals belongs on the shoulders of middle- and lower-level managers. Charts. References. –Carroll, Archie B. and Hoy, Frank; *Jrnl of Business Strategy,* Winter 1984, 4(3): pp. 48-57. Avail. ABI 84-03881

Strategic management, Social policy, Social responsibility, Social issues

Integrating Strategic Management and Social Responsibility (134)

Economic or traditional strategic planning decisions can have global repercussions and create enormous problems. The successful resolution of these problems ultimately requires formal integration of social issues into the strategic management process. Such an approach will decrease the possibility that unintended, socially disruptive outcomes will occur. Although, in practice, there is little linkage between strategic and social assessment, the integration of traditional economic and emerging social concerns is feasible. This involves recognizing strategy as a management process. A look at 3 companies indicates how firms can enhance performance through improved strategic management by: 1. recognizing the chief executive officer's ultimate responsibility for corporate strategy formulation, 2. communicating top management's commitment to social responsibility to all levels of the organization, 3. using sophisticated environmental scanning techniques, and 4. generating and using social reporting systems. References. –Daneke, Gregory A. and Lemak, David J.; *Business Forum,* Summer 1985, 10(2) -3: pp. 20-25. Avail. ABI 85-34407

Strategic management, Social impact, Social responsibility, Economic trends, Theory, Strategic planning, Minnesota Mining & Manufacturing-St Paul, General Electric-Fairfield Conn, ARCO

Internal PR Efforts Further Corporate Responsibility: A Report from Dow Canada (135)

Credibility is an asset that is difficult to evaluate, but it is an important asset to any publicly held company. Public relations (PR) professionals are aware that it is impossible to build a strong base of corporate credibility unless management colleagues are aware of their endeavors. Dow Chemical Canada has taken a long series of steps internally to encourage basic changes in operating philosophies. The groundwork for the philosophical change was based on 5 postulates for creating a management environment to promote socially responsible corporate performance: 1. Social responsibility must be a firm, deep-seated belief of management. 2. Management must be consistent in its support of social responsibility. 3. Social responsibility programs must be a long-term commitment. 4. Management must practice what it preaches. 5. The approach should be framed in terms of the incentive. Credibility is an essential part of Dow's growth strategy. It is based on gaining management's respect for the capabilities of the PR functions. – Stephenson, D. R.; *Public Relations Qtrly,* Summer 1983, 28(2): pp. 7-10. Avail. ABI 83-22867

　　Dow Chemical-Midland Mich, Case studies, Canada, Chemical industry, Public relations, Corporate responsibility, Social responsibility, Management development, Employee morale, Programs

The International Infant Formula Controversy: A Dilemma in Corporate Social Responsibility　　　　(136)

One of the most controversial issues ever to confront industry has been the infant formula problem in less developed countries (LDC). Producers of infant formula were faced with a boycott which began at the grass-roots level and ultimately involved many corporations, organizations, and nations. Nestle S.A. (Vevey, Switzerland), one of the largest producers of infant formula, was the target of the international boycott. This discussion is aimed at analyzing the way the controversy changed industry or corporate strategy with respect to the marketing of breast-food substances, particularly in LDCs, and how it presented an international dilemma in the marketing of such products. The international protest movement against infant formula will probably have more far-reaching consequences than merely changing the industry's marketing policies. Ultimately, better sanitary conditions in LDCs and higher quality research on the feeding of infants could result. References. –Baker, James C.; *Jrnl of Business Ethics (Netherlands),* Jun 1985, 4(3): pp. 181-190. Avail. ABI 85-21877

　　LDCs, International, Marketing, Corporate responsibility, Nestle-Switzerland, Food processing industry, Case studies

Investing in Social Welfare - How One Detroit Bank Does It　　　　(137)

There are now 4 groups that determine the success of the corporate manager: 1. the shareholders, 2. the customers, 3. the employees, and 4. the public. The public's expectations of business were changed during the post-war era. Business was faced with the expectation that it should devote much of its time and talent to solving all manner of social problems. A popular line of reasoning was that business had created social problems and, therefore, had a responsibility to devote time and talent to the solution of such problems. There were many suggested tasks, including: 1. providing jobs for the hardcore unemployed, 2. cleaning up the environment, and 3. revitalizing decaying neighborhoods and central cities. For Detroit, New Detroit Inc., a coalition of business, labor, government, and community leaders, addresses a broad range of socioeconomic problems. A public/private, nonprofit corporation was also created to consolidate private sector economic development programs; this corporation is the Detroit Economic Growth Corp. There could be more government regulation if the corporations do not behave in a socially responsible manner. –Surdam, Robert M.; *Directors & Boards,* Summer 1982, 6(4): pp. 18-21. Avail. ABI 82-20348

　　Social responsibility, Corporate responsibility, Banking industry, Case studies, Donations

Irving Shapiro-Chairman & Chief Executive Officer E.I.   (138)
duPont de Nemours & Co.

Irving Shapiro's appointment in 1973 to be duPont's chairman and chief executive officer (CEO) surprised the entire business community. Unlike his predecessors, Shapiro is a lawyer, a Jew, and a Democrat; he attributes the appointment to his views. Shapiro feels that CEOs must use their expertise to improve society. In his case, that meant utilizing his background as a government lawyer to help forge closer corporate and personal links with the Federal government. His business acumen is formidable, but it is his visibility and public participation which have put him in the forefront of industry's shift to social activism. Shapiro feels that, aside from businessmen's obligation to apply their talent to social problems, from a business viewpoint it is necessary for them to do so. Government is now a silent, unrecruited partner in business, and businessmen must involve themselves with it. Shapiro is noted for his behind-the-scenes influence in the Carter Administration, and for his 2-year chairmanship of the Business Roundtable.
—Anonymous; *Industry Week*, Oct 27, 1980, 207(2): pp. 50-52. Avail. ABI 80-22315

Du Pont-Delaware, Case studies, Corporate responsibility, Social responsibility, Public policy

Issues Management: Conflicting Interests Within a   (139)
Multidivisional Organization

Nabisco Brands Inc. has manufacturing operations in 36 countries and 25 US states. The company employs 55,000 people worldwide and markets cookies, crackers, snack foods, nuts, margarines, gelatins, and confections in more than 100 countries in the free world. As an integral part of the food industry, Nabisco Brands is constantly bombarded with international, federal, and state public policy proposals which affect its corporate interests and management prerogatives. This highly decentralized multidivisional corporation has faced conflicting problems such as the sugar issue of the 1981 Farm Bill and sodium labeling. Issue management is a relatively new discipline and one that is increasing in importance to corporate US. Business managers must be able to see beyond the scope of a particular function, company, or industry. A broad-based background and understanding of the business/government relationship is required of today's business managers.
—Anderson, Wayne C.; *Vital Speeches*, Mar 1, 1984, 50(10): pp. 308-311. Avail. ABI 84-10717

Corporate responsibility, Public policy, Issue, Management, Nabisco Brands-New York, Case studies

The Japanese Blackade? An Absence of Japanese   (140)
Advertisers in Black Magazines Raises Serious
Questions

Virtually none of Japan's manufacturers include blacks in their media and advertising strategies, and less than 0.5% of their magazine advertisements are placed in black publications. The absence of Japanese advertisers in black magazines is of concern to owners of black media, who have tried to present a case to the Japanese for pursuing black consumers. They point to black purchasing power and the chance to build goodwill in this segment of the population. Explanations for the Japanese market strategy include a preference for general rather than segmented marketing, lack of advertising research on the black community, and ignorance of the value of the black market. Frank Mingo of Mingo-Jones Advertising believes that the Japanese are nationalistic and isolationists, but not humanitarian, and esoteric notions of corporate responsibility have no effect unless they can see a direct benefit to themselves. Because the Japanese are cautious and conservative, any change in market strategy toward blacks will probably come slowly. –Schultz, Ellen; *Madison Avenue,* Sep 1985, 27(9): pp. 62-66. Avail. ABI 85-31524

Blacks, Magazines, Advertising, Market segments, Japan, Market strategy, Imports

Journalists and Businessmen Have a Lot in Common: (141) They Are Distrusted by the Public

Corporations are creatures of the state, and the public, through its legislatures, charters corporations and determines - and may change - the rules by which they operate. The same is true of the press. It is perceived that businesspeople and journalists lack human qualities and are blinded by their quests for money and objectivity. Businesspeople and journalists must work together. Business schools should have courses that teach some journalism so that students understand the difficulties reporters and editors face. Likewise, business education should be supported in journalism schools. Although it sounds idealistic, business and journalism should find ways to work together to engage in debate, exploration, and contemplation. Journalists are urged to reinstate the dignity, beauty, and the power of the written word. –Hockaday, Irvine O., Jr.; *Vital Speeches,* Feb 1, 1985, 51(8): pp. 244-246. Avail. ABI 85-09807

Journalism, Business, Social responsibility, Public opinion, Press

Latin American Subsidiaries and Social Responsibility (142)

Most countries are examining more closely the manner in which corporations assume their responsibilities to society. Corporations in most capitalistic industrialized nations are increasing their involvement in social responsibility activities and are periodically reporting on the socially oriented activities in which they are involved. In order to gain information on the current state of social responsibility involvement of foreign affiliates in Latin America, a mail and personal interview survey was conducted among respondents with business experience in that area. Areas of the survey included: environment and energy, treatment of minorities, employee welfare and training, community involvement, and disclosure of strategies. Results indicated that: In their annual published reports, affiliates report very little about activities in preservation of environment and conservation of energy. Some affiliates have policies with respect to fair treatment of minorities and also take initiative in employee training and welfare. All respondents indicated community involvement, but of a passive nature. Over 50% of affiliates are publicly disclosing such information as codes of ethics and exports. It appears that affiliates of large multinational firms are inclined to be active in social involvement. Table. References. —Whitt, John D.; *Arizona Business,* Apr 1981, 28(4): pp. 19-23. Avail. ABI 81-12962

Latin America, Multinational corporations, Foreign subsidiaries, Social responsibility, Surveys, Corporate responsibility

Lessons of Leadership: "Thanks, Dad-and Thank Mom, too" (143)

John C. Emery, Jr., is chairman and president of Emery Air Freight Corporation, the nation's largest air freight forwarder, and a firm founded by his father. The legacy given him was to seek out the high expectations, and the firm may hit the billion-dollar-mark in 1984. Emery believes in free enterprise and better pricing for the public through the absence of governmental restraints. He has played a major role in deregulation by successfully arguing against the rule preventing freight forwarders from chartering aircraft, and continues to work for deregulation in other areas. His management philosophy is a behavioral technique, calling for praise of good performance and the downplay of criticism. He believes strongly in corporate morality and integrity, as well as corporate responsibility. He does not underrate his own contributions, yet credits his father's imaginative role in founding a new business. Emery does not accept the status quo. He believes there are always ways to be better, simpler, and more effective. —Louviere, Vernon; *Nation's Business,* Jul 1980, 68(7): pp. 44-48. Avail. ABI 80-21200

Case studies, Air freight service, Air transportation industry, Leasing, Chief executive officer

The Limits of Business Self-Regulation (144)

Opponents of government regulation have called for business self-regulation as a means of promoting corporate social responsibility. However, businesses typically have failed in efforts at self-regulation, since the outcome (in terms of benefits to society) is a public good subject to the free-rider problem. In the absence of coercion, individual firms will not want to contribute to the costs of producing a public good if other self-interested firms can benefit from these contributions without making any of their own. Thus, if all firms behave in a rational and self-interested manner, the public good will not be advanced. In the US, the problem of self-regulation is compounded by the fragmentation of the business market, making it impossible for any firm to know how another firm will behave. Some European countries have relied upon a peak business organization to coordinate collective business self-regulation as a successful alternative to government regulation. However, given the individualistic US political culture and the structure of US government, it is unlikely that a business-wide peak organization could be established in the US. References. —Maitland, Ian; *California Mgmt Review,* Spring 1985, 27(3): pp. 132-147. Avail. ABI 85-22801

Self regulation, Corporate responsibility, Social responsibility, Corporate, Behavior

The Line Between Banking and Commerce (145)

With companies like Sears and Merrill Lynch now offering banking services, the line between banking and commerce is fading. Today, banking includes all regulated financial institutions. Banking is regulated by social legislation to maintain social objectives. Nonbank banks must accept the social responsibilities inherent in a banking charter. If nonbank banks do not accept these social challenges, banks should not be required to bear the brunt. If nonbank banks do accept the social constraints and cross over into banking, banks should be allowed to expand into other fields. Consumer activist groups are concerned with the following issues: 1. life-line banking, 2. dissemination of pricing and rate information at branch level, 3. standardized disclosure forms for basic accounts, 4. elimination of noncost barriers to checking accounts, 5. comparison of savings account yields, and 6. service charges. –Edwards, Raoul D.; *United States Banker,* May 1985, 96(5) (NE Regional Edition): pp. 4,6. Avail. ABI 85-20154

Banking industry, Deregulation, Banking law, Bank services, Social responsibility, Financial institutions

Linking Public Affairs with Corporate Planning (146)

In order to cope effectively with frequently disruptive societal and political factors, corporations are developing an administrative area called "issue management," a component of which is the inclusion of public affairs issues in established decision-making processes and managerial functions. An analytical framework for this component is presented, based on on-site, structured interviews with managers of 25 large corporations in the grocery products manufacturing industry. The managers produced information on methods of communication of public affairs issues, coordination of issues, introduction of issues into division plans, preparation of the corporate plan, and strength of linkage. Major recommendations included the establishment of an issue-scanning capability and communication network, active participation by top management in setting policies and standards and structuring the organization, and the crucial role of division managers, who must internalize the public affairs issues and incorporate them into division plans. Chart. Tables. References. –Fleming, John E.; *California Mgmt Review,* Winter 1980, 23(2): pp. 35-43. Avail. ABI 81-04664

Social responsibility, Functions, Corporate planning, Public, Issue, Identification, Communication, Organizational behavior, Divisions

Lobbying, Ethics and Common Sense (147)

Government is relaxing restrictive business practices and pulling back from the social arenas, an occurrence business has lobbied in favor of before Congress for many years. Business is being asked to recognize it is something quite different from what it was 20 years ago. The voice of business is growing stronger in state capitals and in Washington, and it is taking a broad view of industry's role in society. Executives are finding it is important to combine maximizing profits with upgrading quality of life. They are also realizing that business cannot have it both ways-little government restrictions and little community involvement. Roberto Goizueta, chairman of The Coca-Cola Co. states big business must sacrifice short-term profits for long-term societal benefits. George Allen, president of Fawcett Publications, a unit of CBS, believes the heart of the business decline in America is the insistence on short-term profits at the expense of long-term planning. He further states businesses have become banks and they have forgotten what they were originally chartered for. —Spitzer, Carlton E.; *Public Relations Jrnl,* Feb 1982, 38(2): pp. 34-36. Avail. ABI 82-08237

Corporate responsibility, Social responsibility, Ethics, Social policy

Making Decisions in the Public Sector (148)

The methods employed in the public sector for reaching a decision are different from those used in the private sector. There is a need for better training in the area, although in both sectors, decision making is a required management skill and should involve a series of rational and predetermined steps. Some of the important contrasts between the 2 sectors include: 1. The private sector can relate the effectiveness of decision making to quantified criteria such as profitability, but the public sector must also take into consideration the social responsibility factor. 2. The private sector generally makes decisions in secrecy, where the reverse is mainly true of the public. 3. Professionalism has been more characteristic of the private rather than the public sector. Consultation is more a part of traditional practice in private-sector decision making, and rewards are more of a financial nature. The public sector manager must often make decisions while reconciling conflicting objectives. There is a slowly growing awareness in the public sector for required training in the decision process, but the private sector has long recognized that need. Decision making is a multidisciplinary activity, and the public sector must learn to treat it as such. Chart. —Leigh, Andrew; *Personnel Mgmt (UK),* Dec 1983, pp. 28-31. Avail. ABI 84-03339

Managers, Decision making, UK, Public sector, Management training, Management development

Management Applications of Catastrophe Theory (149)

Although it may be years before management scientists will be able to actually produce working models of catastrophic change, knowledge of the theory can aid managers in developing rich insights into the behavior of complex organizations. Catastrophe theory employs control variables and behavior variables to define the system being simulated. Three cases are used to illustrate the application of catastrophe theory to management: venture management, research and development support, and corporate social responsibility. However, it should be noted that these 3 cases represent only hypothetical examples of typical corporate behavior. Second, the systems being represented by these models are more complex than can be portrayed fully in this or any conceptual framework. Nonetheless, catastrophe theory offers management scientists a unique technique of modeling discontinuous forms of organizational behavior. Better understanding allows better prediction and control of organizational behavior. Diagrams. —Halal, William E. and Lasken, Robert A.; *Business Horizons,* Dec 1980, 23(6): pp. 35-42. Avail. ABI 81-00106

Mathematical models, Catastrophes, Theory, Management, Concepts, Applications, R&D, Corporate, Social responsibility, RCA-New York

Management's Key Strategic Issues in the Turbulent (150) Eighties: Part II

The dynamic environment of the future requires managers to be able to deal with uncertainty. Companies will anticipate and participate in the society surrounding it in the 1980s. The General Manager of a company must have a personal commitment to environmental issues and must delegate management of internal operations to a senior management team to provide the General Manager time to work on the external business environment. The General Manager also must devote more time to social, political, and regulatory issues. Although managers may feel unqualified in the area, corporations now have social, moral, and ethical obligations to fulfill. During the 1980s, there will be more cooperation of business and government. Information will be an important resource in the future, with management skills in the information-intelligence process becoming critical. Corporate planning will become more involved with factors such as changes in the external and internal environment. Styles of management will change, causing changes in management training and development. References. – McKenna, Patrick J.; *Canadian Manager (Canada),* May/Jun/Jul 1981, 6(3): pp. 4-7. Avail. ABI 81-14178

Management, Uncertainty, Changes, Corporate responsibility, Social responsibility, Information management, Corporate planning, Management training, Management development

Managerial Values in the '80's (151)

Managerial effectiveness involves the productive use of resources and attempts to make work enjoyable and worthwhile. It can be a lifeline through whatever personal values, objectives, and moral or political values one holds. The social responsibility of business is to increase its added value by using all the resources so well that more socially valuable resources are produced. Although values change, businessmen's responsibility to create added value will not change. Ineffective management wastes resources and impoverishes the nation. –Reddin, W. J.; *Canadian Manager (Canada),* Nov/Dec 1980, 5(5): pp. 7. Avail. ABI 81-00658

Managers, Management, Values, Predictions, Social responsibility, Resource management, Effectiveness

A Manager's Guide to Making Social Responsibility (152) Work and Pay

Companies, in order to be good corporate citizens, must be prepared to accept total corporate social responsibility. Such responsibility must be a part of corporate policy, not a public relations activity. Top management must actively include social responsibility issues in daily work activity in order to give employees a good example. Corporations must constantly monitor the important social issues of the communities in which they are located, because recently those issues have become more important to the success of companies than the internal workings of the company. The successful company will maintain a checklist of general issues, charitable actions, community relations policies, employment policies, safety and health areas, training and education systems, and employee privacy of information. – Anonymous; *International Mgmt (UK),* May 1981, 36(5): pp. 38-40. Avail. ABI 81-13550

Social responsibility, Corporate responsibility, Chief executive officer, Guidelines, Performance

Managing Corporate Citizenship (153)

Corporate responsibility relates to involvement in social issues that have an impact on the health and welfare of a community, and the public has come to expect corporations to justify their existence with contributions of their resources. The bigger the corporate citizen and the greater its success, the higher will be society's expectation of its contribution. If a social responsibility program is to achieve the desired aims for the corporation and the community, it must be integrated into the business and managed professionally. IBM UK Ltd. is an example of a company on the leading edge of corporate responsibility. It applies its resources - cash, management expertise, and technology - to 3 major problems where it feels qualified to help. These problem areas are: 1. work creation, 2. educational programs, and 3. community welfare, focusing on the disabled. Each area has an issue manager responsible for research, preparation, and implementation of an action plan, and specific criteria are applied to project selection. New corporate responsibility programs are announced and explained to all employees to secure their understanding, support, and involvement. —Peach, Len; *Personnel Mgmt (UK)*, Jul 1985, 17(7): pp. 32-35. Avail. ABI 85-29446

IBM United Kingdom Holdings-UK, Case studies, UK, Social responsibility, Corporate responsibility, Donations, Community support, Computer industry

Managing Large Egos (154)

Good research groups attract creative people who often have substantial egos. Managers are challenged to form such individuals into effective units. Good creative scientists acknowledge the difficulties of their tasks and should be modest about their chances of success. One of the major dilemmas of the research manager is to avoid the destructive competition that may be at play among the scientists working on a given project. Bell Labs, for example, uses an appeal to social responsibility and lets scientists know that the corporation is bigger than any single individual. It also tries to make researchers feel special by using good administrative support and technical memoranda written at the initiative of the individual researcher. Research managers must develop rapport with their staff, but they must take care not to be perceived as competing with them. Researchers must be given full credit for their accomplishments; the manager should be a catalyst stimulating their creativity. —Wolff, Michael F.; *Research Mgmt*, Jul 1982, 15(4): pp. 7-9. Avail. ABI 82-18069

Research, Management, Skills, Creative, Scientists, Engineers, R&D

Managing on the Ethics Frontier (155)

The concept of social responsibility, particularly as it relates to safety and environmental issues, is an increasingly common topic of debate, which can perhaps be better handled by philosophy and religion than by economic theories, computer language, and accounting manuals. A manager's first lesson must be that a business firm has the power to shape society and in turn is shaped by that society. Therefore, a good manager must learn to detect and anticipate social forces, rather than waiting for them to appear. Environmental management skills occur on 3 levels: the individual company level, the public policy level, and the ethical/moral level. In the first, the key is positive social responsiveness. In the second, learning how to relate to government and elected officials is essential. Learning that all business decisions have ethical and moral overtones is the key to the third. Examining their own consciences, realizing that value clashes occur, and speaking out concerning the ethical stance of the company are all actions concerned executives can take. An internal audit of ethical performance can also be taken and corrections made. The reward for prompt and sure ethical responsibility is often enhanced prestige in the public eye, whereas hesitation or inaction can cost dearly. –Frederick, William C.; *Managing,* 1982, (1): pp. 35-37. Avail. ABI 82-12407

   Corporate responsibility, Social responsibility, Ethics, Skills, Public policy, Public relations, Manycompanies

Managing Relations with Government and Society - The   (156)
Business Perspective

The future of democracy depends upon the style and quality of management. A narrow and authoritarian view of business management will lead eventually to a centralized state bureaucracy. An enlightened and knowledgeable approach by management that is designed to secure the voluntary consent of employees will safeguard the future of democracy. At Carroll Industries Ltd. (Dublin, Ireland), management has changed greatly in 5 years. Management seeks to view the business in a holistic way and is interested in setting goals and pursuing strategies that reconcile the concerns of direct and indirect stakeholders. Accounting systems have been changed in order to reveal to society the real performance of the business and the real shares held by stockholders. Management seeks continually to involve itself with external affairs because factors outside the business often have greater significance for the business than do internal factors. Management strives to achieve an essential coherence in the approach to things arising from this holistic view, which minimizes ambiguity and facilitates open and honest dialogue. –Carroll, Donal S. A.; *Long Range Planning (UK),* Apr 1983, 16(2): pp. 10-14. Avail. ABI 83-13457

   Public sector, Private sector, Relations, Social responsibility, Managers, Skills, Information, Economic planning, Strategic, Planning, Ireland

Managing Social Issues in a Time of Change   (157)

The Northwestern National Bank of Minneapolis (Minnesota) has developed an Employee Task Force program, through which volunteer employees are assigned to study and recommend positions and courses of action for the bank to take on pressing social issues. The 3 priority items selected to receive initial task force attention are: 1. urban development, 2. constituent rights, and 3. privacy. Membership was open to employees at all levels, except senior management. A chairperson was also appointed to supply leadership and ensure sufficient staff support for the task force. During the first stage of the process, task force members met every week for 2 hours-1 hour on bank time and 1 hour on their own time-for several months. Management emphasized that all recommendations made by the task forces would be taken seriously and, if possible, implemented. As a result of the program, management discovered that the task force's viewpoints and insights greatly clarified and sharpened management perspective on the issues. —Zippo, Mary; *Personnel,* Sep/Oct 1981, 58(5): pp. 43-45. Avail. ABI 81-25046

Case studies, Banks, Policy making, Social responsibility, Social issues, Employee, Task forces

Manufacturing and Technological Strategy (158)

In today's world, managing manufacturing in mature industries seems to be characterized by poor financial performance, insufficient capacity, depreciated and worn-out equipment, outmoded skills in the work force and in middle management, adversary labor relations, and a pattern of regularly replacing plant managers. The symptoms of duress in manufacturing facilities that were once successful are strikingly similar. Typically, there are 5 basic problem areas in mature manufacturing industries: 1. financial, which involves financing major re-equipping and retooling needed to lower costs, improve quality, and modify product mix, 2. strategic, 3. social responsibility in considering relocation or closing up plant, 4. human resource management, which involves retraining, reeducating, or replacing a considerable portion of the work force, and 5. manufacturing strategy, which focuses on structural problems. In mature industries, the need to adopt a strategic approach to manufacturing is becoming more important. Mature industries need a manufacturing strategy audit and review and a reformulation of the critical task of manufacturing. —Skinner, Wickham; *Jrnl of Business Strategy,* Fall 1980, 1(2): pp. 69-72. Avail. ABI 81-02536

Manufacturing, Industries, Maturity, Life, Cycles, Companies, Problems, Alternative, Solutions, Strategic, Financial, Strategic management

Mark Hyman: Commitment To Black Awareness (159)

Mark Hyman Associates (Philadelphia, Pennsylvania) is a black-owned-and-operated public relations firm. The firm has advised many companies in the areas of black awareness and career motivation. Among those companies are the Philadelphia Electric Co. (PECO) and Bell Telephone Co. of Pennsylvania. With Hyman's advice, PECO sponsored a 24-panel exhibit that demonstrated contributions in America of black inventors, physical scientists, and engineers. Some 500,000 people, mostly school children, have seen the exhibit at the Afro-American Historical and Cultural Museum. For the Bell Company, Hyman suggested a series of 60-second radio spots to tell of black achievements before the discovery of America. A companion book was also published. Both these programs will inspire black children by making them aware of these examples of black achievement, and contribute to the goodwill enjoyed by the company. —Warren, J. Hugo, III; *Public Relations Jrnl,* Sep 1982, 38(9): pp. 12-13. Avail. ABI 82-23507

Public relations, Case studies, Blacks, Business ownership, Minorities, Social responsibility

Marketers Can Become Social Activists with These Guidelines (160)

The maintenance and growth of economic and sociopolitical systems in the US require that marketers become social activists. Socially responsible marketing action must be taken to solve these problems. Ten propositions have been formulated to help set the guidelines for corporate behavior in this area: 1. Marketing must make a total commitment to meet the needs of more people. 2. Marketing must introduce new products that function better than their predecessors. 3. The least possible amount of scarce natural resources should be used. 4. Distribution system improvements must be made so more people can buy more of everything. 5. Effective information should be provided through the mass media. 6. Marketing communications should be directed only to target audiences. 7. Marketing and advertising executives should be sensitive to the effect they have on social forms. 8. Marketers must realize their responsibility to society. 9. Marketers need to use the Net Economic Welfare (NEW) socioeconomic measures instead of gross national product (GNP). 10. The higher the price the lower the consumer satisfaction and well-being. —Samli, A. Coskun and Sirgy, M. Joseph; *Marketing News,* Apr 1, 1983, 17(7): pp. 5-6. Avail. ABI 83-10511

Marketing, Personnel, Ethics, Social responsibility, Social, Activists

Marketing CPA Services: Communications (Written)   (161)

The American Institute of Certified Public Accountants (AICPA) Rule 502 states that a member shall not seek to obtain clients by advertising or other forms of solicitation that are false, misleading, or deceptive. Practice development methods should be informative and objective, in good taste, and professionally dignified. One method of communication is the use of a directory. There are few directories that list details about professionals and professional services in communities. A readily available and reasonably priced directory might be successful in reaching individuals and small businesses. Educational television may be used by an organization. A less obvious way of marketing may be that of sponsoring a program. This sponsorship would also fulfill a firm's social responsibility. Additional methods of written communication may include: endorsements, institutional advertising, magazine advertising, newspaper advertising, personal notes, and point of purchase displays. The use of reminders for medical appointments might be transferred into the accounting field with reminders to individuals concerning taxes or other related services. —Whisnant, Susan R.; *CPA Jrnl,* Apr 1983, 53(4): pp. 96-99. Avail. ABI 83-12631

Marketing, CPAs, Accounting firms, Market strategy, Methods

Marketing for Human Needs in a Humane Future   (162)

Since its inception some 70 years ago, marketing has developed into an extremely powerful technology. However, looking honestly at its central paradigms, there can be little hope about marketing's potential in a world moving towards humaneness, sharing, and nonacquisitiveness. Marketing is basically a neutral force that can lead to good or evil. A restructuring of marketing awareness can invest the discipline of marketing with a brilliant, certain future. New paradigms could become the basis of how marketing is portrayed in books and journals, taught at universities, and understood by practitioners. They could also reconstitute the conceptual framework within which additional research and investigation could be carried out by marketing scholars. The paradigms presented are designed as tentative propositions which will hopefully incite further ideas and discussion.

Marketing is what practitioners make it, and marketers share the accountability of guaranteeing the survival of their profession. References. —Dawson, Leslie M.; *Business Horizons,* Jun 1980, 23(3): pp. 72-82. Avail. ABI 80-13397

Marketing, Social responsibility, Models, Changes

The Maturing of Church Corporate Responsibility (163)
Programs
The most significant expressions of activism, in terms of influencing social, economic, and political policies, are institutional and conceptual activism. Major churches have their own action groups, and perhaps the most influential and widely respected is the Department of Social Development and World Peace of the US Catholic Conference. The Urban Industrial Mission in South Korea is another significant expression of institutional activism. However, conceptualization is more important than activism. In this regard, the Roman Catholic Church stands out due to its precision and sensitivity in the formulation of social and economic policy statements. Institutionalism and conceptualization of activism cannot be separated, and business and churches must communicate with each other in order to achieve higher degrees of social responsibility. —Armstrong, A. James; *Business & Society Review,* Summer 1985, (54): pp. 6-9. Avail. ABI 85-33830

Religious organizations, Corporate responsibility, Activists, Social policy, Statements, Ethics

Men, Women and Social Responsibility (164)
For some time, public relations has been regarded as a profession that offers substantial opportunities to women workers. Females have played an important role in the recent development of public relations. A study was conducted to explore male/female attitudinal differences concerning social responsibility values. Subjects were 105 public relations practitioners in Atlanta, Georgia. Subjects completed a questionnaire containing a social responsibility measuring scale. Results of the survey indicated only minimal differences in social responsibility values between men and women. A well-developed social conscience was evident among respondents of both sexes. Tables. Graph. —Wright, Donald K.; *Public Relations Jrnl,* Aug 1983, 39(8): pp. 27-29. Avail. ABI 83-22519

Public relations, Professional, Women, Roles, Attitude surveys, Social responsibility, Statistical data, Volunteers, Studies

Modern Values and Corporate Social Responsibility (165)
Corporate social responsibility (CSR) is a doctrine fusing social values with efforts to maximize profit goals. Most current approaches to CSR begin from the legitimacy-accountability theme which contends that the power and authority possessed by corporations depend on the perceived value of corporations by those affected. The classical view of accountability advocates putting return to shareholders and economic efficiency first, while operating within the legal and economic rules of the game. The activist view sees corporations are possessing great socioeconomic power to do good and evil. Corporations have broad social responsibilities and must be monitored by the general public. The balanced managerial view proposes that generating an acceptable return is the corporation's first duty, followed by investing in

social purposes which allows it to retain its legitimacy. Short-term cash profits are traded off in return for long-term profitability resulting from social investment for rational purpose. It is implemented as an internal, line management responsibility. CSR has also been implemented via external methods, like social audits, disclosures in footnotes of financial statements, diversity in board members, etc. —Bock, Robert H.; *MSU Business Topics,* Spring 1980, 28(2): pp. 5-17. Avail. ABI 80-11194

> Corporate responsibility, Social responsibility, Accountability, Social accounting, Social goals, Economic justification

Moving Social Responsibility down a Peg   (166)

Most chief executives believe that corporations have a social responsibility to the community and society. This is evident by the establishment of such units as corporate social responsibility offices, departments of social planning and analysis, and offices of social-issues management. Unfortunately, this concern for social responsibility has not descended to line and middle management. Part of the problem may be caused by senior management's inability to communicate effectively the rationale for and extent of its commitment to social responsibility. All levels of management should try to educate employees about the importance of evaluating the social consequences of their activities. An effective information program should have the following strategies: 1. integration of social-impact analysis into long-range planning, 2. social accountability centers created for after-the-fact evaluation, and 3. performance measurement standards at the individual and organizational-unit levels. To develop commitment to social-impact management, superior performance must be rewarded by money and recognition. —Sethi, S. Prakash; *Public Relations Jrnl,* Aug 1982, 38(8): pp. 25-27. Avail. ABI 82-22366

> Social responsibility, Corporate responsibility, Line managers, Corporate, Strategy, Public relations

Multinational Corporations and Third World Capitalism   (167)

Economic institutions and prevailing ideas about them run a typically uneven race that is always in progress. The institutional changes almost unfailingly move faster, which means that the ideas lag. A current case in point is that of multinational corporations. Two related questions are raised. One concerns whether operations of the multinational corporation are in the interests of third world countries, and the other concerns whether it is in the interest of the US to encourage their foreign activities. The principal conclusion of an analysis of these issues is that the direct investment of US multinationals has had a powerfully benign effect on Third World countries, promoting extraordinarily high rates of economic growth wherever they are allowed to do so. A related conclusion is that foreign direct investment has been a far more important promoter of growth than has foreign economic aid. Investment in less developed countries should not be unduly hampered, either by taxes or other domestic regulations. Table. Equations. Appendix.

References. —Ulmer, Melville J.; *Jrnl of Economic Issues,* Jun 1980, 14(2): pp. 453-471. Avail. AEE 80-19619

Multinational corporations, Third world, Capitalism, Economic trends, LDCs, Corporate responsibility, Growth rate, Economic impact, Economic justification, Foreign investment, Foreign, Relations

The Multipurpose Corporation (168)

The multipurpose corporation, one which is primarily designed to meet demand at a profit but does not use the "bottom line" as the sole criterion for investment decisions, reflects a rising awareness that economics can no longer be divorced from other societal dimensions. Social responsiveness may rest partially upon decentralization of the business corporation; this decentralization recognizes the limits to economies of scale and is being acknowledged by: 1. a flattening of corporate hierarchies, 2. the recognition that small work units are advantageous, and 3. the success of the "matrix" type of organization. Renowned futurists' visions of the business corporation assume a "paradigm shift", or the management of change. Three requisites must be met: synthesis and "wholism", cooperation of business and government, and the harmonious blending of corporate short-term objectives and societal long-term best interests. —van Dam, Andre; *Business Qtrly (Canada),* Winter 1980, 45(4): pp. 79-81. Avail. ABI 81-05593

Multiple, Functions, Social responsibility, Decentralized

NAIW Told Why U.S. Corporations Fall Short on Some (169) Social Issues

Society's expectations of corporations have changed since World War II; now corporations are expected to: 1. stand behind their products and services, 2. help on issues of environmental protection, and 3. participate in the educational and cultural support activities of society. These issues were once considered outside the corporate agenda. Despite the change, society is still using the 1945 and 1950 model of what a company is and expecting that model to produce responses to new broader social issues. Under the new agenda, power will have to be shared. Those employed in large corporations today do not see themselves as communities organized in reaching a goal, but as entities that are competing with one another, even while trying to help the corporation achieve its goals. Until the issues of power, money, and community and individualization are addressed in large corporations, the external or social agenda issues will not be treated properly. Individuals can play a role in the conversion process by exposing the problem, helping to devise viable alternative solutions, and working inside their own organization for a consensus-driven change. —Lyons, Lois J.; *National Underwriter (Life/Health),* May 19, 1984, 88(20): pp. 2,43. Avail. ABI 84-19370

Corporate responsibility, Roles, Social issues

The National Small Business Panel: Proposal for a (170) Computerized Data Base for Small Business Research

Currently, there exists no broad base of research on small business. For example, small business owners have no way of determining how a successful small business differs from an unsuccessful one. An attempt is made to reduce the numerous definitions of small business to one. A panel was organized to include a representative sample of all small businesses in the nation. The initial stage of the National Small Business Panel project would consist of a board of experts to advise on the operation of the panel, an advisory committee, and a temporary executive staff. The total size of the panel would be large enough to provide a statistically significant finding for most studies. Nine areas of research were chosen including accounting problems and practices, management problems and practices, profitability, and social responsibility of small business. Data collected would be made available with user priority being determined by the policies of the permanent advisory committee. —Brannen, William H.; *Jrnl of Small Business Mgmt,* Jul 1980, 18(3): pp. 1-7. Avail. ABI 80-18901

Data bases, Research, Small business, National, Panels

A Need-Hierarchy Framework for Assessing Corporate (171) Social Responsibility

A conjugate theoretical framework of the socially responsible organization is presented, using a need-hierarchic construct. A wide-ranging definition recently offered by Carroll for the concept of corporate social responsibility (CSR) is: The social responsibility of business encompasses the economic-legal, ethical, and discretionary expectations that society has of organizations at a given point in time. A microanalytic foundation for organizational analysis is proposed, using a paradigm derived from need theory. A taxonomic construct to assess corporate performance is presented, and a yardstick to monitor its social responsibility is proposed. The conceptualization of CSR is more easily motivated and operationalized in the context of an organizational-need hierarchy. Maslow categorized needs into 5 broad groups: 1. physiological, 2. safety, 3. affiliative, 4. esteem, and 5. self-actualization. The lower level needs deal with corporate profitability and survival. The socially responsible organization is the self-actualizing organization, having satisfied prepotent needs. Table. References. —Tuzzolino, Frank and Armandi, Barry R.; *Academy of Mgmt Review,* Jan 1981, 6(1): pp. 21-28. Avail. ABI 81-03781

Corporate responsibility, Social responsibility, Organizational, Needs, Hierarchies, Organizational behavior, Needs analysis

New Company Watchdog (172)

A new position is emerging in the corporate world: that of issues manager. It is the issues manager's job to alert top management to the political, social and economic issues that will affect the company, determine which are most pressing, and suggest ways of dealing with them. Five years ago, only a few companies had such a position; now at least 70 major companies have an issues manager in one form or another. The position has drawn people from such diverse careers as law, public relations, economics, and journalism. Among their tasks are: 1. lobbying for or against legislation, 2. writing speeches for top management, 3. directing issue advertising for the company, 4. writing articles, 5. organizing task forces within the company, and 6. engaging in discussion with anti-corporate activists. Newcomers to issues management are offered 2 pieces of advice on how to succeed. First of all, they should get the active support of top management. Secondly, they should become involved in the legislative process early. —Perham, John; *Dun's Business Month*, Dec 1981, 118(6): pp. 88-89. Avail. ABI 82-00719

Social responsibility, Political, Social issues, Management, Corporate, Environment, Manycompanies

New Corporate Programs in the Public Sector (173)

Corporate leaders are uneasy over what they perceive as a governmental move to shift social responsibility to business. Ironically, many Americans who have come to rely upon government as the main provider of social services, also feel that same government is inefficient and unresponsive in doing so. It is suggested that private sector initiatives can be just as effective as government programs. This relates not so much to the role of funding social programs, as to providing them. Companies such as Honeywell Corp. and Procter & Gamble have already established programs which work for the benefit of the community as a whole. President Reagan has created a task force on private sector initiative, whose mission is: 1. to identify existing examples of successful private programs, 2. to encourage more creative and effective use of business resources, 3. to encourage partnerships to identify needs, priorities, and resources, 4. to identify government obstacles to private initiatives, and 5. to propose practical options based on its findings. —Baroody, William J., Jr.; *Directors & Boards*, Winter 1982, 6(3): pp. 22-25. Avail. ABI 82-08830

Corporate, Programs, Public sector, Private sector, Social responsibility, Social services, Corporate responsibility

The New Federalism: Some Bottom Line Considerations (174)

President Reagan's "New Federalism" is optimistically based in part on citizen, non-profit, and corporate voluntary efforts. However, the central question is whether voluntarism can begin to fill the funding gap being created in Washington. Those most affected have already answered that it cannot because of the enormous size of the gap. Most local and national non-profit groups get some type of corporate assistance, but in the past, few companies approached giving the allowable 2% of their gross income as a beneficial tax write-off. Congress has now raised the write-off to 10%. Companies must give more if the quality of life in communities is not to deteriorate further, but increased giving should be done under more strict ground rules. However, companies should not give more just because governments are not meeting their responsibilities to the public. Instead, companies should give more because private enterprise needs a progressive social context in order to realize maximum growth and profits. Companies should expect a detailed accountability for donated funds. The performance of individuals, money, and other resources must be measured against the outcomes so that funding for a specific program can be increased, lowered, or terminated. —Pratson, Frederick J.; *Managing*, 1982, (2): pp. 4,37. Avail. ABI 82-19416

Volunteers, Corporate responsibility, Social responsibility, Accountability

The New Meaning of Corporate Social Responsibility (175)

Corporations have traditionally fulfilled social responsibilities through philanthropic contributions to their host communities. However, cultural enhancements to communities are no longer sufficient to promote a quality of life which supports community and business development. Continued economic growth requires that business address social problems such as unemployment and the reindustrialization of the US, which government alone cannot cure. The primary social responsibility of business is to generate enough capital to support future economic growth and to create the jobs of the future. Business profits have become the primary source of capital formation, since rising consumption has decreased the funds available for investment. Business profits and social responsibility have been viewed as fundamentally incompatible. However, solutions to social problems must be profit-making if they are to be financed on a continuing basis. References. —Drucker, Peter F.; *California Mgmt Review,* Winter 1984, 26(2): pp. 53-63. Avail. ABI 84-11835

Social responsibility, Corporate responsibility, Social policy, Capital formation

A New Militancy (176)

Over the past few years, organizations that had previously kept a low profile have been adopting more aggressive strategies in advocacy and corporate image advertising. This new corporate militancy is a reaction to concerns about business influence on public policy and a distrust of corporate leaders. The public's perception of a company arises from the company's actions and messages, which are influenced by the purpose of the company and its relationship to society. Many executives do not perceive the role of their companies in society. As a result, their organizations are unable to set ethical standards needed to ensure public credibility. In the 1980s, corporations have come to be perceived as barriers to achieving quality of life. To overcome this image, corporations must understand their social responsibilities. As a citizen of society, corporations must provide goods, services, and jobs in a way that reflects contemporary expectations. —Judd, Larry R.; *Public Relations Jrnl,* Nov 1984, 40(11): pp. 15-16. Avail. ABI 85-03166

Social responsibility, Advocacy, Institutional advertising, Corporate image

The New Voluntarism (177)

A kind of new voluntarism has evolved, in which businesses loan the time and expertise of their employees to another organization for a specified period of time at no cost to the recipient. A United Way brochure describes the benefits of such an arrangement to the various parties involved: 1. The company receives recognition for its commitment to the community. 2. The employee gains leadership skills, community contacts, and experience in working with people in all types of jobs. 3. The community receives more for its charity dollar because it does not have to use its funds for salaries. These loaned executive programs are not just for nonprofit organizations. Levi Strauss volunteers both manpower and monetary assistance to smaller businesses as a public relations gesture. Chairman of the board Walter A. Haas, Jr., views voluntarism as an issue of company self-interest. He cites voluntary affirmative action and environmental control programs, which can protect companies from government regulation. References. —Beattie, Elisabeth L.; *Business & Economic Review,* Apr 1985, 31(3): pp. 22-23,28. Avail. ABI 85-18079

Volunteers, Public relations, Executives, Charitable foundations, Corporate responsibility

Nurturing Private-Sector Initiatives (178)

US businesses are reevaluating their role in the community. Although corporate executives are not elected officials responsible for the needs of a specific constituency, many chief executive officers are taking a fresh look at the role of the corporation in community service. These executives are starting to explore new alternatives to attend to the difficult task of assuring that the company's business activities make social sense. The business community must take the lead in establishing community partnerships in which all elements of the community are represented. Such a partnership would provide a forum for determining local needs and devising collective ways of addressing them. The President's Task Force on Private Sector Initiatives is urging business to provide both financial and voluntary support for community projects undertaken by community partnerships. Many business associations and individual corporations are urging their executives to become more involved. Executives are beginning to realize that there is no conflict between profits and social responsibility. —Verity, C. William, Jr.; *Industry Week,* Jul 26, 1982, 214(2): pp. 67-68. Avail. ABI 82-20134

Business, Government, Relations, Corporate responsibility, Manycompanies

Of Saints, Sinners and Socially Responsible Executives (179)

On the issue of corporate responsibility, it is a common belief that society has parallel responsibilities to the corporation, particularly in the area of establishing clear and consistent rules about what the corporation should do. This widespread position about the question of social responsibility: 1. seriously understates the ambiguity inherent in the relationship between the corporation and society, 2. exaggerates the dependency of business on other social institutions, and 3. encourages the denial of personal executive responsibility for corporate actions.A more useful image of the socially responsible executive is one of intense but potentially constructive role conflict. The executive's personal and subjective resolution of conflicting demands from society is the very essence of managerial leadership in the area of corporate responsibility. Morality may be viewed as a basic control mechanism for social system functioning. "Social system preaching" plays an important role in this control, and managers must be forceful in disclosing the rationale for their decisions that affect the public directly. References. — Waters, James A.; *Business & Society,* Winter 1980, 19(2) /v20n1: pp. 67-73. Avail. ABI 80-13731

Corporate responsibility, Social responsibility, Organizational behavior, Executives, Roles

Ohio's Public Insurance Information Program (180)

The Ohio Insurance Institute (OII) was formed in 1968 and the Ohio Insurance Information Service was merged into it. The purpose of the OII is to promote the welfare of the public and the insurance industry through: 1. research development and distribution of factual information, and 2. cooperation with governmental agencies and educational institutions. To implement these objectives, 3 divisions were created: Public Information, Research and Education, and Government and Industry Relations. OII's Public Information Division attempts to maintain public confidence in the insurance industry and to preserve Ohio's favorable climate for insurance

operations. OII programs are directed at the general public, the legislature, and the news media, and they have been especially effective in newspaper, radio and magazine advertising campaigns. In Education, OII has designed educational programs for high school teachers and pupils to improve their understanding of the business. The Ohio Insurance Guide, published annually, is a major research project and includes extensive Ohio insurance data. The Government and Industry Relations Division provides insurance information to the Ohio General Assembly and Ohio legislators in Washington. OII also works closely with the Insurance Federation of Ohio.
—Winchell, John C.; *CPCU Jrnl,* Mar 1980, 33(1): pp. 30-38. Avail. ABI 80-07637

Ohio, Insurance, Institutions, Public relations, Consumer, Education, Social responsibility, Advertising, Research, Consumerism

On Corporations and Communities (181)

The shrinking role of government and the heightened regulation and social awareness of the 1960s and 1970s have contributed to a growing role of business in society. Most business leaders today no longer see community activities as discretionary charitable donations. They realize their activities are investments that will have positive impact on their businesses' long-term profitability, success, and growth. Some of the corporate programs today include: 1. $4.7 million provided by Amoco to nonprofit organizations in Chicago, Illinois, to retrofit structures for energy savings, 2. a loan by Geico Insurance of computer specialists and equipment to help the Washington, DC, government clean up voter registration roles, 3. help from 33 Baltimore, Maryland, construction companies to clear out backed-up storm drains at no cost to the city, and 4. Memphis, Tennessee, marketing executives from Holiday Inns, Federal Express, and Plough volunteering to plan a marketing campaign to lure white students back to public schools. Marketing is the one area within a corporation best suited to help select, plan, implement, and communicate these and other types of community activities. Marketing can provide research expertise and help ensure that the activity fits into the corporation's total strategic picture. —Schofield, Elvin J.; *Marketing Communications,* Feb 1984, 9(2): pp. 64. Avail. MC 84-09632

Corporate responsibility, Social responsibility, Marketing

Operations Research and Society (182)

The problem of complex decision making is addressed from the aspect of the impact of technological progress and modern mathematical methods on decision making in government and industry. Many of the problems arising in these areas are the result of too little technology or wrong applications, not of too much technology. The computer has been one of the most important products of the past quarter century, and this technological development has both advantages and disadvantages. Some recommendations governing the future use of technology include: 1. Better knowledge must be gained of the possibilities and dangers of technological progress and computer application. 2. Checking of decision making should be better organized, especially at the preparatory stage. 3. Operations research people should be aware of the social responsibility for what they are doing. 4. Parliamentary control in many nations could be strengthened by better information systems and more supporting staff. Technological tools must be used to benefit mankind, as they can both reduce and enlarge freedom and individual rights, depending on how they are utilized. – Zoutendijk, G.; *European Jrnl of Operational Research (Netherlands),* Nov 1980, 5(5): pp. 302-308. Avail. ABI 80-22951

Technology, Computers, Operations research, Society, Computer based modeling, Political, Decision making, Control

Organizational Growth: Big Is Beautiful (183)

The observation that bigger is better for the business enterprise is a controversial one. An attempt is made to: 1. review growth as an organizational phenomenon and a near universal goal, 2. discuss the supposed association between size and organizational performance, and 3. develop an argument that growth and absolute size should be legitimate goals of an organization whether or not size can be meaningfully related to performance. While it is clear that the size of the organization is not related to performance, financial and otherwise, there are many nonfinancial advantages that accrue to the larger organization, such as: 1. pure clout, 2. larger executive salaries, 3. recognition, and 4. ability to afford specialists in all fields. There is also a downside to bigness, though. For example, larger firms are subject to closer scrutiny, greater social responsibility is expected of them, and problems of coordination and allocation of resources become more complex. Charts. References. –Dalton, Dan R. and Kesner, Idalene F.; *Jrnl of Business Strategy,* Summer 1985, 6(1): pp. 38-48. Avail. ABI 85-30674

Corporate management, Strategic management, Business growth, Organizational change, Organization development, Competitive, Matrix, Models, Organizational behavior, Acquisitions & mergers

Parents, Kids and Companies: New Rules for Business (184)

The US family has changed greatly in structure: More married women work outside the home, and there is an increase in the number of single-parent families. The number of workers who must seek daycare centers for their children is growing rapidly along with the growth of dual-career families, and firms who wish to recruit women employees will have to increase compensation benefits revolving around childcare. Such action will enhance the corporate image as well as decrease turnover. Childcare assistance models vary in terms of financial commitment made by the firm. Among the companies offering seminars to teach parents about daycare opportunities are Southwestern Bell, J. C. Penney, and Levi Strauss. Northwestern Bell and Control Data have opted to join together to provide convenient offsite daycare facilities in the Minneapolis, Minnesota area. Connecticut General Life rents on-premises space to a daycare center catering to its employees. –Schram, Rosalyn Weinman; *Personnel Jrnl,* Jun 1981, 60(6): pp. 436,438. Avail. ABI 81-14776

Working mothers, Child care, Corporate responsibility, Social responsibility, Manycompanies, Employee benefits

Perceptions of Socially Responsible Activities and   **(185)**
Attitudes: A Comparison of Business School Deans and
Corporate Chief Executives

A major group of external stakeholders in business comprises deans of collegiate schools of business. The perceptions about corporate social responsibility held by top corporate executive officers (CEO) and those held by business school deans were compared using questionnaire data supplied by 203 deans and 116 CEOs. The respondents indicated the degree to which they believed the US business community supported 15 activities commonly associated with corporate social responsibility. They were also asked to indicate their degree of agreement with 22 philosophical statements regarding social responsibility. Significant differences between the 2 groups were found for only 2 statements arguing for business assumption of social responsibility. The deans were more likely to agree that social responsibility is needed to balance corporate power and that business should be expected to solve some of society's problems. They perceived less corporate support for socially responsible activities than did the CEOs. The deans appear to be more pragmatic and pessimistic compared to the idealism and optimism expressed by many of the CEOs. Tables. References. —Ford, Robert and McLaughlin, Frank; *Academy of Mgmt Jrnl,* Sep 1984, 27(3): pp. 666-674. Avail. ABI 84-27785

Social responsibility, Business schools, Executives, Studies, Statistical analysis

A Personal Performance Review of the Board   **(186)**

Over the past 10 years, corporate governance has come under sharp public scrutiny. While the board of directors can be considered responsible for corporate wrong-doings, it is also the guiding force for firms that are trusted and respected. Based on misperceptions of runaway corporate power, a number of measures have been proposed to promote social responsibility in corporate governance, including: 1. establishing national corporate charters, 2. requiring boards to be made up entirely of outsiders, and 3. giving representatives of community and labor constituencies places on boards. Generally, existing regulatory and competitive forces ensure that board members are responsive to the long-range interests of their firms and the various constituencies these firms affect. Drastic reform measures are unnecessary. Boards with interest-group directors would be in perpetual conflict because such directors would be unfamiliar with firm operations and ill-equipped to consider the long-range interests of all. Boards should strive to improve their public image through enhanced corporate disclosure and public communication. —Shapiro, Irving S.; *Directors & Boards,* Summer 1984, 8(4): pp. 20-24. Avail. ABI 84-35451

Boards of directors, Outside directors, Qualifications, Roles

Personnel Practice in South Africa: How British   **(187)**
Companies Rate

A recent survey was conducted to determine if British company personnel management practices are directed towards significant change in South Africa and if they are any different than those of other companies operating there. The survey was conducted by questionnaires given to 181 managers from 24 British, 18 American and 121 local South African companies. Results indicate that: 1. UK personnel managment practice is not particularly different from that of South African companies. What differences there are suggest that British companies are utilizing traditional personnel practice rather than initiating new approaches in South Africa. 2. British companies are attempting to develop and recruit skilled manpower and thereby increase manpower utilization efficiencies. However, they do not seem to be emphasizing social responsibility, black advancement, or conflict resolution. Personnel management is directing efforts toward immediate and medium-term benefit, as opposed to long-term survival and prosperity. Tables. References. —Templer, Andrew; *Personnel Mgmt (UK)*, Aug 1980, 12(8): pp. 28-31. Avail. ABI 80-19079

South Africa, UK, Companies, Personnel policies, Personnel management, Racial discrimination, Social responsibility, Corporate responsibility, Studies

Peter Drucker: Nobody Says It Better (188)

At a recent symposium on social responsibility and business, management expert Peter Drucker contended that the greatest current need is for capital formation. Business is most effective in attacking social problems by using trained people and the profit motive. Drucker prefers to think in terms of leaders rather than businessmen. According to Drucker, leaders understand issues and deliberate rather than make decisions. Drucker shows appreciation of Japanese senior management's tendencies to stay out of day-to-day business operations and focus on developing human resources. Drucker perceives the current US switch from a "labor intensive" to an "information intensive" economy as one of change, but not necessarily a breakdown. —Anonymous; *Training*, Feb 1983, 20(2): pp. 61-62. Avail. ABI 83-07173

Social responsibility, Management styles, Capital formation, Technological change

Philosophical Context of Banking in the 80s (189)

The most important variable in these uncertain times is the quality of the person who is making decisions about waiting or going ahead with pursuit of opportunities accompanying change. The quality of this decision-making depends greatly on values which fortunately seem to be coming back in style now as a way of life. Leaders of the community must not overlook their responsibilities to society. They must turn from the era of both individual and corporate narcissism, and must be concerned with broad issues. Bankers must realize innovation will be critical in the days ahead. To keep and to attract the best people, bankers must provide a sense of social responsibility. In other words, bankers must be bankers in the best sense of the word rather than money-lenders. This is not a revolutionary shift in attitude, but rather a kind of enlightened self-interest. Nothing could be less responsible to society than going broke in the name of social responsibility. However, it is possible to be a part of the community, acting honorably and ethically, yet still being prosperous. —Mangels, John D.; *Bankers Monthly*, Nov 15, 1981, 98(11): pp. 21-22. Avail. ABI 81-28275

Banking, Banking industry, Business conditions, Social responsibility

Planning for Corporate Social Actions (190)

It is imperative that a company's actions in social areas be planned if the firm is to: 1. make a maximum contribution in these areas, 2. avoid criticism from the many diverse groups it must respond to, and 3. continue to reach its long range goals. Three important questions require a framework for analysis: 1. How is the responsibility to take action on a specific issue determined? 2. What elements must be considered when planning social responses? 3. Given several alternative socially impacting projects, how is the question of choice between alternatives resolved? It must first be determined whether a responsibility really exists in a certain situation. Second, after an assessment of all interest, it should be ascertained if the action is desirable and whether benefits outweigh costs. If costs can be acceptably distributed, it must be decided whether there is the managerial competence to do the job. Last, a company must decide if an act is the best use of its resources. Charts. References. —Jackson, Donald W., Jr. and Aldag, Ramon J.; *Managerial Planning,* Sep/Oct 1980, 29(2): pp. 28-33. Avail. ABI 80-18469

Planning, Corporate planning, Social responsibility, Corporate responsibility, Decision making models, Social accounting

Point of View: The Corporate Role in the Not-So-Great (191) Society

The Reagan Administration has called upon corporate and private contributions to fill the void arising from budget cuts in social programs. However, a corporation's sense of social obligation depends upon its perspective of compliance to, adaptation to, and anticipation of changing societal needs. These 3 motivating factors commonly are bound together by self-interest; a corporation will increase its social responsibility when its interests coincide with society's interests. A corporation's willingness to provide social services depends upon the public's ability to communicate needs to the corporation and the corporation's idea of a solution to provide it with the most benefits. Many think that if a social issue is complex, if the issue is accompanied by a diverse constituency, and if the benefits to the corporation are short-lived, corporate support is unlikely. Corporate involvement in social projects most likely will occur when the issue involved is manageable. References. —Rivlin, Catherine A.; *California Mgmt Review,* Summer 1983, 25(4): pp. 151-159. Avail. ABI 83-24937

Corporate responsibility, Public interest, Social responsibility

The Poletown Dilemma (192)

When General Motors Corp. (GMC) decided to accept the Detroit City Council's terms for acquiring an assembly plant cite at Poletown, issues were raised concerning a corporation's responsibility to the community in which it operates. The Michigan Supreme Court held that the city council's action was a legitimate use of eminent domain. The dissenting opinion in that case noted that the corporation had been permitted to act as a sovereign for the benefit of its private purse. One course of action in situations such as these is to present problems and proposals for solutions to representative groups such as labor organizations, the community's political leaders, and social welfare organizations. A corporation can meet its objective of social accountability by following a course that includes: 1. defining the terms it deems tolerable to lessen the harm to the community, 2. disclose these terms to all social communities involved, and 3. solicit the participation of all groups involved. References. —Auerbach, Joseph; *Harvard Business Review,* May/Jun 1985, 63(3): pp. 93-99. Avail. ABI 85-19684

General Motors-Detroit, Plant location, Eminent domain (LAW), Condemnation (RE), State court decisions, Implications, Corporate responsibility, Case studies, Social responsibility, Guidelines

Political Risk Problems Must Be Dealt With-Now! (193)

The prevalence of wars, riots, embargoes, sabotage, hostage situations, and terrorism is giving rise to a new specialized type of insurance. Companies are being formed for the express purpose of providing coverage against international instability and related problems. Among factors contributing to this world climate are the following: 1. Western powers are no longer able to influence emerging Third World countries. 2. Due to linkage, once seemingly isolated events such as those in Afghanistan and El Salvador can no longer be ignored. 3. Wall Street keeps steady pressure on to minimize political surprises. 4. Insurers have a corporate responsibility for lives and safety of personnel. Since the government's record of accuracy in predicting foreign political climates is something less than spectacular, that responsibility will fall increasingly upon the shoulders of the risk manager. Companies should review several political scenarios to assess their might-have-been impact on company operations. —Anonymous; *Risk Mgmt,* Jun 1981, 28(6): pp. 44-45. Avail. ABI 81-17854

International, Political, Risk management

Pressures Build to Offer Lifeline Banking (194)

Consumer activists, legislators, and regulators are expressing concern about the consequences of financial service deregulation. Among their worries are: 1. new or increased service charges on low-balance deposit accounts, 2. branch closings in low-income areas, 3. service reductions, 4. excessive holds on deposited items, and 5. inaccurate or misleading disclosure and advertising of account terms. Consumer groups charge that those most adversely affected by these conditions are low-income groups, the elderly, and the young. The steps advocated to stop or at least bring such practices under control are called "lifeline banking" and are modeled in some cases after measures taken in some states to guarantee basic utility services to certain public groups. Institutions must now reevaluate their basic offerings and determine whether: 1. fees can be justified, 2. charges are fully disclosed when new accounts are opened, 3. community needs have been considered in designing services, and 4. the opportunity for developing low-cost services for low-income groups has been considered. Tables. —Brantley, R. Lamar; *Savings Institutions,* Jan 1985, 106(1): pp. 90-91. Avail. ABI 85-08839

Bank services, Bank service charges, Low income, Customers, Social responsibility

Private Management and Public Policy (195)

In examining the involvement of corporate management in areas of social concern, the first step is to define the appropriate scope of corporate responsibility. This includes primary involvement-the essential tasks of establishing a facility, procuring supplies, engaging employees, and conducting the marketing and manufacturing activities-as well as secondary involvement. Secondary involvement includes consequential effects resulting from the primary considerations, such as earning opportunities and the impact of these opportunities on the community. The goals and criteria to guide a manager in these areas are found within the framework of public policy, which includes everything from the text of regulations to public opinion and emerging issues. The manager must base policy on an awareness of social concerns and intentions as they relate to both primary and secondary involvement. Generally, public policy for the firm must be developed when there is a gap between the actual performance of a firm or industry and the performance which is expected by the public. Greater attention to this fact by business would reduce the need for government regulation. References. –Preston, Lee E. and Post, James E.; *California Mgmt Review,* Spring 1981, 23(3): pp. 56-62. Avail. ABI 81-19653

Public policy, Corporate responsibility, Social responsibility, Regulation, Compliance, Costs

The 'Promises, Promises' Era Is Turning (196)

The 1970s was an age of promises made by corporations. In fact, in the context of all corporate actions and expenditures, public interest or public policy-related activities still are a small part of the financial pie, although a number of individual companies are doing very good work. Another negative element is that, in many large companies, there is still considerable doubt that spending large sums on community involvement is wise. There are several trends for corporate social responsibility that can be identified for the rest of this decade: 1. More and more corporations will establish departments to handle social responsibility as a major function. 2. The handling of charitable contributions will alter dramatically. 3. Voluntarism will start to find expression in corporate activities. 4. The most promising area of activity will be the government-business partnership at the local level. 5. The idea of social responsibility will impact areas of the private sector other than publicly held corporations. 6. Social responsibility will become worldwide. 7. The study of corporate social responsibility will emerge as an important part of formal business education. 8. Social policy, futurism, and corporate planning will mesh. –Dennis, Lloyd B.; *Public Relations Qtrly,* Winter 1981/1982, 26(4): pp. 13-17. Avail. ABI 82-11255

Social responsibility, Corporate responsibility, Predictions, Donations, Social policy

The Public Interest Goes International (197)

American activist groups, which have largely focused on the domestic social performance of major corporations, are now turning their attention more intensively on international trade and investment operations. This interest is symbolized by the recent launching of Multinational Monitor, a new monthly magazine published by Ralph Nader's Corporate Accountability Research

Group. This magazine represents the globalization of US activist demands for corporate responsibility and accountability and offers a continuing vehicle for comparable groups around the world to exchange information and publicize firms that are the targets of their campaigns. The agenda of the new magazine is the usual litany of charges against multinational corporations. Activist groups are also directing their attention to the governmental and international financial institutions with which private corporations and banks often work. One of the impacts of this new activist focus is to challenge public institutions which have seldom been a source of controversy. —Barovick, Richard L.; *Business & Society Review,* Summer 1980, (34): pp. 53-54. Avail. ABI 80-19213

> Corporate responsibility, Accountability, Advocacy, Public interest, Multinational corporations, International, Agencies

Public Interest Accounting: A Look at the Issues   (198)

When members of a profession become involved in public-interest activities, it is far more than a public relations campaign. This involvement is the cornerstone of a vocation's claim of professionalism. The Commission on Standards of Education and Experience for Certified Public Accountants has cited 7 characteristics as being representative of a profession. The accounting profession fulfills all but 2 of the characteristics quite well. The criteria not fulfilled are an acceptance of social responsibility and the advancement of the social obligation. A group called Accountants for the Public Interest (API) has been organized to address public-policy issues. The fundamental issues that remain unresolved are: 1. nonadvocacy, 2. conflict of interest, 3. quality of work, 4. competition, 5. professional liability, and 6. confidentiality. These issues need to be resolved before API can gain commitment and support from the major certified public accountant firms and the profession. API is one means through which accountants can express their social concern by helping to solve social problems. References. —Skousen, Clifford R.; *Accounting, Organizations & Society (UK),* 1982, 7(1): pp. 79-85. Avail. ABI 82-11682

> Public interest, Social accounting, Social responsibility, Accounting firms, CPAs, Independence, Conflicts of interest, Competition

Public Invisibility of Corporate Leaders   (199)

Corporate executives have great potential for inspiring leadership, yet they fail to present themselves as persons who truly care about the world in which they live. The popular notion is that executives would rather see the world blow up than jeopardize their profits. To dispel this notion, they need to let people see what kinds of human beings they really are, what they believe in, and what they hope to accomplish through their business activities personally and for society. Talented business executives should: 1. integrate their communal and business lives, 2. develop an appetite for being in the public eye, 3. speak publicly about human needs and values as well as economics when discussing business policies, 4. initiate company programs that grow out of personal interests and speak publicly about them, 5. develop a sense of style or flair when conducting business, and 6. persuade the stockholders of the importance of managers being human beings with deep concerns about the health and welfare of their fellow citizens. In so doing, they will change the public perception of who business leaders are and provide effective leadership for the nation. —Finn, David; *Harvard Business Review,* Nov/Dec 1980, 58(6): pp. 102-110. Avail. ABI 80-22230

Corporate management, Executives, Image, Public opinion, Leadership, Social responsibility

Public Policy, an Opportunity for Business (200)

A blending of the economic and social policy of past years started in the early 1980s, according to research by Yankelovich, Skelly & White. The national focus following the end of World War II was almost entirely economic, but a social agenda became dominant in the 1960s. However, a number of events in the 1970s, such as recurring recession, raised some questions concerning the wisdom and cost of achieving every social goal. The resulting new pragmatism should present opportunities for business to improve productivity and stimulate economic growth. Private business will also take on many of the social responsibilities that once fell to government-run programs. This situation offers a chance for business to shed its bad guy image and to emerge as the nation's public-policy champion. The role of the public relations professional in business policymaking will expand as a result. —Blatherwick, Gerald D.; *Industry Week,* Jun 11, 1984, 221(6): pp. 10. Avail. ABI 84-22960

Public policy, Social responsibility, Public relations

Public Policy: Becoming a Better Advocate (201)

The way in which US corporations use the media to advocate their positions on public policy issues influences the public's perception of those corporations. However, many advocacy campaigns have mixed results because of the ineffective use of issue advertising. There are 3 ways to improve the quality of advocacy campaigns. The first approach is to create a positive corporate image by promoting ideas and debate on important public policy issues. The campaign does not have to be directly related to the company's operations and should be educational rather than adversarial. The 2nd approach is to use effective sources, such as multiple, recognized authorities. The 3rd approach is to be creative to reflect commitment to the issue in question. The best issue campaigns are developed in-house by people who understand the issues involved. Top management should seek approval and involvement from the board of directors when considering advocacy campaigns. The support of the directors and the use of outside advice lend objectivity and credibility to issues advertising. —Sethi, S. Prakash; *Directors & Boards,* Fall 1984, 9(1): pp. 12,14. Avail. ABI 84-37393

Corporate responsibility, Advocacy, Public policy, Advertising campaigns, Quality, Guidelines, Boards of directors, Roles

Public Relations-An Integral Part of Your Management Team (202)

Public relations (PR) is an important aspect of organizational decision making, and PR practitioners can make valuable direct contributions to the decision-making process. In order for PR persons to become part of the management mainstream, they should: 1. Gain management's support and understanding. 2. Become issue-oriented. 3. Learn to think like managers. Four important relationships are those which exist between PR and marketing, advertising, personnel, and the legal department. PR can make several kinds of contributions to marketing via cooperation, while overall corporate communications is the hottest area of cooperation for advertising and public relations. In order to ensure employment policies and practices consistent with overall corporate image and social responsibility, personnel and PR must cooperate. However, legal departments and PR often find themselves in competition for the ear of top management. References. – Aronoff, Craig E. and Baskin, Otis W.; *Business,* Nov/Dec 1981, 31(6): pp. 16-22. Avail. ABI 82-03362

Public relations, Organizational, Decision making, Roles, Management decisions, Corporate management, Marketing management

Public Relations and Business Schools (203)
Through the years, the position of Public Relations (PR) has gained in importance; today, it influences corporate policy and public debate issues. During the 1980s, many demands for new skills will occur in PR/public affairs. Skills in public affairs/communications will become increasingly necessary as corporations assume a broader role in society. Some existing educational and training programs help prepare corporate managers in PR/public affairs. PR issue management aspects are offered in some advanced management courses. However, few, if any, business schools offer PR or public affairs as a separate course. Generally, PR education lacks the respect accorded other professional training programs. Thus, overview units must be prepared that can be worked into existing public policy courses or other appropriate parts of the curriculum. Public policy has been viewed too narrowly by educators. Public policy and PR must be perceived in a broader sense, to constantly review issues which can impact a company concerning its: 1. operations, 2. products, 3. reputation, and 4. profits. Business schools are thus challenged to meet the needs of a new business era. –King, Kerryn; *Vital Speeches,* Feb 15, 1982, 48(9): pp. 271-274. Avail. ABI 82-06937

Public relations, Business schools, Public policy, Higher education, Corporate responsibility

Public Relations in the Third World: The African (204) Context
American public relations (PR) practitioners have a role that is very different from that of their Third World counterparts. In the West, it is generally assumed that the PR practitioner will be socially responsible. In the Third World, however, PR practices are designed to be consistent with political ideologies, levels of development, and sociopolitical controls. To be socially responsible, the PR officer in a developing nation is expected to be a team player on the side of government. In politically unstable Africa, government PR is used to present an image of a unified country. Western PR practitioners in the Third World need to reorient traditional, Western principles to that environment and get firsthand experience with the culture, the value system, and the political system of the society with which they are dealing. Practitioners also must be aware that communications systems in the Third

World are not likely to function as efficiently as they do in the West. —Pratt, Cornelius; *Public Relations Jrnl,* Feb 1985, 41(2): pp. 10-16. Avail. ABI 85-10608

Public relations, Practices, Roles, Third world, Social responsibility, Corporate responsibility

Public Relations Entails More Than Press Agentry (205)

The need for effective communication is as great in the non-profit sector as it is in the business world. Public relations (PR) is a management function. It should be a comprehensive program that is part of policy-making, planning, and problem solving. Voluntary agencies and hospitals have not been quick to recognize this need, and agency boards must be convinced. One reason for the limited implementation of PR as a management function has been a lack of professionalism in the field. The PR practitioner must be management material and must also have a sense of social responsibility. The PR person needs a professional understanding of marketing and advertising, as well as strong writing and editorial skills. The PR practitioner must also be capable of advising and counseling management. The PR function should be a separate function and not involved with fund raising and volunteer services. —Scanlon, Walter F.; *Fund Raising Mgmt,* Dec 1980, 11(10): pp. 34-37,42. Avail. ABI 81-00934

Nonprofit organizations, Public relations, Programs, Standards, Problem solving, Accreditation, Social responsibility

Public Relations Challenges (206)

According to the most recent study in a series of 5-year surveys of Fortune 500 public relations executives, the biggest challenge facing the executives is developing and maintaining a positive corporate image. Other challenges cited include improving employee communication, marketing communication, and government relations. Although most of the 163 respondents believe top management is showing more respect for the public relations function, a more long-term orientation is needed to cope with today's rapidly changing environment. The challenges public relations executives face have changed since 1963. The first survey reported marketing communication as the biggest challenge. Many trends influence the public relations function. These trends include concerns about the company's role in society, the growing number of small businesses, and an increasingly educated workforce. In addition, employee involvement in corporate management is increasing. Tables. —Strenski, James B.; *Public Relations Jrnl,* Nov 1984, 40(11): pp. 41-42. Avail. ABI 85-03173

Public relations, Goals, Surveys, Internal public relations, Community relations, Consumer relations, Social responsibility

Public Rights and Corporate Social Responsibility: A (207) Profitable Marriage

The consumer movement will continue to have profound effects on business in the 1980s. Business had initially responded to consumerism by developing strategies to meet directly the challenge of consumers and business continued as usual. This approach reflected the needs of business more than the solutions to the consumer problems. Business leaders have now found that support for consumers' rights does not always compromise company objectives. The growth of the new business profession-consumer affairs-is also indicative of the impact of consumerism on business. Business must begin its response to the consumer movement by sensitizing itself to the attitudes of its customers. This is especially important in the retailing industry where complaint handling can be a very useful tool. This should include some form of complaint analysis with direct feedback to management. Good complaint handling has other advantages as customers will often turn to litigation when there is no impartial forum where they can bring their complaints. A number of companies have created and developed consumer affairs departments as a mechanism for dealing with customer problems, placing this area on the same plane with sales, design engineering, and marketing. Other approaches that can help meet the challenge of the consumer movement include: 1.scheduled dialogue sessions to listen to consumer and special interest groups, 2. the creation of public advisory panels, and 3. the appointment of public members to corporate boards. – Haney, Camille; *Retail Control*, Mar 1980, 48(7): pp. 16-27. Avail. ABI 80-07572

Corporate, Social responsibility, Public, Rights, Consumer attitudes, Consumerism, Complaints, Handling, Consumer credit, Consumer relations

Public Service Needed, Now More than Ever (208)

Years ago, Louis Dublin felt that the life insurance industry could assist national health and welfare organizations. This resulted in the public service program cosponsored by the National Association of Life Underwriters (NALU) and the American Council of Life Insurance. For 27 years, the NALU has honored local life underwriter associations for their public service programs. Community service programs are greatly needed today for various reasons, some major ones being the aging of the US population and the entrance of Third World minorities into the US. The changing American family is also creating needs for such programs. More women are joining the marketplace, and there is an increase in teenage alcoholism, drug abuse, and pregnancy. Government does not have the resources to deal effectively with these problems; thus, the local insurance agent must do something. Because insurance is service-oriented it is related to community involvement and responsibility. –Schweiker, Richard S.; *National Underwriter (Life/Health)*, Sep 28, 1983, 87(39A): pp. 6,22. Avail. ABI 83-28174

Insurance agents & brokers, Community relations, Social responsibility

Public Versus Business Expectations: Two Views on (209) Social Responsibility for Small Business

To address the social responsibility of small business and make comparisons between small business and big business with respect to the nature and fulfillment of social responsibility, a questionnaire was constructed based on results of Erika Wilson's survey (1980), and was used in a random telephone survey in a midwestern city. Responses were solicited from 51 business owners/operators, and 65 individuals not directly related to a business. Results indicate that business owners/operators tend to have a more complete understanding of their social responsibility than does the general public. Responsibility to the customer was the component of social responsibility mentioned most often by both groups. Non-business individuals were more likely to agree that there is no difference in the responsibilities of large firms and small ones. Both groups felt that the small business sector adequately fulfilled its social responsibility, although the small business owners seem to have less confidence in their performance than does the general public. The change in attitudes on the part of both groups may be due to businesses' greater concern about social responsibility or to individuals' increasing realism in their expectations. Tables. References. –Chrisman, James J. and Fry, Fred L.; *Jrnl of Small Business Mgmt,* Jan 1982, 20(1): pp. 19-26. Avail. ABI 82-07155

Social responsibility, Small business, Attitude surveys, Corporate responsibility, Social research, Statistical data, Expectations

Public/Private Sector Relations (210)

Public administrators can meet community needs more effectively by realizing the positive influence of the private sector. In recognizing the significant value of interaction with the private sector, public managers must: 1. realize the scope and utilization of public/private-sector initiatives, 2. understand the impact of these initiatives on the domains involved, and 3. develop a plan of action. The scope of public/private-sector interaction must embrace government, nonprofit organizations, and business. The domains involved in public/private-sector initiatives depend upon an individual manager's perspective. Each manager reviews and analyzes a proposal from a different perspective. Public managers should organize a framework in which to view a public/private-sector initiative during its conception and implementation. The initiative should: 1. be an agreement to assess the needs and goals of the community, 2. fit into the community structure, and 3. be viewed as a method for action and innovation. A planning model for a public/private-sector initiative includes several stages for developing a successful initiative. –Adams, Salisbury M.; *Bureaucrat,* Spring 1983, 12(1): pp. 7-10. Avail. ABI 83-13092

Public sector, Private sector, Cooperation, Social services, Social responsibility

Reagan's Second Thoughts on Corporate Giving (211)

Early in his administration, President Reagan asked the American Enterprise Institute (AEI) to determine how neighborhood groups, churches, families, voluntary and ethnic groups, corporations and labor unions could help deal with such problems as youth unemployment, health care, and child welfare. AEI's response was a report released this summer entitled Meeting Human Needs: Toward a New Public Philosophy. The report says that the gigantic social services bureaucracy, whether funded by government or the private sector, is top-heavy and ineffective. Efforts to help those in need should instead focus on employing the potential of what AEI calls mediating structures - churches, family units, grass-roots neighborhood groups, and other groups that fall between the individual and the huge institutions of modern society. However, President Reagan was not enthusiastic about the report. Between requesting it and receiving it, he had already named another group to deal with the same issue, the President's Task Force on Private-Sector Initiatives. The Task Force has recommended that by 1986 every company in the US give 2% of pretax net income to nonprofit groups doing public service work. —Olasky, Marvin N.; *Fortune,* Sep 20, 1982, 106(6): pp. 130-136. Avail. ABI 82-22994

Social responsibility, Corporate responsibility, Government, Social policy, Social goals

Reassessing the Role of Public Responsibility (212) Committees/Profile of Public Responsibility Committees/Top Issues on the Committee Agenda

In a recent interview, Vernon E. Jordan, Jr., a partner in Akin, Gump, Strauss, Hauer & Feld and a director of public responsibility committees for several companies, defined public responsibility as concern for such areas as the environment and the community that are outside a company's traditional bottom-line concerns. Public responsibility committees are an outgrowth of social circumstances in the 1970s. Major issues faced by these committees include affirmative action, occupational health and safety, and pollution. Worker retraining and the related issue of maintaining employment in the US are also areas of concern for corporate citizenship. Proper staffing, commitment by the chief executive officer to the public responsibility committee, and enthusiasm by the committee's chairperson are vital to the effectiveness of such committees. Future issues for these committees are likely to include undocumented workers and wellness concerns. A profile of public responsibility committees and future issues for committees as perceived by members are included. Tables. —Anonymous; *Directors & Boards,* Spring 1985, 9(3): pp. 22-27. Avail. ABI 85-18628

Boards of directors, Committees, Social responsibility, Corporate responsibility, Manycompanies, Manypeople

Reforming Corporate Governance/Difficulties in (213) Overseeing Ethical Policy

Corporate boards have failed to take responsibility for guiding and overseeing the ethical behavior of firms. Despite trends toward increasing use of outside board members to ensure board objectivity, corporations have continued to place self-interest above public interest, and boards have not been held accountable for corporate wrongdoings. Nader proposes several steps that could improve the governance function and accountability of corporate boards: 1. Board members should be elected for full-time positions to oversee specific areas of responsibility. 2. Boards should have special staffs to investigate corporate operations and ensure that critical information reaches board attention. 3. Through the establishment of cumulative voting procedures and more systematic corporate disclosure, board members would be encouraged to take their positions more seriously. 4. Firms should have a corporate ombudsman who would take serious matters of employee and shareholder concern directly to the board. Andrews comments that social responsibility rests with a firm's chief executive and is beyond the scope of the board. References. —Nader, Ralph and Andrews, Kenneth R.; *California Mgmt Review,* Summer 1984, 26(4): pp. 126-137. Avail. ABI 84-29477

Boards of directors, Responsibilities, Obligations, Corporate, Reforms, Ethics, Behavior, Corporate responsibility, Social responsibility

Regional Differences Fuel the Corporate-Public Policy Debate   (214)

The US is a collection of distinct regions that operate from unique values and attitudes that frequently surface in the form of regional public policy. An understanding of the underlying attitudes that shape a region's public policy and that influence corporate policy can be critical to the public relations manager, whose job is to help manage the corporate public policy debate. Research conducted for a Fortune 100 corporation attempted to determine whether attitude differences existed between senior corporate policymakers at company headquarters in one region and public opinion leaders in another region. A survey was completed by 72 representatives of key groups of opinion leaders, activists, and senior executives and managers. The results of the study indicated significant differences between opinion leaders and corporate executives. Further, the degree to which the 2 sets of attitudes converge or diverge on given issues determines to a great extent corporate public relations policies and strategies. Table. —Rada, S. E.; *Public Relations Qtrly,* Summer 1983, 28(2): pp. 29-31. Avail. ABI 83-22872

Attitude surveys, Policy making, Executives, Public opinion, Public relations, Energy, Social responsibility, Quality of life

Regulation and the Sociopathic Firm   (215)

The sociopathic firm is marked by the same characteristics as denote the sociopathic person: 1. low regard for others, 2. little respect for conventional morality, and 3. high need for immediate gratification. The sociopathic firm is the result of improper corporate socialization. In an economy evolving toward corporate viability based on social responsibility and responsiveness to external constituencies, the sociopathic firm jeopardizes its survival by focusing on irresponsible actions to boost short-term profits. Moreover, it fails to learn from past mistakes. Regulation has proved a poor vehicle for socializing the sociopathic firm because of the slowness of the bureaucratic process in setting and enforcing regulations and because of the lack of consistency in the reasonableness of regulatory requirements. To promote cooperative and adaptive social learning on the part of regulated firms, both the structure of regulatory agencies and their approach to regulation must change. References. —Daneke, Gregory A.; *Academy of Mgmt Review,* Jan 1985, 10(1): pp. 15-20. Avail. ABI 85-08154

Social responsibility, Corporate responsibility, Accountability, Regulation, Organizational behavior, Socioeconomic factors, Social psychology

A Regulatory Compliance Model   (216)

A model has been developed to estimate the likelihood of a profit-making firm's compliance with government regulation. The scope is limited to those regulations which attempt to internalize social costs (social responsibility regulations). The equation leads to a calculation of probability of compliance only for a single firm and not for all firms in an industry. The model was developed on the theory that a regulation which attempts to induce business to assume social responsibility alters a firm's methods of operation over an extended period of time due to the indefinite duration of the regulation. A decision to comply or not to comply will be viewed by the firm in much the same way it views a decision regarding proposed investment alternatives. Introduction of precision into the making of public policy should result in more efficient regulation and a reduction in costs to the firm. It will introduce greater equity into the policy-making process. Equations. References. –Baron, Barry R. and Baron, Philip; *Jrnl of Contemporary Business,* Second Quarter 1980, 9(2): pp. 139-150. Avail. ABI 80-19453

Regulation, Compliance, Models, Probability, Forecasting, Public policy, Deregulation

Religion: The Spirit or the Enemy of Capitalism (217)

Churches and corporations have traditionally maintained an adversarial relationship whereby churches call for businesses to better distribute their wealth among the poor, and corporate managers continue to control their contributions to society through the market. Churches are limited in their understanding of the corporate world by a militant form of liberation theology that advocates rapid changes in social structures, and by an antibusiness bias. Catholic theologian Michael Novak posits a threefold theory of democratic capitalism that accounts for the interdependence of political, economical, and religious factors of capitalism and illustrates that corporations do aid the human moral endeavor. Religious and business leaders must cooperate through open lines of communications so as to maintain a creative rather than a destructive tension between their separate visions. Churches can take a more active part in influencing democratic capitalism, while business managers can share their knowledge to help churches transform their good intentions into tangible outcomes. References. –Williams, Oliver F.; *Business Horizons,* Nov/Dec 1983, 26(6): pp. 6-13. Avail. ABI 83-32313

Religion, Capitalism, Social customs, Ethics, Multinational corporations, Socialism, Political systems, Social responsibility

A Reply to Professor Kripke: The Negative, Not the (218) Positive, Is the Real Issue of Corporate Governance

Standards of corporate responsibility must be allowed to change in order to meet the legitimate goals which society expects. Some feel that American business has become too professionalized, leaving a vulnerable economy controlled by people motivated only by their own interests and goals. Today's corporate strategy is based upon the premise of realizing maximal return upon investment. Even those corporations looking for long-term as well as short-term interests follow the strategy of selling or otherwise liquidating any unit which is not increasing either corporate growth or cash flow. Thus, the real problem is a new legal definition of corporate responsibility, which will insulate directors from liability to shareholders for adoption of any policy tending to benefit the public interest, as long as it does not adversely affect investors to an unreasonable extent. While some observers feel that case law is moving in that direction, what is needed is carefully drafted legislation to the same effect. References. –Sealy, Albert H.; *Business Lawyer,* Jul 1981, 36(4): pp. 1655-1666. Avail. Business 81-22116

Corporate, Accountability, Corporate management, Boards of directors, Corporate responsibility, Public interest, Social responsibility

Retailer's Social Responsibility: A New Consciousness (219)

Since 1975, when a study was made to assess the social responsibility of retailers, there has been intensive focus on social responsibility in business. The incidence of product recalls and increased regulation could be expected to produce a change in opinion. The same questionnaire was given to a randomly selected sample of retailers, representing more than 90% of the establishments in the region. a 91% level of cooperation was achieved. With 2 exceptions, the changes in responses to the questionnaire were all in a more socially responsible direction. In general, they reflect a growing disapproval of dubious selling practices by retailers. There is evidence of increased concern for long-run customer patronage over short-run profit goals. The uniformity of consensus across retail types is an optimistic sign for the business community and for society. Charts. References. –Dornoff, Ronald J. and Dwyer, F. Robert; *Jrnl of Contemporary Business,* Second Quarter 1980, 9(2): pp. 151-161. Avail. ABI 80-19454

Social responsibility, Retailing industry, Perceptions, Attitudes, Studies, Retailing

Revitalizing Corporate Democracy: Control of (220) Investment Managers' Voting on Social Responsibility Proxy Issues

During the last 10 years, proxy voting on issues involving the social responsibilities of publicly held companies has become a significant national concern. However, the impact on corporate behavior will be small so long as significant changes do not occur in the voting behavior of financial institutions that serve as trustees of the enormous amounts of capital. These trustees rarely vote in favor of social responsibility issues, and instead vote with management. Proxy issues concerning social responsibility will be seriously considered by corporate management only when the power of these trustees in the corporate political process is understood and corporate democracy is restored. Corporate democracy could be furthered by facilitating participation in proxy voting by beneficiaries of pension plans and other trust accounts. One way to bring necessary changes about would be to initiate statutory, regulatory, and institutional reforms to improve the efficacy of social responsibility proxy voting. References. –Curzan, Myron P. and Pelesh, Mark L.; *Harvard Law Review,* Feb 1980, 93(4): pp. 670-700. Avail. Harvard 80-06671

Social responsibility, Proxy solicitation, SEC proxy rules, SEC 34, Corporate responsibility, Proxy statements, Institutional, Investors, Voting, Stockholders, Fiduciaries, Pension funds, Reforms

The Righteous and the Powerful: Differing Paths to (221) Social Goals

A growing number of church-related institutions are influencing the behavior of corporations in complex ways. Church intervention in economic affairs generally takes one of 2 forms: 1. direct pressure and confrontation, or 2. rapprochement and alleviation of the problem. The halo effect of the good-versus-evil character of confrontations between business and the church often makes business defensive. Analysis of church activism reveals 3 problem areas: 1. exaggerated and strident demands by activists, 2.

dominance by a minority within the church of the activist movement, and 3. the difficulty in determining priorities for intervention. —Sethi, S. Prakash; *Business & Society Review,* Summer 1985, (54): pp. 37-44. Avail. ABI 85-33836

Religious organizations, Activists, Conflicts, Boycotts, Corporate responsibility, Social responsibility

The Rise of the New Organization (222)

As more business functions become automated, creation will be a more important aspect of work. Author Isaac Asimov believes people and companies will be judged on their contributions to the betterment of society, and management styles will reflect this service standard. The need for flexibility, creativity, and entrepreneurship will become more demanding because increased production automation will free people for planning, problem solving, human relations, research, and meetings. More people will work at home, and management in the workplace will be more people-oriented. In the best scenario, people will live longer productive lives and pursue multiple careers. Managers will relinquish order-giving roles for those of teacher, consultant, counselor, and facilitator. A renewed work ethic will include a stronger stress on accountability. In the emerging environment, the multipurpose organization will demand managers capable of specifying multiple goals, weighting and interrelating those goals, and finding synergistic policies that accomplish more than a single goal. —Goddard, Robert W.; *Management World,* Jan 1985, 14(1): pp. 7-11. Avail. ABI 85-03416

Corporate culture, Changes, Predictions, Automation, Employees, Managers, Corporate responsibility, Social responsibility, Implications

The Role of Hospital Administrators in Multihospital (223) Systems

Using data gathered from interviews with 42 administrators in 11 multihospital systems, the role of the administrator was examined. Questions addressed were: 1. What is the most important work performed by the administrator? 2. What similarities and differences are exhibited by them due to the type of multihospital system in which they work? 3. How much of their work is guided by corporate structure, and do they view this guidance as supportive or constraining? 4. Are other factors besides type of multihospital system influencing their work? A sampling of findings includes: 1. Other influencing factors were found to be training and experience, tenure at the hospital, and personal contacts with key people in the hospital and the community. 2. Administrators viewed planning, policymaking, financial management, and human resource management as among the most important work they perform. 3. Differences observed according to type of multihospital system included local versus corporate responsibility for operations, extent of corporate guidance, and physician recruitment difficulty. Tables. Graphs. References. —Kleiner, Stanley G.; *Hospital & Health Services Administration,* Mar/Apr 1984, 29(2): pp. 26-44. Avail. ABI 84-14661

Hospitals, Administration, Roles, Job descriptions, Health care industry, Surveys

The Roots of New Federalism (224)

The purpose of President Reagan's New Federalism is to change the relationship between the citizen and government, returning to the framework like that of the early days of the Republic. To appreciate the historical significance of Reagan's approach, it should be remembered that the US form of government was founded on a blend of 2 contradictory principles. Federalists thought a strong national government was essential, while Anti-Federalists believed the Republic could be sustained only if the national government was weak and political power localized. In practice, the modern liberal theory of federalism has clear and serious shortcomings. Reagan's appreciation of these shortcomings and his basically 18th century view of community lie at the heart of his New Federalism. If the recent trend that has eroded individual responsibility and neighborliness in US society is reversed, it will cause major changes in government and a basic reassessment of individual and corporate responsibility. —Butler, Stuart M.; *Cornell Executive,* Spring 1983, 9(2): pp. 12-15. Avail. ABI 83-28399

Federalism, Political power, Political systems, State government, Local government

Runaway Inflation: Formula for Economic Holocaust (225)

For the nearly 50 years since the Great Depression, the fear of a falling economy and the dire consequences that go with it has been a major concern of US public policy. Although there has been some abatement with the present Administration, signals are again producing evidence of that fear. Hyperinflation is fast becoming a serious economic problem; and runaway inflation is the economic equivalent of a holocaust. Inflation is an economic phenomenon, as well as the final result of a system of social thought and practice. Now is the time for re-examination of Depression-born justification for current policy. As a result of nearly 50 years of government expansion: 1. non-governmental institutions have been limited, 2. development has been hindered, and 3. innovation has been repressed. The US society has become dependent on poorly working government programs. The solution to runaway inflation is a counterrevolution, a massive resumption of social responsibility by non-governmental institutions. New leadership is needed, with a new social strategy that works largely outside the political system. — Cornuelle, Richard; *Industry Week,* Sep 7, 1981, 210(5): pp. 106-109. Avail. ABI 81-22149

Hyper, Inflation, Economic policy

Saints and Sinners? Church-Sponsored Critics of Private (226) Enterprise Gain a Following

The Interfaith Center on Corporate Responsibility (ICCR), an offshoot of the National Council of Churches, is organizing a church investor activism movement which criticizes corporate behavior in a wide range of activities from nuclear power to doing business with South Africa. Despite its limited budget of $300,000 and its small size, the ICCR has brought many issues before corporate leaders and the public, often winning supporting votes from various lobbying groups with which it has a common cause. The ICCR sees its role as being loyal critics of the system, not anticapitalists, and seeks to discuss issues with management.Tim Smith, the ICCR's executive director has had more than casual contact with supporters of Marxist guerilla groups. In his early days, he worked on the Southern Africa Magazine. Further, the ICCR does not criticize doing business with the USSR. Currently, church groups are backing such resolutions as getting Consolidated Edison to close down 2 reactor units located close to Manhattan and proposing that Coca-Cola get its foreign subsidiaries to observe human rights. —Boland, John C.; *Barron's,* May 5, 1980, 60(18): pp. 11,22-28. Avail. ABI 80-10184

    Corporate responsibility, Social responsibility, Interest groups, Activists, Lobbying, Accountability, International trade

A Sampling of Twenty-Five Codes of Corporate Conduct: Call for a Renascence (227)

The Foreign Corrupt Practices Act of 1977 (FCPA) has had a significant impact on existing corporate ethics literature. Ten major themes appear in the samples of codes presented here. After the predictable themes of honesty and integrity and compliance with the law per se, are themes which are directly related to concerns expressed in the FCPA. Of the dominant, specific issues treated in the codes that were reviewed, the issue of political contributions made from corporate funds numbered first as a topic of concern. The next most important issue appeared to be kickbacks and bribes. These are specifically mentioned in the FCPA as crimes. None of the topics seems to have emerged as industry's own struggle with the issues unique to for-profit institutions. Not even the issue of a new mode of government interference has prompted corporate management to renovate their codes. Few of the codes examined linked corporate ethics to profitability. The decade ahead should see boardrooms formulate active codes rather than codes which merely react to the next regulatory crisis. Tables. References. — Holt, Robert N.; *Directors & Boards,* Summer 1980, 5(2): pp. 7-17. Avail. ABI 80-17108

    Foreign Corrupt Practices Act 1977-US, Corporate responsibility, Social responsibility, Ethics, Codes, Manycompanies, Long term planning, Profitability

Sanctions, Incentives, and Corporate Behavior (228)

Insight into effective incentives and sanctions to promote corporate social responsibility is gained through examination of: 1. cases in which corporations have changed their behaviors and the reasons they have changed, and 2. other cases in which corporate behavior change has not occurred. Corporations have been motivated to pursue short-term results with quick payoffs rather than long-range objectives that would benefit business and society together. Media pressures and personal liability pressures can be used to divert corporate attention from short-term profit maximization. Sanctions must be stiff, sure to be enforced, and swiftly applied in order to influence corporate behavior. Corporations must provide incentives for their managers and employees to achieve objectives for social responsibility, e.g., stock-option or profit-sharing plans that give managers a stake in the long-term success of the firm. The use of sanctions and incentives as counterpressures to irresponsible corporate behavior can improve the financial as well as the social performance of business. —Jones, Peter T.; *California Mgmt Review,* Spring 1985, 27(3): pp. 119-131. Avail. ABI 85-22800

    Corporate responsibility, Social responsibility, Incentives, Sanctions, Corporate, Behavior

Says Business Must Help Make Government Work (229)

Paul S. Wise, retiring president of the Alliance of American Insurers, urges the private sector to assume a much stronger role in making government work. Business leaders must be more involved in addressing the lack of leadership and the failure of the process. Insurers must be involved with the insurance regulatory systems, the judicial system, the fiscal system, the monetary system, the bureaucracy, and other parts of the total economic and political process. An effective trade association can have a major impact on the processes of government. To be effective, the trade association and the industry it represents must always seek first to identify with and serve the public interest. The Alliance of American Insurers employs coalition strategies to overcome the fragmentation of the political process. In public policy forums, policyholders expect the association to provide leadership on liability, availability, and pricing issues. —Anonymous; *National Underwriter (Property/Casualty),* Jun 1, 1984, 88(22): pp. 20. Avail. ABI 84-19439

Insurance industry, Interest groups, Corporate responsibility

A Serenade to the US Corporation (230)

Some observers feel that antibusiness groups in the US will not be satisfied with anything less than disappearance of corporations. It is suggested that a corporate philosophy be developed which is based on understanding and fulfillment of society's reasonable expectations. Such an attitude would ultimately profit both the corporation and society. Defining the proper corporate role is difficult. However, a good starting point would be setting the first priority as providing needed goods and services, then seeking to do so in a profitable and self-sustaining way. Profit and return on investment should not be seen as the name of the game, but merely a score of the game. The business news media will be essential to any change in the public's perception of corporations, as it must accent stories of "serve others" developments within the corporate realm. This might lead to a partner relationship between government and business, rather than the current adversary situation. —Hutchinson, Charles T.; *Business Horizons,* Jan/Feb 1982, 25(1): pp. 15-18. Avail. ABI 82-04861

Corporate responsibility, Social responsibility, Planning

The Seven Deadly Sins of Corporate Doubletalk (231)

In the face of increasing pressure from constituent groups concerned with a variety of social issues, companies sometimes react by taking the offensive, with methods that may work for the short term but may cause greater damage in the long term. Some companies try to ignore the social problem completely, but this can help to motivate the opposition and strengthen their battle against the company. Some companies respond by trying to place the blame elsewhere, but this can backfire when others ultimately determine that the company was at fault. Many companies try to discredit outside critics, but this tactic is rarely helpful. Some companies respond to criticism by firing those whom they perceive as troublemakers, but this may result in other employees discussing more openly the company's illegal or unethical practices. Other issue-avoidance tactics used by corporations include: 1.

suppressing information, 2. responding with a public relations campaign, and 3. denying the charges. —Alexander, Larry D.; *Business & Society Review,* Winter 1984, (48): pp. 41-44. Avail. ABI 84-08186

Social responsibility, Social issues, Corporate responsibility

Should Corporations Exercise Their Freedom of Speech Rights? (232)

The US Supreme Court has made decisions in the last 5 years that have expanded and clarified business' First Amendment freedom of speech rights. Management has an important responsibility to properly exercise the corporation's free speech rights. A 2-step analytical framework is developed to help the manager to determine when a corporation should exercise its First Amendment rights. First, the corporation must determine whether it should pursue only the interests of the shareholders or the interest of society at large, and then decide if it should respond only to shareholders or to society at large. The result is 4 schools of thought regarding the role of a corporation in society. These schools are: 1. inherence, 2. enlightened self interest, 3. invisible hand, and 4. social responsibility. The 2nd step is to assess the factual situation with regard to a particular speaking engagement confronting the manager. The 4 schools each have factors to consider when assessing the situation. Charts. References. —Hatano, Daryl G.; *American Business Law Jrnl,* Summer 1984, 22(2): pp. 165-187. Avail. ABI 84-33493

Freedom of speech, Court decisions, First Amendment-US, Corporate responsibility, Social responsibility

Should Government Audit Corporate Social Responsibility? (233)

If industries begin to take initiatives toward alleviating societal problems rather than wait for governmental rules and regulations, constructive, cooperative results can be achieved. By translating corporate social responsibility into pragmatic community programs and by being willing to be publicly accountable for performance, industry can assure a proper balance of power with government agencies. By its actions, industry can also help bring a splintered nation together again. Rather than be evaluated by a government-derived "Social Performance Index," industry can begin coordinating its own urban investments with governmental efforts to revitalize particular communities. Business executives and elected officials need to arrive at a mutual understanding of what constitutes corporate public and social responsibilities and replace the traditional adversary relationship with cooperative communication and mutual planning. —Spitzer, Carlton E.; *Public Relations Review,* Summer 1981, 7(2): pp. 13-28. Avail. ABI 82-00674

Social responsibility, Corporate responsibility, Social, Performance, Indexes, Proposals, Industry, Government, Cooperation

Social Demands as Strategic Issues: Some Conceptual Problems (234)

Companies today are operating within a larger social system that makes demands on the organization beyond the production of goods and services. Managers, who probably will have to respond to these social and environmental demands at a level beyond their own social commitments, face the problem of responding to those demands while operating successfully in a competitive economic environment. It may be advantageous to treat these demands as strategic issues. The evolutionary nature of social demands as described by the lead-lag methodology of Ackerman and Bauer (1976) is extended. However, there are still problems with measurement, uncertainty, and common measures. In the end, management will have to rely on its own informed judgment in making any decision. References. – Arcelus, Francisco J. and Schaefer, Norbert V.; *Strategic Mgmt Jrnl,* Oct/Dec 1982, 3(4): pp. 347-357. Avail. ABI 83-08469

Strategic management, Social responsibility, Social accounting, Social issues, Measurement, Decision making, Interest groups, Goal programming, Forecasting techniques, Strategic, Planning

Social Forecasting for Corporate Priorities (235)
When mathematical and mechanistic models failed to predict oil price hikes, high inflation, and other vital events, the UK's Henley Center began to use social forecasting to bring about better predictions. The Center compiled a major data-base of attitudinal data, and now matches attitudes with economic and other data on social circumstances. A similar service is offered by Inbucon, called Corporate Priorities. Inbucon's program is based on social survey research and is supported by more than a decade of experience in the US. Inbucon's program measures, monitors, and even predicts national issues having an impact on business. The Corporate Priorities Program is utilized by companies in numerous ways, such as: 1. in corporate planning, 2. employee policies (i.e., labor relations, communications, programs adapting to advanced technology), 3. marketing, and 4. public relations and community affairs. In the US, Bank of America was able to improve its standing in the community via sensitive response to Corporate Priorities research findings on corporate secrecy and disclosure. In the UK, despite its youth, the program is already making a contribution to corporate decision-making. Charts. –Kellaway, Alec and Richardson, Clara; *Personnel Mgmt (UK),* Sep 1980, 12(9): pp. 42-45. Avail. ABI 81-08613

Social, Forecasting, Corporate, Policy, Corporate planning, Public opinion, Social, Trends, Corporate responsibility, UK

Social Limits to Planning (236)
The planning paradigm of participation, continuity, and holism proposed by R. L. Ackoff is reviewed in terms of the practical problems of trying to implement these ideal principles. His proposal of utilizing the paradigm to design ideal-seeking systems is compared with the market-based approaches of M. Friedman. The comparison draws on F. Hirsch's critique of the efficiency and moral content of the market and utilizes that critique on Ackoff's proposed alternatives. Hirsch's major challenge was to market-based approaches, and his analysis suggests that Ackoff's concerns about planning as a means of resolving social problems are correct. Their resolution ought to be based on a recognition of costs, an adequate conceptualization of the exercise of power in decision making processes, and the design of processes that produce outcomes that can be justified morally. References.

—Bevan, R. G.; *Jrnl of the Operational Research Society (UK),* Oct 1980, 31(10): pp. 867-874. Avail. ABI 80-20990

   Social policy, Planning, Decision making, Processes, Social responsibility, Market economies, Principles, Theory

Social Needs as Business Opportunities: An Interview   (237)
with W. C. Norris

William C. Norris runs Control Data Corp. (Minneapolis, Minnesota) with the twin goals of keeping the company profitable over the long run and contributing to society in general. A sampling of his comments and views gained through an interview includes: 1. Control Data finds business opportunities in addressing unmet needs of society, unlike the narrower view of corporate social responsibility. 2. The first steps a large firm can take in addressing society's unmet needs can be small ones, such as helping small companies get started. 3. Cooperative programs are good for large corporations, but many avoid such ventures, using such excuses as potential antitrust problems when they are really unwilling to share power. 4. A large firm investing in an innovative small firm would do well to be satisfied with being a minor partner and not risking too much money; if the firm achieves outstanding success, the contributing firm could consider buying out the enterprise. Norris has put this philosophy to work in such areas as the development of the PLATO computer-based teaching machine, in which Control Data invested at least $900 million over 20 years. —Anonymous; *New Mgmt,* 1984, 2(2): pp. 38-43. Avail. ABI 84-36265

   Chief executive officer, Control Data-Minneapolis, Corporate, Strategy, Development, Impacts

Social Policy at Enterprise Level: Managerial   (238)
Responses to Employment Prospects

UK employment has experienced a major structural change due to the sharp contraction in manufacturing as compared to services. Semi-skilled and unskilled employees suffer the most displacement. Factors that include a slowing in the growth of demand for services put a check on the growth of employment in services. The reduction or, at most, maintenance of staff, coupled with hiving-off and contracting out to smaller firms, will have substantial social policy consequences for organizations in both the private and public sectors. Self-employment and part-time employment are growing as employment patterns change. The increasing entry of married women into the workforce will help alleviate shortages of people with particular capabilities. Firms must be willing to: 1. help employees spin off products and ideas dropped by the firms, and 2. help small firms develop. References. —Thomas, Raymond E.; *Jrnl of General Mgmt (UK),* Summer 1984, 9(4): pp. 3-16. Avail. ABI 84-30810

   Social policy, Employment, UK, Social responsibility, Economic structure

Social Proxy Fights Spice Up Annual Meetings   (239)

Proxy resolutions addressing social issues once were ignored by corporations, but the Securities & Exchange Commission (SEC) ruled in 1972 that resolutions relating to a company's business could not be arbitrarily excluded. Since then, proposals relating to a number of social issues have been regularly added to proxy statements; they also have been regularly voted down by overwhelming majorities. However, such issues continue to attract attention. Support for such issues is now coming from institutional investors such as pension funds, foundations, and church groups. According to the Investor Responsibility Research Center (IRRC), in 1982, some 109 resolutions were voted on by corporate shareholders, and 74% of them received more than 3% of the vote. The IRRC (Washington, DC) recently distributed a questionnaire which was returned by more than 70 institutional investors. Some 52% of these institutions supported votes on a variety of social issues. —Moskowitz, Milt; *Business & Society Review,* Spring 1983, (45): pp. 23-24. Avail. ABI 83-15139

SEC proxy rules, Proxy statements, Shareholder meetings, Social responsibility, Shareholder relations

Social Regulation of Business Activity: Reforming the (240) Corporate Governance System to Resolve an Institutional Impasse

Debate over the proper goals of corporate activities and the promotion of these objectives is longstanding. Three issues must be considered: 1. Profit maximization is more and more at odds with the standards by which US society judges the contribution by corporations to the public welfare. 2. Government regulations have not forced corporations to consider values other than corporate profit, while the same regulations have caused large, unneeded costs to be inflicted on the economy. 3. The failure of government regulations to achieve their goals may unnecessarily centralize and politicize economic decisions, cause a loss of respect for government authority, and diminish the rule of law. The dangers posed by this regulatory crisis are discussed in terms of the threat to corporations, to the rule of law, and to social cohesion in general. The various elements of the regulatory crisis are: 1. changing expectations by society, considering resource limitations and other factors, 2. patterns of corporate behavior, considering corporate inertia and various managerial perspectives, 3. the role of corporate law, and 4. hostility by corporations to governmental regulations. Inherent problems with regulations are elaborated. The proposed solutions are: 1. a new standard of "altruistic capitalism" for corporate behavior, and 2. use of an elite National Directors Corps by which corporate boards of directors would seek to promote altruistic capitalism. References. —Weiss, Elliott J.; *UCLA Law Review,* Feb 1981, 28(3): pp. 343-437. Avail. UCLA 82-00820

Social responsibility, Corporate responsibility, Social, Regulation, Regulatory reform, Corporate, Reforms

Social Responsiveness, Corporate Structure, and (241) Economic Performance

The issue of the social responsibilities of business has become a subject of intense interest. Recently, the term social responsiveness has been applied as a substitute for social responsibility. Murphy (1978) marks 1974 as the beginning of the Era of Corporate Social Responsiveness. In this era, corporations have begun to react to fundamental concerns about their role

2

62

in society. An examination is conducted of the empirical research on the manner in which business has responded during the era of corporate social responsiveness. Focus is directed on 2 primary issues: 1. the relationship between social responsiveness and changes in organizational structure, including corporate goals, and 2. the relationship between social responsiveness and the economic performance of organizations. This review suggests that business had recognized the importance of social responsiveness and is attempting to modify organizational activities to adapt to this concern. However, social responsiveness is subordinated to the primarily economic corporate goals. Table. References. –Arlow, Peter and Gannon, Martin J.; *Academy of Mgmt Review,* Apr 1982, 7(2): pp. 235-241. Avail. ABI 82-14383

Social responsibility, Corporate responsibility, Goals, Organizational, Structure, Studies, Social issues

Social Responsibility and the Industrial Marketer (242)

Increasingly, industry's social responsibilities are an issue of concern. Much of this concern has arisen from media discussions and reports regarding the impact of actions taken by certain industries and individual companies on society or sections of it. Industrial marketing, in particular, has a responsibility and needs to utilize specific skills for considering the consequences of marketing actions. For example, although technological advancements may indicate that a product is hazardous, the product's manufacturer may choose to limit the response to this knowledge to the alternatives of plant closure or minor adjustments to the product. No "universal laws" exist that specify what to do in such a situation. Company management must determine the responsible action to take and implement that action. A major problem of social responsibility is determining how responsible a company should be. The problem is an individual one, and a personal one; and such a decision from a single manager could impact the company and society, as well as have an effect on his own job and career. References. –Blois, K. J.; *Management Decision (UK),* 1980, 18(5): pp. 246-253. Avail. MCB 81-19152

Social responsibility, Industrial, Marketing, Industrial markets, Manufacturers, Social change

Social Responsibility: How Companies Become Involved (243) in Their Communities

President Reagan is asking private industry to assume some of the burden of helping the disadvantaged and aiding US cultural institutions. Business donations can be classed in 3 categories: monetary, products and other noncash items, and service or voluntarism. Charity clubs, cash contributions, and matching gifts are forms of monetary giving. Many corporations directly or indirectly sponsor community programs such as job training and health programs. Product donations are not as popular as monetary giving because many companies do not realize that their products could make excellent charitable gifts. The contribution of time and experience includes such things as free professional services, discounts on services, volunteer sabbaticals, volunteer projects, and civic voluntarism. Individual voluntarism can be encouraged through support and example-setting by management. The personnel department can: 1. act as a liaison between departments and volunteer programs, 2. keep records on employees' volunteer hours, and 3. appraise management's encouragement of and participation in community affairs. Business support of community activities improves workers' attitudes because it recognizes workers' personal values and encourages them to act upon them. References. –Lawrence, Melanie; *Personnel Jrnl,* Jul 1982, 61(7): pp. 502-510. Avail. ABI 82-18216

Social responsibility, Community relations, Corporate, Strategy, Programs, Donations, Volunteers, Personnel management

Social Trends Set UK Managements a Fierce Challenge   (244)

Economic forecasting has fallen into some disrepute, but social forecasting is still a novelty among most businesspeople. Any company strategy plan must contain not only profits forecasts, but must also consider: 1. political implications, and 2. social trends. The New Agenda is a book derived from a survey of 30 leading experts in UK management. The fundamental message of this work is that "people matter most." While this has always been true, British managers have done little about it until recently. It is not easy to discern the sociological long wave within the overall pattern when dealing with the immediate impact of economic, political, and new technological trends. It is important not only to recognize social changes, but to plan for them and to see beyond the problems the hope of future development and growth. The role of business, in trying to transform these difficult problems into something positive, can be expressed in 4 roles or duties in the areas of: 1. success, 2. taxation, 3. unemployment and direct action, and 4. practical suggestions. Reference. –Kinsman, Francis; *Accountancy (UK),* Oct 1984, 95(1094): pp. 139-140. Avail. ABI 85-01243

Social issues, Trends, Impacts, Industry, Changes, UK, Social responsibility

South Africa: The Industry's Stake   (245)

Foreign chemical companies doing business in South Africa are determined to stay, despite: 1. recession, 2. racial violence, 3. the reduced value of South Africa's currency, and 4. pressure at home to divest because of apartheid. US firms in other industries, including Pepsico, Coca-Cola, Apple Computer, Ford Motor, and General Foods, are withdrawing partially or altogether. The United Nations Commission on Transnational Corporations notes that South Africa's chemical industry, which employs some 100,000 people, is growing twice as fast as the entire economy. However, business is poor, with producers of consumer items hit the hardest. To date, the Reagan Administration's sanctions have had virtually no effect on chemical industry trade with South Africa. European chemical companies, which have a greater stake in South Africa than do US firms, adhere to the European Economic Community's code of conduct, while US companies generally follow the Sullivan Principles, which now ask participating firms to use their influence against apartheid. Tables. —Bluestone, Mimi and Shuttleworth, Geoffrey; *Chemical Week,* Sep 25, 1985, 137(13): pp. 49-53. Avail. ABI 85-32597

South Africa, Foreign investment, Chemical industry, Manycompanies, Statistical data, Business conditions, Pharmaceutical industry, Social responsibility, Political risk, Multinational corporations

Sowing New Seeds for Corporate Responsibility (246)

US corporations are in a position to use their resources for the development of programs that meet the major needs of society in the areas of health, human services, and education. In return, these programs can offer profitable business opportunities. Most corporations currently invest only a small percentage of their vast resources in such programs. However, Control Data Corp. (Minneapolis, Minnesota) has established a social responsibility strategy that includes: 1. poverty area plants, 2. better, more available, and less costly education through computer usage, 3. health programs that emphasize wellness and lifestyles by computer education, 4. urban revitalization, 5. rural area development of farms and businesses, and 6. small business assistance programs. US firms are judged largely on year-to-year performance, but are facing foreign competition that is less concerned with short-term performance; consequently, US executives are reluctant to undertake long-term, high-risk innovations. However, as the profitability of existing programs becomes apparent, other corporations will realize the soundness of the strategy and begin addressing unmet social needs. —Norris, William C.; *FE: The Magazine for Financial Executives,* Jul 1985, 1(7): pp. 16-23. Avail. ABI 85-27895

Corporate responsibility, Social responsibility, Donations, Employment, Case studies, Control Data-Minneapolis, Computer industry, Education, Social issues

Speaking Out Can Be Good for Your Corporate Health (247)

International Telephone & Telegraph (IT&T), W. R. Grace, and Mobil use corporate advertising to assure that the public's perception of them is based on deliberate and well thought-out advertising that can help to balance the negative stories that sometimes appear. IT&T has the lowest profile. Its television spots concentrate on the new products and ideas that are produced by IT&T companies. Print advertisements support the television campaign, but the company does not believe in advocacy advertising and so all ads avoid controversy. Mobil depends heavily on paid issue advertising in print media. Television networks have not yet accepted issue advertising because of the requirement to provide free rebuttal time for controversial statements. W. R. Grace & Co. does both image and advocacy advertising. Chairman J. Peter Grace became personally involved in the company's issue advertising when then-President Jimmy Carter advocated increasing the capital gains tax from 48% to 52%. W. R. Grace spent some $400,000 placing ads in major publications, and the capital gains tax was lowered to 28%. — Mehlman, Barbara; *Madison Avenue,* Feb 1983, 25(2): pp. 72-80. Avail. ABI 83-08426

Corporate, Advertising, Public relations, ITT, Mobil Oil-New York, Grace-New York, Social responsibility, Case studies, Corporate image, Advertising campaigns, Political, Advocacy

A Special Kind of Service (248)

The National Association of Life Underwriters (NALU) and the American Council of Life Insurance (ACLI) co-sponsor a public service program. Local life underwriter associations also have public service programs which will continue to grow in importance. Local problems are best addressed by local government, organizations, and individuals. Furthermore, the federal government has reached its limit of resources that could be applied to service programs. Entitlement programs cost $367 billion today. The need for public service programs in the community is greater than ever before and will increase. Insurance products are service-oriented and appear to go hand-in-hand with community involvement and a sense of responsibility to one's fellow man. Those in the insurance industry are in a position to donate time, money, enthusiasm, and creativity. –Schweiker, Richard S.; *Life Association News,* Nov 1983, 78(11): pp. 132-136. Avail. ABI 84-00615

Associations, NALU (INS), Insurance industry, Life insurance, Underwriting (INS), Social responsibility, Social policy

Specialists View Industry Social Responsibility (249)

During a meeting of the Insurance Industry Consumer Affairs Exchange, a panel examined corporate social responsibility in the role of the insurance industry. Anne Impellizzeri, vice-president of corporate public involvement at Metropolitan Life, noted 8 main resources the industry can employ to foster involvement in social programs including: 1. its products, 2. investments in business developments, 3. jobs generated by insurance company business operations, 4. purchasing decisions, 5. time and talent, 6. support for public policy, 7. "in-kind" contributions, and 8. financial contributions. James Alexander, a consultant on corporate philanthropy and community relations, noted that the American public expects private industry to help offset cutbacks in federal social programs imposed by the Reagan Administration. The effectiveness of corporate social philanthropy can be great if it is open about its objectives, biases, and limitations. The insurance industry should provide leadership in the area of corporate social involvement. –Jones, David C.; *National Underwriter (Life/Health),* Oct 2, 1982, 86(40): pp. 30. Avail. ABI 82-25403

Insurance industry, Social responsibility, Corporate responsibility, Insurance companies, Public policy

Specialists View Industry Social Responsibility (250)

According to Anne Impellizzeri of Metropolitan Life, consumer affairs activities are the heart of insurance industry corporate social involvement. There are 8 main resources the insurance industry can use to foster involvement in social programs. The 4 that are economic in nature are insurance products, investments, jobs generated, and purchasing. The 4 social involvement sources that are in the public service area are insurance time and talent devoted to public leadership, support for public policy, in-kind contributions, and financial contributions. According to Dorothy Light of PRUPAC, many "fires" have been set on the consumer front for the insurance agency by such public awareness groups as senior citizens and Mothers Against Drunk Driving. Regulators and state legislators have also set their share of fires. The insurance industry must respond with increased corporate social involvement to counter criticisms that have been leveled against it. Many social groups will be looking to the industry to provide capital to finance their social programs. —Jones, David C.; *National Underwriter (Property/Casualty),* Oct 8, 1982, 86(41): pp. 36,43. Avail. ABI 82-25853

Social responsibility, Insurance industry, Corporate responsibility

Specialty Market Outlook-1982 (251)

Underwriting losses for 1981 hit an all-time high of $6 billion, for a percentage loss of 5.7%, second highest in history. However, investment income grew to $13.4 billion. Specialty insurance is expecting much the same for 1982. Many large standard companies are departing from standard underwriting practices to concentrate on market position maintenance and "bottom line" profit. An expert panel of 31 specialty insurance and brokerage executives discussed the specialty market's outlook. A sampling of comments includes: 1. Overcapacity in property-casualty and reinsurance markets has meant reduced rates, and competition caused by lack of business activity is preventing profitability. 2. Rate-cutting is most active with large accounts. 3. Less competition on specialty product rates makes them almost adequate, but their future is uncertain. 4. Social responsibility classes will never achieve profitability because of the necessity of low rates. 5. The trend of mergers between large and small houses will continue. 6. New state laws have restricted non-admitted markets, but some have clarified procedures, and specialty admitted carriers have gained new freedom of operation. 7. Most specialty houses reported growth during 1981, and they are being increasingly used to get reduced rates. 8. Some refuse standard class rejections, and others consider professional and retroactive liabilities, tough umbrellas, and new product lines. Most specialty companies expect growth in 1982. —Clapp, Wallace, L., Jr.; *Rough Notes,* Mar 1982, 125(3): pp. 24-33. Avail. ABI 82-08847

Property insurance, Casualty insurance, Insurance industry, Forecasts, Recessions (ECON), Business conditions, Specialty, Nonstandard, Markets, Excess, Surplus, State laws

State of the Union-1982 (252)

In 1981, a new spirit of partnership was introduced between Congress and the Administration, as well as between the federal government and the state and local governments. During 1981, the foundation was laid for the US' economic recovery and a change in government that returns its services to the people. The current economic program calls for reduction in the growth rate of government spending and a 3-year tax-rate reduction to stimulate the economy and create jobs. This program has lowered inflation, taxes, and interest rates, and increased public confidence in both government and business. Further, federal regulation growth has been cut by half. While the federal government moves to reduce waste and fraud, the private sector is voluntarily taking on social responsibility. New legislation will improve and develop depressed urban areas. Special economic incentives in urban enterprise zones will help attract new business and jobs to US inner cities and rural towns. The federal government is also moving in areas of: 1. women's rights, 2. crime, and 3. pollution. Foreign policy will improve in strength, fairness, and balance. The new budget is aimed at a strong national defense system and reliable social programs. Together, the people and the government will preserve the union. –Reagan, Ronald; *Vital Speeches*, Feb 15, 1982, 48(9): pp. 258-262. Avail. ABI 82-06933

Economic conditions, Economic recovery, Economic policy, Federal, Budgets, Deficits, Social policy, Welfare, Fiscal policy

A Strong Case for the Agency System (253)

There have been many attacks on the agency system, however, there is a strong case for the system's existence. The agency system is the way life insurance companies market via sales units or agencies and provide product and home office expertise to them. The system is impacted by the attitudes of regulators, legislators, and consumers, and it must be proven viable to eliminate negative agent attitudes, as well as to survive. Without the support, service, and expertise of an agent, consumers purchasing insurance on their own would not likely create a financially-secure program. The same professionalism is vital for insurance as it is for many other industries, such as medical and legal. No other distribution method can match that accommodation to individual needs and unique situations. However, the agency system does have some difficulties due to attitudinal problems; yet with professional and knowledgeable agents, trained by a supportive company, these problems can be resolved. Agents and companies that support one another create a strong loyalty and a high morale that results in better serving the public and in fulfilling industry's responsibility to society. –Levine, Norman G.; *National Underwriter (Life/Health)*, Sep 17, 1982, 86(37A): pp. 6,14-17,59,61. Avail. ABI 82-24652

Insurance agencies, Insurance agents & brokers, Life insurance, Life insurance companies, Insurance industry, Insurance policies, Attitudes, Employee morale, Social responsibility

The Student Seminar as an Effective Public Relations Technique (254)

The traditional methods of "telling the corporate story" often reach a high concentration of the local populace, while advocacy advertising reaches an extensive national audience but has limited impact. A corporation/university student seminar reaches a very small number of individuals in comparison to other public relations approaches, but the exposure is intensive. The students benefit through course credit and an exposure to the realities of the corporate world. The effectiveness of this method of telling the corporate story can be measured better than perhaps any other approach due to the greater applicability of before/after surveys with a distinct group of recipients compared to advertising or community involvement. A survey of participants in such a seminar indicated that this kind of course can help in changing attitudes toward a company's social responsibility efforts. However, the success of such a course can vary from year to year; this suggests that the nature of the presentation and the individual executives selected to talk with the students can be factors in the course's success. –Fry,

Fred L. and Hartman, Richard I.; *Public Relations Qtrly,* Winter 1980, 25(4): pp. 23-26. Avail. ABI 81-05468

Corporate, Public relations, Students, Seminars, Attitude surveys, Social responsibility, Business, Regulation

Sugar Babies and the Sisterhood-A Business Case Study (255)

Using the Harvard Business School case method of teaching business administration, a dramatization of a classic business situation is presented. A discussion takes place among top managers of a Midwest corporation which produces baked goods. The matter under discussion is an objection raised by an organized group of minority stockholders to the use of television advertising aimed specifically at children. Among the different points discussed are: 1. the basic legal responsibility of the corporation in restricting its advertising and/or balancing its direct advertising with health and nutritional disclosures, 2. steps previously taken by the corporation in voluntary compliance with industry guidelines for responsible children's advertising, 3. tactics undertaken by competitors in the same area, 4. industry reaction to the position taken by the Federal Trade Commission, and 5. the consequences of ignoring the minority stockholders' objections. —Dickson, Douglas N.; *Across the Board,* Jan 1982, 19(1): pp. 40-46. Avail. ABI 82-03206

Television advertising, Restrictions, Children, Social responsibility

Survey by ORC Reveals Practitioners' Views on Major Issues (256)

Opinion Research Center (ORC) undertook a study to appraise corporate performance in key issues areas. Respondents were 189 members of the Public Relations Society of America, 556 executives in major companies, 502 executives in mid-size companies, and 103 Washington opinion leaders. They were asked to rate the business community's performance on such issues as: 1. protecting health and safety of employees, 2. working toward fair international trade policies, and 3. preserving world peace. A significant level of agreement was found among all 4 groups. However, a number of public relations executives thought the business community had no responsibility for a number of key issues. Public relations practitioners seem to lag behind executives in awareness of key issues and in an appreciation of the role business can play in helping solve social problems. Tables. — Anonymous; *Public Relations Jrnl,* Aug 1984, 40(8): pp. 29-30. Avail. ABI 84-32219

Public relations, Executives, Attitude surveys, Corporate responsibility

Taking Aim in the 80's (257)

The battle for markets will be fiercer than ever in the 1980s, and according to author Philip Kotler, most firms are quite unprepared to face the coming marketing challenges. Kotler believes that only a handful of firms are "master marketers," with this group including Xerox, International Business Machines (IBM), McDonald's Caterpillar, and Eastman Kodak. He views the coming decade as one in which firms will have to reconcile the demands of company profitability, social responsibility, and customer satisfaction. He believes that good marketing consists largely of "riding the trends," a task which will be difficult in the 1980s. Companies must anticipate changing trends and competitive efforts as much as possible. Firms are often in the position of seeing the need for a change in strategy but, at the same time, finding themselves unwilling to alter company structure. Many examples of good and clever marketing can be found. For example, the Japanese have been successful in penetrating the US market. Toyota was successful in obtaining previous Volkswagen customers in the US. —Hollier, Derek; *Chief Executive Monthly* , (UK), Apr 1980): pp. #35-37. Avail. ABI 80-11672

Marketing, Market research, Market strategy, Trends, Predictions

The Ten Commandments of Corporate Social Responsibility   (258)

Corporations often fail to respond properly to social issues. Companies may try to discredit their critics, ignore major social issues, and counter with public relations campaigns, but these tactics do not work. Alternative constructive actions can be used to handle social issues. Presented are Ten Commandments for Corporate Social Responsibility. They are: 1. Take corrective action before it is needed. 2. Work with affected constituents to resolve mutual problems. 3. Work to establish industrywide standards and self-regulation. 4. Publicly admit mistakes. 5. Get involved in appropriate social programs. 6. Help correct environmental problems. 7. Monitor the changing social environment. 8. Establish and enforce a corporate code of conduct. 9. Take needed public stands on social issues. 10. Strive to make profits on an ongoing basis. Tables. —Alexander, Larry D. and Matthews, William F.; *Business & Society Review,* Summer 1984, (50): pp. 62-66. Avail. ABI 84-30016

Social responsibility, Guidelines, Pollution control, Social issues

They're Listening with Different Ears   (259)

Dwindling resources, environmental concerns, inflation, and recession have combined to put new pressures on the public relations effort. New research has indicated that each public issue has a very different pattern of support and opposition and that demographic characteristics show little about the feelings of those being surveyed. While demographic factors do have some impact on attitudes, the membership of a respondent in an attitudinal segment is much more important.A recent research study by Natural History magazine examined specific current issues, revealed public attitudes toward responses to environmental challenges by US industry, and measured respondents' attitudes toward specific companies' reactions to the energy crisis. The research also attempted to isolate changing attitudes. The findings of the study indicate the need for a rational approach to communications with the many subgroups that exist in the US. Graph. Table. —Valandra, Kent T.; *Public Relations Jrnl,* Jun 1980, 36(6): pp. 22-25. Avail. ABI 80-14307

Public opinion, Public opinion surveys, Corporate responsibility, Social responsibility, Environmental accounting, Studies

A Threat to Innovation and Risk-Taking   (260)

Unless corporate leaders take steps to help the public accurately perceive risks in the industrial world, the public's misunderstanding of industrial hazards will generate attempts to eliminate risk. This will lead to suppressed innovation and eventually to a lack of growth. It is difficult for industrial leaders to explain complex scientific information to the media, which perpetuates public concern. To form public perceptions based on substance, executives need to first recognize the problem, then to be seen and heard in many places. They must take the initiative with their industry's key constituencies, which include the government, universities, and the media. To provide the media with the proper information, industrial leaders should take the lead in communication, volunteer information, and emphasize their accessibility. Dow Chemical Co. (Midland, Michigan) has established a media hotline, sends scientists around the US to answer public concerns, and is helping create a Science Communications Center at University of Missouri. These programs are aimed at improving the quality of information made available to media. –Lundeen, Robert W.; *Directors & Boards,* Spring 1985, 9(3): pp. 28-32. Avail. ABI 85-18629

Case studies, Dow Chemical-Midland Mich, Chemical industry, Social responsibility, Corporate image, Media, Public relations, Risk, Boards of directors, Manypeople

Toward Public Relations Theory   (261)

Public relations is composed of a multitude of people performing a wide variety of communication tasks. Considerable confusion surrounds perceptions of the public relations functions. To clear this misunderstanding, the public relations profession must strive for its own unique core of knowledge and philosophy. The best definition of today's public relations would be "management of interdependence." This concept can be approached by way of 3 principles that suggest the scope and breadth of a theory of postmodern public relations. These principles involve: 1. the nature of social interdependence, 2. the management of interdependence, and 3. the communication-mindedness of the people responsible for managing this evolutionary process. These principles indicate the direction in which public relations practice should be going and help to eliminate superficiality, ambiguity, and the lack of focused flexibility. –Wolter, Louis J.; Miles, Stephen B.; and Awad, Joseph A.; *Public Relations Jrnl,* Sep 1983, 39(9): pp. 12-16. Avail. ABI 83-27243

Public relations, Consultants, Roles, Responsibilities, Innovations, Communication, Social responsibility

Trends in Shareholder Activism: 1970-1982   (262)

For 14 years, public interest resolutions have appeared on the proxy statements of US corporations. An attempt is made to review and assess the history of the public interest proxy resolution. Public interest proxy resolutions originated in the social activism of the 1960s and gained political and ideological strength from the drive for increased public controls over the corporation that dominated the political agenda for much of the 1970s. Since 1977, both the public interest movement and organized labor have suffered a series of major political setbacks. The issues of corporate accountability and responsibility have lost much of their urgency. The US is now more interested in making the large corporation more productive and internationally competitive. References. –Vogel, David; *California Mgmt Review,* Spring 1983, 25(3): pp. 68-87. Avail. ABI 83-14838

Stockholders, Activists, Social responsibility, Manycompanies, SEC regulations, Unions, Proxy statements

TVA at Age Fifty - Reflections and Retrospect (263)

The Tennessee Valley Authority (TVA) turned 50 years old in 1983. The TVA's effects and consequences on political and organizational life in the US and abroad may be discerned by studying 4 themes of the TVA: 1. its legacy, 2. the TVA idea, 3. its ironies, and 4. its lessons. The TVA was a technical challenge that made contributions to management practices and introduced the concepts of grass-roots democracy and cooptation. The TVA idea, an enduring perception of organizational purpose, contributed to TVA's staying power over the years. The 5 elements of the TVA idea include a sense of social responsibility, unified regional development, and a decentralized administration. However, internal and external developments created some uncertainties in TVA's future. TVA's power program is an example of the paradox created when TVA lost control over some elements while trying to control others. The lessons to be learned from TVA's experience include the idea that complex organizations will always face problems. TVA is also illustrative of the bureaucratic growth process, showing that bureaucracies are both hard to live with and hard to live without. References. —Neuse, Steven M.; *Public Administration Review,* Nov/Dec 1983, 43(6): pp. 491-499. Avail. ABI 84-04872

TVA, Public works, Employment policies, Regional, Development, Case studies

The Understanding of Scale (264)

How management deals with change today affects the context of future reality. Management skills will influence the policies of financial institutions and the public policies institutions must tolerate. Present decision making is expected to have impacts in the future on: 1. the prestige and esteem the organization earns from individuals and institutions on whom it depends for survival and return on investment, 2. multiple levels and across functional lines within the institution, and 3. senior management decision making. Management needs to be provided with: 1. a framework to identify the realities of change, 2. systems purview to align internal policies with the nature of society, and 3. a process that will fit today's institutional practices to the future. The future and a person's role in it involves both skill and scale. Scale is basic to an understanding of the present and the future. We need to put our organizations into perspective with society. —Jones, Barrie L.; *Vital Speeches,* Jan 15, 1980, 46(7): pp. 216-219. Avail. ABI 80-04247

Public relations, Decision making, Scale, Social responsibility

Unilever Shows That It Cares (265)

Sir David Orr, chairman of Unilever, is an outspoken critic of the multinational world and demonstrates a conscience for the social consequences of advertising and big business. The firm spends L300 million annually on theme advertising and thus is anxious both to emphasize the positive effects of advertising and warn against its abuse. Of course, Orr's primary concern is the health of Unilever itself. He is a believer that the ingenuity of advertising can save resources, and he points to seat-belt campaigns of the government as an illustration of this capability. He is conscious of the difficulty many people have in just obtaining the necessities of life, and he has a profound sympathy for the problems and needs of developing countries. He is in favor of the codes of conduct embraced by many multinational firms except for the fact that their multiplicity is self-defeating. He cautions that every code must be 2-sided, to reflect not only responsibilities of the firm, but of the host nation as well. Today, when multinationals must deal with mounting political pressures, he considers the self-critical attitude of the group a healthy one. —Lester, Tom; *Marketing (UK)*, Apr 30, 1980, 1(3): pp. 32-33. Avail. ABI 80-12511

Unilever-Britain-Neth, Advertising, Personal, Profiles, Case studies, Marketing, Social responsibility

Untangling the Muddled Management of Public Affairs   (266)

Businesses have tended to be more responsive to market constituencies - suppliers, distributors, and customers - than to their broader public constituencies made up of special interest groups, local communities, labor organizations, and public officials. However, public interest in business affairs and accountability has increased, requiring that businesses manage public affairs more effectively. Case studies of several firms in the forest products industry demonstrates the necessary ingredients for effective public affairs management. Attempts to influence the public will not be sufficient; dialog with public constituencies and understanding of their concerns is required. Organizations must be able to read their environments and establish effective mechanisms for information gathering. The organization must be structured to be environmentally sensitive. Public affairs expertise must be integrated and coordinated throughout the organization, particularly into business decision making as part of the corporate culture. Charts. References. —Sonnenfeld, Jeffrey; *Business Horizons*, Nov/Dec 1984, 27(6): pp. 67-76. Avail. ABI 85-02967

Public interest, Social responsibility, Corporate, Public relations, Community relations, Constituents, Corporate culture, Structure

Updating Social Responsibility   (267)

The role of business organizations concerning communities' needs is being questioned by the public, and people are losing trust and confidence in banks and in other major institutions. The social fact which likely underlies the trends and situations in this society is the separation and alienation of individuals from the various institutions upon which they depend. The challenge lies in developing effective ways of re-establishing appropriate and relevant ties of mutual expectations and obligations; the essence of social responsibility lies in explicitly considering the social and public consequences of private marketing or economic decisions and actions, and ensuring that banks do not interfere with the satisfaction of customers' other needs and wants. Many banks have experimented with voluntary programs - socially responsible activities involving such diverse efforts as improving the quality of housing, educating people on the role of business, supporting the arts, sponsoring seminars, and working with grass-roots groups to solve community problems. References. —Levin, Alfred E.; *Canadian Banker & ICB Review (Canada)*, Oct 1982, 89(5): pp. 56-61. Avail. ABI 82-28930

Banks, Social responsibility, Corporate responsibility, Financial institutions, Government, Intervention

Variations in Corporate Social Performance (268)

Past studies on social responsibility have not explained the sources of variation in socially responsive activities of firms. The purpose of this study is to explain the relationship of factors affecting the socially responsive activities of banks in Texas. The objectives were to develop models of the variable(s) that explain variations in socially responsive activities and to test for interdependency among the variables. The independent variables were: 1. organizational size, 2. organizational income, 3. managerial values, 4. organizational charter, 5. nature of stock ownership, 6. corporate market share, 7. minority population, 8. degree of local ownership, and 9. the size of the community. The dependent variables were 4 socially responsive activities: 1. intensity of minority employees, 2. intensity of female officers, 3. loans for low-income housing, and 4. loans for minority enterprises. The findings of the study suggest that: 1. No single set of independent variables explain variations in each of the socially responsive activities. 2. Socially responsive activities tended to be independent of each other, except for a significant positive correlation between intensity of minority employees and loans for minority enterprises and a strong negative correlation between intensity of minority employees and intensity of female officers. Tables. References. —Kuntz, Edwin C.; Kedia, Banwari L.; and Whitehead, Carlton J.; *California Mgmt Review*, Summer 1980, 22(4): pp. 30-36. Avail. ABI 80-22672

Corporate responsibility, Social responsibility, Variation, Variables, Banks, Commercial banks, Texas, Studies, Bank loans, Employment, Minorities, Women

Verity's Truth Center for Enlightened Business (269)

Generally, business is seen more as a contributor to public problems than a part of the solution. Business, in reality, exists only because and as long as society permits it to. The public attitude toward business is a reflection of the public's determination of how well business serves all of its needs, not just some of them. At Wright State University (Dayton, Ohio), a study is being conducted concerning the establishment of a National Center for Corporate Responsibility. The Center, as currently conceived, would include representatives from business, government, labor, public interest groups and other interested constituencies. The center would be joined to a network of cooperating regional centers that would operate independently but would collaborate in addressing a number of areas. These areas of concern would include: 1. research, 2. standards, 3. curriculum, 4. a clearinghouse of state-of-the-art business information, 5. services to local communities, 6. reporting, and 7. consulting. —Verity, C. William, Jr.; *Business & Society Review*, Winter 1984, (48): pp. 60-62. Avail. ABI 84-08190

Corporate responsibility, Social issues, Accountability

Voluntarism Means Doing the Job Without Uncle Sam (270)

In an interview, C. William Verity, Jr., Chairman, President's Task Force on Private Sector Initiatives, states that the time has come for communities to examine what their real needs are and then see what they can do to be certain that those are the real needs. Only then should they act on them. Further, voluntarism involves all elements of the private sector, including religious organizations, civic groups, unions, educators, and others. Verity believes the principal purpose of business is the provision of products and services at a profit so that one can perpetuate the organization and do the things that are needed by society. However, businessmen now realize that the environment for enterprise that exists in communities is very significant in determining how successful they can be. Verity sees little politics involved in resolving community issues at the community level. In the community, individuals are concerned with what the problem is. Verity sees his own Middletown (Ohio) Model as representative of such community action succeeding. In addition, Verity supports the concept of the Enterprise Zone approach to business, which encourages companies to establish plants in depressed zones through tax incentives and other concessions. —Anonymous; *Iron Age,* Mar 1, 1982, 225(7): pp. 25-28. Avail. ABI 82-09773

Volunteers, Corporate responsibility, Social responsibility, Task forces

Wanted-Management Skills in the New Style (271)

European managers are aware of a change-a move toward social responsibility. Technology and communications are presenting conflicting demands, new ideas, and new values. Recession has spotlighted weaknesses of European industry. An increasingly greater percentage of the Gross National Product (GNP) goes to welfare, and fewer financial resources are available for the research and development (R & D) to help Europe keep up with Japan, the US or newly industrialized nations. The 1960s' baby boom has resulted in youth making up 42% of the total unemployed. Mass communication has led to individual groups demanding less pollution, better working conditions, and more disclosure of corporate information. Big business, trade unions, and government are involved in a power play about money, and about the size and division of GNP. The survival of business is at stake. Other trends in Eurobusiness are a shift to services from products, and more bureaucracy. Future Euromanagers will have to give increased attention to motivation and job satisfaction. Business schools need to emphasize practical matters, analytical tools, and how to deal with the social and political pressures outside the organization. Tomorrow's managers must be flexible, skilled in communications and negotiations, knowledgeable about differing cultures, and they must be willing to learn in the face of change. The shape of Europe will be affected by the quality of its managers. —Sedlacek, Jerry F.; *Manchester Business School Review (UK),* Summer 1981, 5(3): pp. 2-5. Avail. ABI 81-20476

Europe, Managers, Social change, Impacts, Skills, Communication

The Way We Weren't (272)

President Reagan's basic political commitment is quite clear: he wants to get the government off the backs of the people by giving some of the federal government's power to the states and the private sector, in the belief that free people achieve the most when they are unrestrained by government. The president's perspective is historically honorable. Throughout history, the US people have clearly understood that both the private and public sectors have certain responsibilities, but there has never been a consensus on how to divide the responsibilities between the 2. In assuming greater social responsibility, government has both addressed current needs and commanded great political power. Getting government off the backs of the people is simply not possible given the American experience and the current consensus. Several conservatives have even implied that the call for a radical return to a reliance on the private sector is hypocritical, ignores reality, and is ultimately self-defeating. —Silbey, Joel H.; *Cornell Executive,* Spring 1983, 9(2): pp. 10-12. Avail. ABI 83-28398

Free enterprise, Private sector, Economic aid, Political power, Economic policy

West Coast Life's Corporate Conscience (273)

West Coast Life has become active in the sponsorship of an organization called Aid for the Adoption of Special Kids (AASK). The insurer's involvement is 2-fold: 1. President John Metzger serves as chairman of the San Francisco (California) Bay Area "Adopt a Family" program. 2. The firm is sponsoring parenting seminars. The company has been eager to help AASK in every phase of its work in finding homes for these children. It is also planning with the University of California (Berkeley) a sports clinic, proceeds from which will go to help AASK. The firm offers some guidelines for firms adopting corporate involvement projects: 1. Be certain the project has a direct relationship to insurance, not an obscure one. 2. Make sure agents and offices can benefit directly and become the point of contact for more information about the project. 3. Find an organization that will participate locally. 4. Contact the local Chamber of Commerce for assistance. 5. Make sure that agents, offices, and the home office are informed and prepared well in advance of the effort. —Maher, Thomas M.; *National Underwriter (Life/Health),* Dec 11, 1982, 86(50): pp. 38. Avail. ABI 83-01876

Insurance industry, Case studies, Life insurance companies, Corporate responsibility, Social responsibility, Programs, Personal, Profiles

West German Banks Defend Their Industrial Shareholdings (274)

Under West Germany's universal banking concept, banks hold sizable stakes in companies borrowing from them and accept some social responsibility for the well-being of these companies. It is possible that the West German Bundestag could amend the Banking Act, forcing banks to reduce their holdings in West German companies to 25% plus one share. The one share gives banks voting privileges and has taxation benefits as well. The holdings of major banks now are usually in the 25%-30% range, with a few exceptions. The Economics Minister, Count Otto Lambsdorff, favors reducing the banks' share to 15%, while coalition party members favor a reduction as low as 5%. Last week the Association of German Banks (BVB) issued a constitutional challenge to any law mandating share divestiture. West Germany's spectacular industrial success may be due in part to the close ties of banks and industry. One factor in the banks' favor is the social responsibility they have accepted along with the shares. —Anonymous; *World Business Weekly (UK)*, Nov 3, 1980, 3(43): pp. 49-50. Avail. ABI 80-21784

Germany, Banking, Banks, Stockholders, Shareholders equity, Divestiture

What Companies Are Doing to Make Themselves Good   (275) Neighbours

The corporate view of itself as the community has been superseded by one which sees a company as the guest of the community in which it is located. Companies are taking an interest in improving community lifestyle, rather than existing outside of the local community. Employees are encouraged to become active in local programs, and some companies require such activity. Other corporations are taking a more active role in environmental areas, voluntarily helping to improve the land around plant operations and implementing pollution control programs. Companies now see themselves as working with government and local leaders to create programs which meet needs not already addressed by other projects. These are then turned over to local community control once the project is running smoothly. Case studies are reviewed for companies in the US, Federal Republic of Germany, and the Netherlands. —Bickerstaffe, George; *International Mgmt (UK)*, May 1981, 36(5): pp. 30-32,35. Avail. ABI 81-13548

Corporate responsibility, Social responsibility, Community, Programs, Manycompanies

What Is True Corporate Responsibility?   (276)

Many people tend to view the corporation as an agent of income redistribution, a community benefactor, and a mechanism for improving the quality of life both on and off the job. It seems that these noneconomic factors have been treated as being paramount. The traditional economic or business functions appear to be viewed as secondary and taken for granted. However, by ignoring the merit of the business firm's economic functions, most corporate social responsibility analyses are fundamentally flawed. The contributions of business to meeting other concerns of society are not trivial, but, a business firm is not an all-purpose mechanism; it is an economic organization created for, and best suited for, economic purposes that are of vital importance to the health and welfare of society. —Weidenbaum, Murray L.; *Regulation*, May/Jun 1980, 4(3): pp. 30-31. Avail. ABI 80-14921

Corporate responsibility, Social responsibility

Whatever Happened to Social Responsibility?   (277)

Traditionally, US corporations saw only financial performance as its criterion for success but in the 1970s, the rising insistence on corporate social responsibility argued that doing good was more important than doing well. In the 1980s, a significant number of companies have learned to do good by doing well. They have gone beyond giving grants to charities and foundations that have no other connection with the company. They have managed to match their business interests with the needs of the community at large. For example, SmithKline, Johnson & Johnson, and other pharmaceutical firms have made large grants to medical researchers, and Delta Airlines has made huge commitments to employment security for its workers. Control Data Corp. has perhaps gone the furthest with its concept of addressing society's major unmet needs as profitable business opportunities. Socially oriented activities must be managed just as other business activities. Among the activities involved in the corporate response to meeting social needs are: 1. combined planning with the recipients of aid, 2. coalition building, and 3. issues scanning. —Fleming, John E.; *New Mgmt,* 1984, 2(2): pp. 44-49. Avail. ABI 84-36266

Corporate responsibility, Social responsibility, Corporate, Activity, Manycompanies, Development

What's Coming Next in Robotics? (278)

The robots now in place on factory floors are crude compared to what is ahead, according to many researchers. Today, machines can be programmed to perform a specific function, such as painting, spot welding, or inspection. In the near future, robots will be more flexible and capable of a variety of operations. Later on, when robots are equipped with all the senses that humans take for granted, the machines will handle more sophisticated tasks. The potential for robotics is restrained only by human inertia, capital formation, social responsibility, and economics. Pioneers are already doing their best to get the robot revolution underway. However, a major obstacle in the way of robot implementation in industry is the fear of job displacement. —Wilson, Marilyn and Rozen, Miriam; *Dun's Business Month,* Nov 1983, 123(5): pp. 70-72. Avail. ABI 83-32599

Robots, Innovations, Researchers, R&D, Industrial, Applications

When Religion and Business Collide (279)

In 1986, US corporations will deal with dozens of shareholder resolutions aimed at raising management's social accountability. Some executives regard such measures as a nuisance, but others see churches and their social concerns as a corporate early-warning system. An April 1985 debate between Timothy H. Smith of the Interfaith Center on Corporate Responsibility and Robert Dean, a former ambassador, highlights some key issues. According to Dean, problems arise when churches become involved in political action programs to better the plight of the poor; churches in Central and South America are carrying hidden agendas when they purport to be looking out for the people. Smith maintains that churches can no longer distance themselves from economics and the marketplace, especially as they are stockholders in US business. Success is reached, says Smith, when church and company find common ground before a shareholder resolution is necessary. Table. —McClenahen, John S.; *Industry Week,* Aug 19, 1985, 226(4): pp. 38-41. Avail. ABI 85-28365

Religion, Influence, Social responsibility, Manycompanies, Religious organizations, Corporate responsibility

Who Are the Truly Needy? (280)

In the 2 years since his election, President Reagan has not yet stated a formal plan to redesign social welfare policy. He did announce intentions to reduce federal monies for social welfare in order to increase defense spending and lower taxes. At the same time, Reagan promised to maintain aid to the truly

needy. This implied that: 1. Some welfare spending was not necessary and could be eliminated. 2. Some social responsibility could be shifted to state and local governments and the private sector. Reagan has called for a narrow definition of deserving beneficiaries, which would aid in the reduction of federal funds for social welfare. The programs he has suggested the states assume, however, are only a small part of social welfare spending and would have little impact on the federal government's financial role. If significant reductions are to be made in federal spending, Reagan will have to fully address all areas of Social Security and health programs. Tables. References.
—Lampman, Robert J.; *Business Forum,* Winter 1983, 8(1): pp. 8-11. Avail. ABI 83-08645

   Welfare, Social policy, AFDC, Transfer payments

Who Cast the First Stone?   (281)

For the past 15 years, church groups and multinational corporations (MNC) have been embroiled in controversy over MNCs' activities in less developed countries (LDC). Complaints about Gulf & Western Industries' (G&W) investment in the Dominican Republic and the boycott of Nestle (which only recently ended) are 2 of the most publicized confrontations between church groups and MNCs. A study of the 2 issues indicates that both parties have made mistakes and that communication and cooperation could have improved both situations. G&W and Nestle should have admitted their mistakes in their LDC operations earlier and should have responded to social pressures more quickly. Church groups should have recognized the efforts G&W and Nestle made to correct their errors. MNC executives need to realize and accept their increasing social responsibilities and need to adopt policies to respond to social pressures quickly, before they become destructive. Such policies should focus on openness, preparedness, integrity, and clarity. Charts. References. —Williams, Oliver; *Harvard Business Review,* Sep/Oct 1984, 62(51): pp. 151-160. Avail. ABI 84-33702

   Multinational corporations, Consumer, Boycotts, Social responsibility, Religious organizations, Activists, Shareholder meetings, LDCs, Corporate responsibility, Gulf & Western Industries-New York, Nestle-Switzerland, Case studies

Who Fills the Vaccuum? Who Picks Up the Slack?   (282)
Replacement Strategies for Phased-Out Federal
Programs

Social responsibility is everyone's business. The withdrawal of federal funding of public programs means that all the other institutions in the society will have to play correspondingly more significant roles in order to pick up the slack. The private business-for-profit sector must play an especially important role, simply because it is one of the institutions most capable of doing so. Six individual perspectives on the subject are offered: 1. Businesses that are not yet contributing to social programs are simply in need of specific encouragement. 2. The handling of charitable contributions will change drastically in the 1980s, and the most promising area of activity will be the government-business partnership at the local level. 3. Business firms should not try to do what the government did, but instead should work equity issues through direct block grants that promote choices. 4. Change is needed in the area of government regulations, which are too prolific, too costly, and often useless. 5. Business firms should initiate needed social programs, but should expect the communities to take over and the programs to become self-supporting. 6. Business should not try to take up the slack because it has neither the resources nor the structure to do so; eventually, the public will again turn to the government to provide services as before. —Mars, David; Emerson, Norman H.; Dennis, Lloyd B.; Biller, Robert P.; Froehlich, Robert J.; Fluetsch, J. Foster; and Kline, Elliot H.; *American Review of Public Administration,* Fall 1981, 15(3): pp. 247-270. Avail. ABI 83-04841

   Federal funds, Programs, Public administration, Corporate responsibility, Social responsibility, Regulations, Public sector, Private sector

Who Should Control the Corporation?   (283)

An attempt is made to bring some understanding to the century-old debate of who should control the large, widely held corporation. Issues related to this subject include how the large corporation should be controlled and which goals should be pursued. Eight major positions are analyzed: 1. government nationalization, 2. attempts to restore direct shareholder control, 3. democratization, 4. regulation, 5. pressure, 6. social responsibility, 7. neglect, and 8. manipulation to induce it to be good. Each position is examined from an organizational rather than a political or ideological viewpoint. Together, these positions represent a portfolio from which society can draw to accommodate social and corporate needs and goals. Table. Chart. References. —Mintzberg, Henry; *California Mgmt Review,* Fall 1984, 27(1): pp. 90-115. Avail. ABI 85-01969

   Management controls, Industrial democracy, Participatory management, Social responsibility

Who's Serious About Corporate Responsibility? (or 187   (284) Ways to Amuse a Bored Cat).

The clamor over government cutbacks in spending has confused many people. Many people believe: 1. that all health/education/welfare/arts funds are being eliminated by the federal government, 2. that "social justice" is being abandoned by the government, and 3. that the reductions must be made up in full by the private sector. In fact, a new public-private partnership is emerging. While the private sector cannot meet fully all needs resulting from cutbacks, business definitely regards social and economic improvements as goals requiring direct and effective action. However, one survey found that fewer than 20% of the people surveyed believe that business is paying its fair share. Indeed, only 6% of all tax-paying businesses in the US give more than $500 to charity in a year. The role of corporate social responsibility must grow to meet future challenges, which will be formidable. Charts. —Williams, Louis C., Jr.; *Jrnl of Communication Mgmt,* 1982, 11(4): pp. 3-6. Avail. ABI 82-26551

   Corporate responsibility, Donations, Charitable foundations, Social responsibility

Why Cooperation Succeeds Where Confrontation Fails   (285)

For 2 decades, the relationship between business and activists from political social welfare and religious groups has been one characterized by confrontation. The widening gap between people in First World and Third

World countries has contributed greatly to this confrontation. Both business and church leaders have been exploring a more cooperative relationship. A sustained cooperative effort to come to grips with the issue of foreign investment in South Africa has encouraged mutual respect between business and church leaders. Also, Nestle and Dow Chemical have had fruitful dialogs on controversial issues with church leaders. Many church people are learning that constructive dialog, rather than confrontation, is more likely to lead to beneficial changes on the part of business leaders. –Pagan, Rafael D., Jr.; *Business & Society Review,* Summer 1985, (54): pp. 27-29. Avail. ABI 85-33834

Religious organizations, Companies, Relations, Corporate responsibility, Social responsibility, Activists, Interest groups

Why Few Corporations Monitor Social Issues   (286)

While many corporations are concerned about social issues, few incorporate them into their corporate planning systems or include issues management in their performance appraisal systems. There are 2 major reasons for this. Business and academe have broken issues down into 3 basic regions: 1. corporate planning and strategy, 2. corporate social responsibility, and 3. public issues management. Business and academe alike have failed to see the interrelatedness of these areas. They have not recognized that ambiguity and uncertainty exist. The other reason for the lack of monitoring of social issues is the number of issues simultaneously facing corporations. The corporations that do monitor issues usually deal with less than 100, but the number is multiplied when the cross-impact of issues is considered. For the companies that can overcome these stumbling blocks, there are many approaches to issues management, including: 1. monitoring published information, 2. establishing issues committees, 3. using company volunteers to identify and track issues, and 4. developing policy papers and in-company briefings. – Goodman, Steven E.; *Public Relations Jrnl,* Apr 1983, 39(4): pp. 20. Avail. ABI 83-13007

Social issues, Issue, Management, Public relations

Why It's Time for CEOs to Defend the Private Sector   (287)

Business in Canada will have to abandon traditional techniques in the 1980s in its dealings with the government. Chief executive officers (CEOs) must respond to social and political forces to assure the viability of their companies. They will also have to acknowledge that they have a responsibility in the determination of the public interest. Nine things are essential for CEOs to discharge their public-affairs functions effectively: 1. They must have an understanding of the public policy implications of what their firms do. 2. They must have timely information about external forces impacting their firms. 3. They must know how the government makes decisions and who policymakers are. 4. They must be able to bring about responses within their firms to the changes in the environment. 5. The public affairs department must have authority, responsibility, and capacity for briefing those approaching the government. 6. This department must advise management on dealing with organizations like trade unions that can promote company interests. 7. The public relations department must have adequate staff and expertise. 8. It must have responsibility for developing the corporate strategy for dealing with the external environment. 9. It must guide company leaders to make positive public contributions. —Gillies, James; *Executive (Canada),* Apr 1982, 24(4): pp. 30-33. Avail. ABI 82-12888

Canada, Corporate, Strategy, Social responsibility, Corporate responsibility, Public interest

Why U.S. Companies Fall Short on Social Issues (288)

According to John P. Mascotte, president, chairman, and chief executive officer of the Continental Corp., one of the reasons that women and minorities have not made more progress in the workplace is that corporations have not been made responsible for implementing change to accomplish the changes that society seeks. It was only in the 1960s that corporations began to be viewed as agents for social change. Today, society expects corporations to accomplish 3 things: 1. provide warranty for their products and services, 2. help on the issues of environmental protection, and 3. participate in the educational and cultural support activities that society is increasingly demanding. Perhaps, a new corporate model is needed. Until the issues of power, money, community, and individualization in the corporate life are addressed, many of the external or social agenda issues will not be treated. The National Association of Insurance Women can play a role in this process by exposing the problem, helping to develop workable alternative solutions, and strive toward change in their own institutions. —Lyons, Lois J.; *National Underwriter (Property/Casualty),* May 25, 1984, 88(21): pp. 38-39. Avail. ABI 84-18402

Social responsibility, Social issues, Social change

2

Philanthropy

Agent Requires Voluntary Responsibility from Athletes   (289)
Leigh Steinberg, an agent who represents professional ball players, feels his
clients have an obligation to their fans to be active in community activities.
Refusing to represent players who will not get involved, Steinberg specializes
in negotiating contracts that stipulate contributions to the players' favorite
charities, with teams often matching the players' contributions. Rolf
Benirschke, place kicker for the San Diego Chargers, works with the San
Diego Zoo, the March of Dimes, Special Olympics, and other charities. Los
Angeles pitcher Tom Niedenfuer donates $100 for his every win or save to
Rancho Los Amigos Hospital, the leading hospital for treatment of spinal
injuries. In addition, Steinberg encourages donations to athletes' alma
maters since those schools often made their professional sports careers
possible. —Jaffee, Larry; *Fund Raising Mgmt,* Sep 1985, 16(7): pp. 34,36. Avail. ABI 85-
30535
   Professional sports, Agents, Charities, Athletes, Social responsibility

Art on Film   **(290)**
Philip Morris Inc. has one of the most unusual public relations programs in
the US in its fine-arts film program. Philip Morris feels that art attracts and
keeps the best employees; because of that, their offices and factories are full
of art. They also sponsor art exhibits in plant communities and other major
cities. They feel that filming the exhibits is a natural extension of the art-
support program. The company's presence in the film is low key and
sponsorship is usually only mentioned in the opening credits. Scripts are
tightly written and top narrators, like Orson Welles and James Earl Jones,
are used. The films are shown on television, in schools and universities, at
civic club meetings, and at resorts and vacation spots. Philip Morris wants
people to be moved and inspired by what they see in the fine-arts film
program. —Saunders, Frank; *Public Relations Jrnl,* Sep 1982, 38(9): pp. 20-23. Avail. ABI
82-23510
   Philip Morris-New York, Case studies, Public relations, Fine arts, Programs, Social
responsibility

Business and the Arts (291)

There is an increasing trend for US business to invest more time and money in the fine arts. Perceptive chief executives realize that a strong corporate involvement in the arts makes managers more sensitive to the world around them, more aware of creativity, and more innovative and imaginative in marketing and business planning. Columbus, Indiana, an industrial city of 35,000, boasts the most concentrated collection of contemporary architecture in the world. More than 40 public and private buildings in Columbus were designed by some of the world's leading architects. The prime mover in this remarkable achievement has been J. Irwin Miller, retired head of Cummins Engine Co. in Columbus. Miller realized that, for Cummins to attract great people, Columbus would have to be exciting, interesting, and culturally advanced. —Doswell, Marshall; *Business & Economic Review,* Oct 1984, 31(1): pp. 15-18. Avail. ABI 84-34648

Arts, Corporate responsibility, Donations

Business and the Arts: A Reciprocal Relationship (292)

There is an increasing realization among managers of US business firms that business and the arts can be beneficial to one another. The level of business financial support for the arts in the US was approximately $250 million in 1978, compared with $20 million in 1967. Critics of business participation in the arts contend that business resources should not be committed to any endeavor which does not directly benefit the enterprise. Most business managers feel that participation in the arts can further the interests of the company in a general, indirect way. Sponsorship of artistic functions gives the company favorable public exposure and promotes an image of social awareness and responsibility on the part of the firm.Business support of the arts has grown from an activity carried on mainly by small locally owned businesses to a major undertaking of many of the nation's largest firms. Art organizations which receive business funds need to be aware that the business usually expects the contribution to be used wisely and efficiently. The art community has the responsibility of making businesses aware of the benefits of support of the arts. Businesses cannot be expected to participate in the arts on the grounds of social responsibility. They can be persuaded, however, when shown that support of the arts can help them reach a potential market of friends, consumers, and employees. Tables. Graphs. References. —Kur, C. Edward and Knudson, Erik; *Arizona Business,* May 1980, 27(5): pp. 8-13. Avail. ABI 80-13830

Arts, Fine arts, Contributions, Companies, Gifts

Business Boost: Sculptors, Singers, et al. Get More Support (293)

More corporations are supporting the arts. Many are following the lead of PepsiCo Inc. (Purchase, New York), which commissioned sculptor Richard Erdman to create "Passage," the largest sculpture ever made from a single piece of marble. Corporate contributions to the arts have risen by about 20% since 1980. The major benefit for the sponsoring companies is better public relations. Corporate support also allows many unknown artists to achieve fame and recognition for their works. For example, PepsiCo's employment of Erdman has led to his getting a chance to show his works at the Weintraub Gallery in New York. Erdman says that corporate sponsors, rather than the government, are best at giving artists the individual freedom they need. Many art groups, therefore, are unhappy with the pending tax reform plan, which could hurt museums and colleges because of the way it treats contributions of property. —Nelson-Horchler, Joani; *Industry Week,* Jul 22, 1985, 226(2): pp. 18,20. Avail. ABI 85-25918

Fine arts, Funding, Corporate, Contributions, Sponsors, Performing arts, Chief executive officer, Corporate responsibility

Business Donations That Don't Help Business (294)

A review of corporate social responsibility programs shows that, although today's problems are different, most of the same institutions or individuals are benefiting from corporate giving. Most of the money goes to 3 main categories: 1. organized charity, 2. education, and 3. community improvement. However, the dramatic social and economic changes that have taken place in the US call for changes in the distribution of these programs' funds. For example, catch-all charities, such as United Fund, could be cut from the donation list in favor of charities that handle specific and current problems. The funding areas of education and community development also need assessment and possible realignment. Corporate cash can be freed for vital purposes, such as to organizations working on social problems, such as inflation and government regulation, whose solutions are essential to business survival. —Hathaway, James; *Business & Society Review,* Fall 1981, (39): pp. 49-52. Avail. ABI 82-03221

Corporate, Donations, Social responsibility, Charities, Community development, Education

Business in the Community: How You Can Make a (295) Difference

Corporate involvement in community life is the subject of intensified study by government, the news media, and the public. A recent survey of corporate executives at companies of different sizes indicated that they consider corporate philanthropy to be an expression of enlightened self-interest, rather than a form of public policy or a substitute for government programs. According to the American Association of Fund-Raising Counsel, charitable contributions from companies totaled $2.9 billion in 1982, compared with $30 million in 1936. Companies considering starting corporate giving programs should consider assigning the project formally to a manager. Such managers should: 1. familiarize themselves with charitable activities in their local area, 2. determine which groups operate efficiently, and 3. develop an understanding of the area's needs. The manager of corporate giving should also meet with those working in the organizations to which the company might donate. Companies might also consider providing: 1. support for cultural events, 2. "in-kind" contributions of office space, or 3. managerial support and low-interest loans. —Dove, Timothy; *Jrnl of Insurance,* Jul/Aug 1983, 44(4): pp. 17-22. Avail. ABI 83-25431

Corporate responsibility, Social responsibility, Donations, Insurance industry, Community relations

Business Responsibility and the Reagan Budget: Can Business Fill the Gap? (296)

Business has, of course, applauded the Reagan administration's budget and tax cuts. Responsibility for many human services is being shifted from the public sector to the private sector. A failure of the Reagan administration and its policies will be seen as a failure for business. Is this burden too much to ask of business? Even with an increase in corporate giving, human services will suffer. Thus, business must take the lead. One way to increase philanthropy is by getting percentage commitments, whereby companies donate a percentage of their pre-tax profits. The keys to effective philanthropy are: 1. philosophy, 2. leadership, 3. focus, 4. partnership, and 5. professionalism. These elements will help fill the needs gap, if not the dollar gap, making business more responsive to its communities. –Dayton, Kenneth N.; *Vital Speeches,* Oct 1, 1981, 47(24): pp. 750-753. Avail. ABI 81-24679

Economic policy, Corporate responsibility, Donations, Social responsibility, Dayton Hudson-Minneapolis, Case studies

The Case for Corporate Philanthropy-The 5 Percent Club (297)

Corporate philanthropy is one way to combat the decline in public confidence in big business. Dayton Hudson Corp. has added a dimension to the concept of corporate philanthropy called Five Percent, in which corporations and businesses in the Minneapolis-St. Paul (Minnesota) area annually contribute 5% of their pretax profits to help meet the needs of communities. Corporate giving can help America solve its greatest problems at the local level where they are readily identified. A corporate philanthropy program in combination with a comprehensive program of community involvement is good for the city, for business, and for free enterprise. Lack of public confidence in business ultimately results in adverse legislation, stringent government regulation, consumer retaliation, and harassment by unreasonable pressure groups. Public confidence can be bolstered through community giving and action. For example, Dayton Hudson has been involved in projects for the retarded, for disadvantaged youth, and for arts, theatre, and music. –Dayton, Kenneth N.; *Vital Speeches,* Aug 1, 1980, 46(20): pp. 619-622. Avail. ABI 80-16755

Case studies, Dayton Hudson-Minneapolis, Corporate, Donations, Social responsibility, Community

Cause-Related Marketing: Case to Not Leave Home Without It (298)

American Express Co. (New York) is successfully using cause-related marketing to promote its products/services and to benefit nonprofit organizations with cash donations and extensive publicity. In cause-related marketing, an extensive advertising campaign highlights the nonprofit group's benefits to the community, how the public can assist the group, and links fund-raising to use of American Express products and services. Fund raisers looking for long-term solutions to fund-raising problems can adapt the American Express approach to meld business with social responsibility.

Steps to take include: 1. Identify where the nonprofit organization fits into the community and what its goals are. 2. Attempt to locate a corporate sponsor that has compatible marketing objectives in terms of target market, corporate culture, and new business plans. Any proposal for a fund-raising venture must reflect a pragmatic fit between the charity's aims and those of the company. All continuing contributions must be related to the business objectives of a company or that company will not respond positively. – Bragdon, Frances J.; *Fund Raising Mgmt,* Mar 1985, 16(1): pp. 42-47,67. Avail. ABI 85-13753

Case studies, American Express-New York, Social responsibility, Nonprofit organizations, Donations, Marketing, Promotions (ADV), Advantages

Charitable Investments   (299)

Many corporations are benefiting from their philanthropic investments by combining charitable contributions with innovative marketing techniques. Corporate contributions all contain some element of enlightened self-interest. Although the result may not be true philanthropy, cause-related marketing will probably continue to be popular. The most ambitious cause-related marketing project to date is the Statue of Liberty/Ellis Island restoration project. The philanthropic objective of preserving a national monument, coupled with the sale of a specific product or service, has generated huge profits and favorable publicity for many corporate sponsors, including American Express Co., Stroh Brewery Co., Coca-Cola Co., Kellogg Co., and Chrysler Corp. dealers. The key to successful cause-related marketing is appealing to the emotions and popular interest of the general public. However, since the not-for-profit demand is self-generating, the private sector cannot continue matching it with contributions. –Kovach, Jeffrey L.; *Industry Week,* Oct 1, 1984, 223(1): pp. 29-33. Avail. ABI 84-34278

Donations, Corporate responsibility, Promotions (ADV), Manycompanies

Civic Causes-Charity Begins at Home   (300)

Although most bankers are willing to be actively involved in civic activities, the time and money entailed can get out of hand if not monitored reasonably. Those civic and charitable endeavors that serve the bank's long-range self-interest are considered a proper use of a banker's time and resources. Banks that work to keep their communities strong are also working to keep themselves strong. Bank officers and boards are often faced with deciding what charities to support. Some banks make up an annual schedule of which charities they want to support and how much they want to give each one-depending on which causes are in the long-term self-interest of the bank. However, as banking becomes a more competitive business and elimination of unnecessary costs and activities becomes mandatory, bankers will be increasingly selective in their choice of charitable contributions and in the way they contribute time and money to the causes they do support. –Nadler, Paul S.; *Bankers Monthly,* Mar 15, 1981, 98(3): pp. 8-11. Avail. ABI 81-09084

Bank officers, Banks, Charities, Social responsibility, Corporate responsibility, Chief executive officer, Responsibilities

Companies Bring Charity Closer to Home (301)

Most companies do not have a specific policy for donating to charitable organizations and are likely to give to the most appealing causes. Larger charities, with their efficient public relations departments that produce professional-looking appeals, are most likely to attract the business manager's attention. However, Roy Evans, community affairs manager for Levi Strauss, claims that, since management cannot spend much time deciding how to spend its charitable budget, a clear policy should be established. Many companies have established policies of giving to charities that benefit their local communities. For example, British Petroleum has set up a program providing support for local educational systems that help prepare 11-16 year olds for adult life. The Charities Aid Foundation has established a service that allows corporations to give to charities flexibly but still avoid paying taxes on the donated money. —MacCarthy, Elizabeth; *Chief Executive (UK)*, May 1985, pp. 26-28. Avail. ABI 85-25467

Corporate, Donations, Programs, UK, Corporate responsibility, Social responsibility, Manycompanies

Computer, Other Services Can Be Business-Donated (302)

There are a variety of non-cash sources of support that can complement traditional grantmaking. An organization in need of transportation services may borrow a truck from a corporation, especially if it is a vehicle not in use by the company in the evening or on a weekend. A corporation could make a major contribution if it extended its computer services to an organization. The computer should meet a valid need within the organization before its use is requested. The services of a voluntary accountant can enable an organization to have a professional review of its bookkeeping procedures, while a law or tax consulting firm may be able to provide free legal or tax services. The use of telecommunications services, such as a WATS line, may be helpful to many nonprofit organizations. Another prime target for the nonprofit organization seeking fund-raising assistance is a person within a business who is responsible for corporate giving programs and corporate community affairs programs. Table. —Plinio, Alex J.; *Fund Raising Mgmt*, Jan 1983, 13(11): pp. 62,64. Avail. ABI 83-04705

Corporate responsibility, Social responsibility, Corporate, Contributions, Donations, Services, Fund raising

Corporate Art Collecting as a Learning Experience (303)

Art collecting and exhibit sponsorship is a growing trend among Canadian corporations and has provided support for artists. A survey of corporate donations officers suggests that the benefits of art collecting and involvement include better public relations and the attainment of marketing objectives. Support of art can also help a corporation portray a specific image. Canadian Pacific has sponsored painters who captured scenes of the Northwest, and the firm is now sponsoring a television series about art. Royal Bank's sponsorship of ArtVenture projects helps student artists exhibit their work and portrays an image of risk-taking for the bank. Art involvement can also give firms exposure, as in Allstate's sponsorship of a traveling exhibition of young artists' works. Some corporations are generating art awareness among employees. Shell Canada has an art committee made up of employees. The exchange between the art world and the business community gives each group a fresh outlook and encourages employees to understand the creative process. —Iley, Sarah; *Business Qtrly (Canada),* Spring 1984, 49(1): pp. 8-12. Avail. ABI 84-26147

Canada, Corporate, Art, Artists, Social responsibility

Corporate Contributions: Altruistic or For-Profit? (304)

Existing literature has centered on 3 rationales for corporate philanthropy: 1. through-the-firm giving, 2. corporate statesmanship, and 3. profit motivated giving. The relationship between giving and advertising expenditures is determined, to examine the profit motivation argument. Corporate philanthropy literature is critically discussed in this research, and the results of an empirical analysis that extends the understanding of this kind of corporate response to the external environment is reported on. Numerous rationales for corporate giving are considered, and finally the possibility that corporate giving is a complement to advertising, and thus a profit motivated expense, is examined. This argument is supported by the empirical analysis. The findings include: 1. Marginal alterations in advertising expenditures and marginal alterations in contribution expenditures are significantly linked. 2. Firms with more public contact spend more on advertising and contributions than firms with little public contact. 3. Changes in contributions, and changes in other business expenses usually considered to be profit-motivated, are highly correlated. Positive analysis of corporate social issues should come before normative discussions in this sensitive area. Tables. Graphs. References. —Fry, Louis W.; Keim, Gerald D.; and Meiners, Roger E.; *Academy of Mgmt Jrnl,* Mar 1982, 25(1): pp. 94-106. Avail. ABI 82-09056

Corporate, Donations, Social responsibility, Tax deductions, Maximizing profits, Behavior, Regression analysis, Advertising, Expenditures

Corporate Giving by Retail Department Stores (305)

With the Revenue Act of 1935, retail department stores were able to deduct up to 5% of net profits from their taxable earnings. Since 1952, the rate of corporate giving by businesses in general has been about one percent of pretax income. Because of slower growth and increased concentration of ownership in the retail department store industry, the national publicly owned store has grown at the expense of the local independently owned store. The question has been raised of whether these new national publicly owned retail department stores will allocate more or less to corporate giving than the local independently owned retail department stores. A survey of corporate giving was designed to answer this question. Respondents in the survey were 32 national publicly owned retail department stores and 16 local independently owned retail department stores. The results of the study indicated, according to percentage of pretax income companies allocated to corporate giving, that the national publicly owned retail department stores gave more than the local independently owned retail department stores.

Table. References. —Barach, Jeffrey and Zimmer, Alan; *Business & Society,* Spring 1983, 22(1): pp. 49-52. Avail. ABI 83-20366

Retailing industry, Donations, Corporate, Contributions, Studies, Social responsibility, Department stores

Corporate Philanthropy: What to Expect (306)

With the prolonged recession deeply affecting earnings, the Council for Financial Aid to Education has predicted an 11% increase in total corporate giving to $3.3 billion in 1982. That is equal to about 10% of the federal government's cuts in social programs and an even smaller percentage of the estimated $50 billion-plus in total charitable contributions. Though some, including President Reagan, assumed that corporate giving would pick up a substantial portion of the extensive federal cutbacks in social programs, business leaders consider that assumption unrealistic and unreasonable. Corporate giving would have to jump from an average of 1% of pretax income to nearly 15% to match this year's federal cuts. A recent survey of more than 200 chief executives by the Council on Foundations indicates that those companies will raise their donations by an average of 28% by 1984. A number of companies are joining together in community groups and pledging at least 2% of their pretax income to contributions. Companies in Louisville, Minneapolis, and Baltimore have set an even higher goal of 5%. More than 500 companies have become involved in such groups, and peer pressure is given credit for the movement's growth. Many companies are also developing formal mechanisms to handle their philanthropic contributions in a more efficient way. Thomas E. Drohan, president of Foremost McKesson Inc. has suggested that companies raise their contributions by pegging them to the 20% portion of the tax cut earmarked for business. – Murray, Thomas J.; *Dun's Business Month,* Jul 1982, 120(1): pp. 55-57. Avail. ABI 82-18294

Corporate responsibility, Social responsibility, Donations

Corporate Philanthropy Head Sees New Directions Ahead (307)

In an interview, James P. Shannon, vice-president and executive director of the General Mills Foundation (Minneapolis, Minnesota), discussed future directions of corporate giving. Shannon is also a director of the Council on Foundations and chairman of the Council's Corporate Philanthropy Committee. The committee seeks to learn of nonprofit businesses' needs for corporate giving and to address private companies' resources and energies for community needs. The prevailing philosophy in US business calls for responsible managers to review corporate resources and pledge to help meet public needs. New networks are developing to facilitate this process. Corporations are increasingly responsive to the needs of the nonprofit sector. Corporate interest in the nonprofit sector has grown to recognize a need to recruit, train, and retain top quality personnel in the nonprofit sector, as well as a need for more creativity and better management. —Plinio, Alex J.; *Fund Raising Mgmt,* Dec 1983, 14(10): pp. 84-85. Avail. ABI 84-01873

Charitable foundations, Nonprofit organizations, Corporate responsibility, Donations, Case studies

Corporate Philanthropy Poised for Takeoff (308)

Between 1936 and 1982 corporate philanthropy increased 10.5% per year from $30 million to $3 billion as corporations recognized that charitable giving is an intrinsic part of corporate activity because it expresses an acknowledged social responsibility. This upward trend is likely to continue. Employees are also encouraged to volunteer and participate in community affairs. Corporate foundations have been developed to channel corporate contributions, acting as buffers between fluctuations in the business cycle and charity recipients. During the 1981-1982 recession, corporate income declined by a third, but contributions did not drop. A change in political and social philosophy was a major reason for this, especially President Reagan's assertion that government cutbacks should be compensated for by corporate and individual philanthropy. Corporate managers realize that a decline in or elimination of corporate contributions would mean more and larger government. Further, the Economic Recovery Tax Act of 1981 (ERTA) encouraged sharp increases in gifts-in-kind. Contributions are now viewed not as charity but as corporate investments in society. Table. –Smith, Hayden; *Fund Raising Mgmt,* Jul 1983, 14(5): pp. 18-24. Avail. ABI 83-19811

Donations, Corporate, Contributions, Excess profits, Corporate taxes, History, Social responsibility

Corporate Philanthropy Comes of Age (309)

As cutbacks in government funding increase, requests for contributions from corporations also increase. Many corporations are looking at their contributions as a way to extend a competitive edge, and some, like American Express, are even making contributions a marketing tool by tying donations to sales promotions. Social responsibility programs are usually administered by public relations (PR) departments, some of which even have contributions managers who have a working knowledge of the community. Some companies involve employees in contributions decision making, and some have specific geographic restrictions or focused areas of interest. Most corporations contribute 1 1/2% of pretax profits. The largest givers are Exxon, IBM, and Mobil, which donate less than 2% of their pretax earnings. Companies keep elaborate records of their contributions, and many are becoming more selective in their giving, hoping to get a return on their bottom line for a contribution. References. –Tilson, Donn J. and Vance, Donald; *Public Relations Review,* Summer 1985, 11(2): pp. 26-33. Avail. ABI 85-26773

Corporate responsibility, Social responsibility, Donations, Public relations, Contributions, Sales promotions, Innovations, Trends

The Corporation - Not a Money Tree! An Insider's View (310) of Business Sponsorship

Nina Kaiden Wright recently shared her expertise and opinions on corporate sponsorship in an interview with Business Quarterly. The amount of donations made to the arts by Canadian corporations has increased drastically in recent years, but the donations are not made carelessly. The corporations have developed criteria for giving and requests are scrutinized carefully. A great deal of research is conducted to determine the value of the funding to the corporation. While there are many projects worthy of support, certain rules should be followed when trying to select a project. The project should: 1. provide common ground for the corporation and the arts institution, 2. make a contribution to the community, 3. fit in with company objectives, and 4. be achievable. Most Canadian firms are only interested in supporting arts that benefit and are located in Canada, but there is growing interest in a broader cultural policy. The arts in Canada would benefit from the infusion of work from other countries. —Sanders, Doreen; *Business Qtrly (Canada)*, Fall 1984, 49(3): pp. 92-99. Avail. ABI 85-05917

Fine arts, Canada, Corporate, Sponsors, Decision making, Corporate responsibility, Funding, Factors

Directing the Flow of Corporate Largesse (311)

The appropriate roles and limitations of governments and the many associations, non-profit institutions, citizen groups, and corporations that make social contributions should be analyzed, and the purpose and nature of corporate philanthropy must be questioned. A business corporation should strive to make its philanthropy a monument to its own best values and the highest quality of thought and action. Corporate philanthropy should become more professional by objectively assessing priorities, better understanding the multitude of issues and groups competing for limited resources, and developing more systematic procedures for program planning and decision making. It is time for some bold and imaginative thinking to determine how business corporations can contribute to community development through daily decisions regarding the well-being of their personnel, the quality of their product, and the uses of their profit. —Joseph, James A.; *Business & Society Review,* Summer 1982, (42): pp. 40-43. Avail. ABI 82-23381

Corporate, Contributions, Social responsibility, Priorities, Corporate responsibility, Roles

Ethical Behavior in Business: A Hierarchical Approach (312) from the Talmud

The Talmud, the compilation of Jewish oral law, includes extensive discussions of business ethics. Four levels of ethical behavior in business gleaned from the words of the Talmud can be distinguished. At the lowest level, the individual is just barely inside the law. The highest level is "the way of the pious." The Talmud also uses a variety of different approaches to deal with someone who has committed a serious moral offense for which prosecution is not possible. Cases from the Talmudic literature are used to illustrate moral and ethical principles at each level and degree of righteousness. Every individual and corporate entity must try to move up the ethics hierarchy. The Talmud negates the validity of the assumption that corporations can employ philanthropy to compensate for their misdeeds. References. —Friedman, Hershey H.; *Jrnl of Business Ethics (Netherlands),* Apr 1985, 4(2): pp. 117-129. Avail. ABI 85-16009

Ethics, Behavior, Social responsibility, Religion

For the Love of Art Business Professionals Play Many (313) Roles

Canada's business professionals - especially accountants, consultants, and lawyers - are prime volunteers for arts organizations, offering management skills and business insight that complements the artistic nature. The depth and nature of involvement varies with the arts organization and the individual. In most cases, professionals get involved in the arts because they have an inherent interest in the medium. Many professionals are motivated by the desire for a change of pace from what they do all day, although most start out in an area that relates to or requires their peculiar skills. Assistance comes in the form of fund-raising, personal contributions, and endowments. Most professional firms like Clarkson Gordon encourage their employees to get involved in community activities, and that is their biggest contribution to the arts. The arts organizations realize the importance of the committed volunteer to its ongoing existence. —Scott, Donald C.; *Business Qtrly (Canada)*, Fall 1984, 49(3): pp. 108-111. Avail. ABI 85-05920

Arts, Support, Canada, Volunteers, Professional, Workers, Services, Corporate responsibility

Foundations of a Better Society? (314)

In 1975 only 273 corporate foundations had $1 million or more in assets, or gave $500,000 or more a year in grants, or both; by 1979, there were 600 such foundations. Since 1979, corporate foundations have been the largest contributors to charitable causes. Company-sponsored foundations have increased because of a new vision among many business leaders of their stake in, and relationship to society. According to W. A. Marcussen, president of the Atlantic Richfield Foundation, corporations are beginning to see that their role goes beyond that of simply making a profit. His view is echoed by E. B. Knauft, vice president for social responsibility, Aetna Life & Casualty Co. The fundamental issue remains, however, of whether corporations are merely searching for today's public relations value, or whether they are truly dedicated to serving public needs. Certainly, it is emphasized, corporations need not contribute to causes which are actively contrary to their own purposes. Corporate giving should not be "disinterested." —Anonymous; *Industry Week*, Apr 20, 1981, 209(2): pp. 49-52. Avail. ABI 81-11176

Corporate, Foundations, Social responsibility, Tax Reform Act 1969-US, Charitable foundations, Donations

Fund Raising's Future Lies with Creative Visionaries (315)

The professional fund raiser's job, particularly for nonprofit hospitals, is a process of raising consciousness of people - boards of directors, chief executive officers, medical staffs - and generating big ideas that inspire people and attract energy in the form of money to build buildings, set up programs, meet payrolls, and fund ideas. It requires design, innovation, assertiveness, and imagination. The not-for-profit hospital of the future will be a market-oriented, high-profit making, entrepreneurial, philanthropic organization if it is to survive. The role of the development officer is to create and implement a capital acquisition strategy that provides the resources to meet the not-for-profit hospital's social responsibility to care for the growing number of poor and elderly people. To do this, development officers with vision will participate in joint ventures that develop new projects, pool capital, and form turnaround teams to help fellow institutions that are in danger of failing. —Kaiser, Leland; *Fund Raising Mgmt,* Mar 1985, 16(1): pp. 34-39. Avail. ABI 85-13752

Nonprofit hospitals, Fund raising, Development, Managers, Innovations

Gift Horses and Hobbyhorses: The Pros and Cons of   (316) Corporate Charity

President Reagan is hoping that private philanthropy could make up for reductions in government spending for social, educational, and cultural programs. That has not been the case, however. Philanthropy by corporations approached an estimated $3.1 billion in 1982, about the same as 1981's total. The recession has reduced companies' ability to give, but chances are that contributions will improve with the recovery now underway. The 1982 donations amounted to an estimated 1.1% of pretax income for the largest industrial concerns and 1.7% for firms in the $25 million-$49 million sales range. Some critics say most corporate philanthropy is too casual and unplanned and that the decision-making structure of corporate giving lacks standardization and objectivity. Further, there is a measure of ambivalence in the corporate community as to whether companies should give anything, which may affect companies' planning of gifts and demands for returns on investments, or at least documentation of results. The experience of Philip Morris, Manufacturers Hanover, and Merrill Lynch in sponsoring the 1983 tour of Vatican art treasures is detailed. —Reynes, Roberta A.; *Barron's,* Mar 28, 1983, 63(13): pp. 38-40. Avail. ABI 83-10231

Corporate responsibility, Donations, Social responsibility

Gifts-in-Kind Organization Gives Something for Nothing   (317)

The National Association for the Exchange of Industrial Resources (NAEIR) is an 8-year-old nonprofit organization that advocates corporate philanthropy through gifts-in-kind (gifts of merchandise rather than money). Charity groups can join for an annual fee of $350, upon which they become eligible for up to $5,000 worth of free merchandise from companies that donate excess inventory (for which they get a significant tax break). In 1984, NAEIR distributed some $40 million in merchandise to its 4,000 members in all 50 states. Currently, about 1,000 active corporate donors contribute products ranging from office supplies to audiovisual equipment to building materials. NAEIR, based in Northfield, Illinois, publishes a 32-page catalog quarterly that lists 332 different products. The group's 1985 goal is $80 million in gifts-in-kind. Corporate donors include Westinghouse Electric Co. and 3M Corp., plus many small businesses. —Jaffee, Larry; *Fund Raising Mgmt,* Jan 1985, 15(11): pp. 50-51. Avail. ABI 85-05149

Nonprofit organizations, Donations, Gifts, Corporate responsibility

The Growing Impact of Business Giving   (318)

In the past 3 years, US corporate giving has risen an average of 16% annually. While tax incentives create a favorable climate for business contributions, numerous other motivations are cited for giving, such as: 1. corporate citizenship, 2. protecting the business environment, 3. contributing to employee benefits, 4. promoting the company image, and 5. meeting personal commitments of company founders. Besides simply deciding to give, corporate executives are being more selective about what and who to give to. For example, 11% of corporate giving is allocated to civic projects. Education and health receive the biggest share, about 70% of corporate contributions, while cultural programs make up about 10% of the philanthropic pie. The remainder goes to other causes and foreign aid programs. With ever-rising costs, shrinking government funding, and growing civic, social, and cultural concerns, business is electing to fill the gap in support. –Tuthill, Mary; *Nation's Business,* Oct 1980, 68(10): pp. 66-70. Avail. ABI 80-20941

Corporate responsibility, Social responsibility, Charities, Donations, Economic impact, Social impact

How Can Canada's Cultural Forces Be Given More Muscle? (319)

Within the last 20 years, administration of Canada's cultural affairs has increased in scope and responsibility to become a big business. Expenditures of federal, provincial, and private sources are between $2-3 billion a year. The cultural executive's role is diverse, involving state-of-the-arts fund raising and dealing with hostile boards of trustees. Without money from the private sector, culture in Canada will wither. Boards of directors that lack innovative ideas and techniques, further jeopardize the preservation and enhancement of culture. The cross-culture conflict in Quebec further exacerbates the problem, therefore, corrective measures are needed. –Swann, Peter C.; *Business Qtrly (Canada),* Summer 1980, 45(2): pp. 54-58. Avail. ABI 81-23499

Canada, Culture, Social responsibility, Corporate responsibility, Arts, Boards of directors, Selection

How Much Must a Bank Simply Give Away? (320)

The public impression that banks are a quasi-public organization puts bankers under pressure to provide funds for charities and major capital projects. The resulting loss of bank profits could have a considerably negative impact. When approached by smaller charities, banks should: 1. adopt a plan of "centralized giving," whereby one person is responsible for all charitable contributions, 2. develop a general policy on giving for the year, and 3. require that all solicitors provide a written statement of the cause, use of proceeds, and general program involved. Banks should consider assisting capital projects only if they are viable in terms of risk, income, and liquidity or on the grounds of long-run self interest in helping the community grow. "Lifeline banking," a program requiring the free provision of certain bank services by law, is a threat to banks. In answer, banks could: 1. switch to a national charter, or 2. trade off for the privilege to sell insurance. –Nadler, Paul S.; *Bankers Monthly,* Nov 15, 1984, 101(11): pp. 10-12,23-25. Avail. ABI 85-04570

Banks, Corporate responsibility, Donations, Bank services

Industry Gives More in Hard Times (321)

Because of the recession, many companies in the chemical process industries are raising their contributions of goods and services to educational, charitable, and other humanitarian organizations. Fund raisers from a growing number of organizations are looking to corporations for help. In the coming years, they will be asked to give even more due to the widening gap between available funding and projected social/cultural needs. Mead, which is representative of donors, is increasing contributions from 1% to 2% of pretax earnings by 1985. Reductions in federal support have spurred corporate contributions to community efforts, and more firms are using gift-matching programs. The theme of employee involvement in charitable programs is a recurring one. Rohm & Haas and Monsanto both have carried out extensive volunteerism programs. Stepped up support by chemical companies has helped many nonprofit groups stay alive. Graphs. –Anonymous; *Chemical Week,* Feb 16, 1983, 132(7): pp. 30-33. Avail. ABI 83-06905

Chemical industry, Manycompanies, Donations, Corporate responsibility

Industry Isn't Rushing into Social Activism (322)

Results of a survey conducted by the Conference Board Inc. indicate that US corporations have not been responding to President Reagan's request to increase contributions to social causes hurt by cuts in federal spending. The survey, which covered more than 400 large companies, found that 60% of those surveyed plan normal increases in their philanthropic contributions in 1982. However, only 6% plan spending increases as a result of federal budget cuts. A separate poll of 137 companies headquartered in large cities found that only 20% plan to boost financial aid to urban programs. In addition, a report on urban public-private partnerships issued by the Committee for Economic Development concludes that, by lowering the tax burden of many companies, the 1981 tax legislation will diminish the need for charitable contributions by companies which had used such donations for tax relief. – Miller, William H.; *Industry Week,* Feb 22, 1982, 212(4): pp. 18-23. Avail. ABI 82-08248

Corporate responsibility, Social responsibility, Private sector, Contributions, Cooperation

Lending People in the Public Interest (323)

The voluntarism that President Reagan has been advocating has long been practiced by many American companies, but no more dramatic example can exist than the ambitious programs that allow employees to take paid leaves of absence to work in social service jobs. In fact, Xerox has a leave program that was set up over 11 years ago. Xerox's leave program, serving as an example, is available for employees who have been working with the company for 3 years. Applications and proposed projects are submitted to a committee, whose 5 members are a cross-section of employees. Of almost 35,000 eligible employees, only 70 submitted proposals in 1981. Fifteen were selected, and those monies spent by the company on the leave are considered corporate philanthropy, eligible for a tax break. On their return, the employees receive their old jobs back or receive comparable ones. Control Data began a similar program in 1977, and it currently has 12 employees on leave. A major problem in the programs has been trouble with the smooth re-entry to work for the program participants, and counseling is being used by some to help. Whatever the case, it requires a strong sense of social commitment for a corporation to set up a social service program. –Tuthill, Mary; *Nation's Business,* May 1982, 70(5): pp. 68-72. Avail. ABI 82-13070

Social responsibility, Corporate responsibility, Manycompanies, Manypeople, Programs, Social services, Volunteers

Making Corporate Responsibility Pay (324)

The term "corporate responsibility" is widely accepted to imply that large corporations, like charitable foundations, should be a principal source of philanthropy. Many political economists argue that the corporation's only responsibility is to provide a profit for its shareholders. Competition, however, is between people, not between products or companies, and the people in an organization create the profit. Those companies that invest some of their earnings in their community are likely to attract better employees, retain employees longer, obtain better performance, and thus show greater profit. Companies must carefully select which organizations it will support in order to avoid supporting organizations that oppose the principles of business. "Corporate beneficence" is an investment in the community that helps maximize corporate profits and reduce adversarial relationships among businesses. –Powers, Robert T.; *Industry Week*, Dec 12, 1983, 219(6): pp. 8. Avail. ABI 84-03136

Corporate responsibility, Profitability, Corporate objectives, Donations

Misdirecting Corporate Philanthropy (325)

The movement to make the private sector, rather than government, primarily responsible for the solutions to social problems has led to calls for increased philanthropy by businesses. Such a move is based on 4 assumptions: 1. that corporations are morally obliged to give, 2. that companies do not give enough, 3. that the "community" should determine the use of contributions, and 4. that larger, more established programs deserve the most support. Each of these assumptions is questionable on one or more counts. While Americans need to unlearn their dependence on the federal government to solve problems, it will not do to place the burden entirely on business. Furthermore, a large philanthropic bureaucracy will be no improvement over a large governmental bureaucracy. Business serves the community best by creating economic activity. To compel business to subsidize the philanthropic bureaucracy will only inhibit the main purpose of business. The government would do better to decrease such barriers to self-help as licensing laws, minimum wage laws, and zoning and building restrictions. – Bandow, Doug; *Jrnl of the Institute for Socioeconomic Studies*, Spring 1983, 8(1): pp. 57-66. Avail. ABI 83-11673

Corporate responsibility, Social responsibility, Donations, Public policy

Non-Cash Support Increasing Says Foundation Head (326)

Corporate philanthropy is the subject of an interview with Robert L. Payton, head of the Exxon Education Foundation. In 1982, the foundation made grants of $27 million, just over half of the firm's total domestic contributions. The foundation staff is unusual in that only 2 of its members are Exxon career persons, with the remaining 5 having backgrounds primarily in education and philanthropy. A representative sampling of Payton's comments includes: 1. Today, there are highly organized and rationalized fund-raising systems, with corporations playing a larger role and endowed private foundations a smaller one. 2. Philanthropy must be carried on with all the professionalism possible, and the corporate giver must be knowledgeable about taxation, traditions, incentives, motivation, and public

policy. 3. There is an increasing need for philanthropy research, and Independent Sector organization has established a research committee to assist people involved in this type of research to get in touch with each other.
–Plinio, Alex J.; *Fund Raising Mgmt,* Sep 1983, 14(7): pp. 86,89. Avail. ABI 83-24420

Social responsibility, Corporate responsibility, Donations

Not Only the Big Boys Play   (327)

Canada's arts organizations are looking to the country's small businesses to expand the base of their support. Thousands of small businesses are being motivated to provide board members and loan space and to give money and goods to performing and visual arts groups. There are many reasons why these companies want to get involved. Lyman Henderson of Davis & Henderson Ltd. thinks that most small firms contribute to the arts because the idea, the project, and the people involved with it excite those who run the business. Corporate supporters also realize the opportunities for business development and enhanced public relations that accompany any civic duty. Small businesses are especially well-positioned to make an impact on their local community. Regardless of how involvement with the arts helps the business, most businesses decide to support the arts because they realize that art helps to shape the communities in which business flourishes. Once a company makes a donation, it usually wants to get more involved because it enjoys the art it sees. –Iley, Sarah J. E.; *Business Qtrly (Canada),* Fall 1984, 49(3): pp. 105-107. Avail. ABI 85-05919

Arts, Funding, Small business, Canada, Corporate responsibility, Manycompanies

Oddball Philanthropy   (328)

When John D. MacArthur died in 1978, his 10 million shares of Bankers Life, which included its subsidiaries and real estate, went to the foundation bearing his name. The MacArthur Foundation's image is that of an offbeat, eccentric operation. MacArthur's son, Roderick, views himself as guardian of the legacy and is critical of the foundation's actions. While MacArthur and his son had their differences, Roderick was appointed one of several co-equal directors of the foundation. With grants of about $50 million each year, the foundation is the second largest philanthropic foundation in the US. The passage of the Tax Reform Act of 1969 forced the divestiture by the foundation of at least 80% of Bankers Life. The handling of that sale in early 1984 led to a lawsuit by Roderick MacArthur against 8 of the other directors, asking that the foundation be dissolved and the assets conveyed to a new one with the same purposes, with Roderick as a director and excluding the others.
–McClory, Robert J.; *Across the Board,* Jun 1984, 21(6): pp. 48-56. Avail. ABI 84-21731

Foundations, Life insurance companies, Personal, Profiles, Grants, Case studies, Social responsibility

On the Charity Circuit   (329)

Cynics often focus on the discrepancy between the expressed intentions of executives who attend charity functions and the reality of less admirable motives. Many major charity dinners are organized around a prestigious honoree whose vendors and associates are then invited to buy tables at the dinner. While popular in New York, Miami, and Las Vegas, these events are disliked by many executives because of their frequency and pressures. However, Minot K. Milliken, vice-president of a textile company and president of the Boys' Club of New York, has identified the motives behind executive involvement in charitable work as the desires to: 1. do some good, 2. demonstrate abilities beyond workaday endeavors, 3. exercise power, and 4. reduce guilt. Roderick Gilkey, an Emory University psychologist, adds that public service helps fulfill the developmental task of achieving "generativity" for men in their 40s and older by allowing them to pass on to others a portion of their learning and gifts. —Kiechel, Walter, III; *Fortune,* Oct 14, 1985, 112(8): pp. 223,226. Avail. ABI 85-32825

Executives, Motivation, Public relations, Charities, Donations, Social responsibility

An Optimist's Challenge to the Independent Sector   (330)
The voluntary sector is today more critical to America than ever before because the nation's international and domestic needs are growing daily, and people are beginning to realize that national resources are finite and that government cannot solve every social ill. We are approaching a sense of urgency and a sense of community, or "communitarianism," as people know that they must share problems and solutions. However, the voluntary sector is in jeopardy, because even though total giving is increasing, private foundations cannot keep up with inflation. The Independent Sector is trying to help increase giving, and the best way to increase giving to any one segment is to increase the size of the whole "pie". Corporations should enact a positive program of community philanthropy on a good-sized scale. The ultimate goal should be the maximum allowed by law as a tax deduction: 5% of federally taxable income. —Dayton, Kenneth N.; *Trusts & Estates,* Dec 1980, 119(12): pp. 19-22. Avail. ABI 81-01556

Third, Voluntary, Sectors, Donations, Corporate responsibility, Social responsibility

Philanthropy: Beyond Good Intentions   (331)
Corporate personnel who make decisions about donating to charity face many dilemmas. A recent survey shows that public relations professionals are important forces in corporate contributions programs. According to a United Way of America report, philanthropic giving will increase from $48.2 billion in 1980 to $90.4 billion in 1988. However, only 9.1% of all US corporations give more than 2% of their net income to charity. Moreover, although corporate giving is increasing, it cannot compensate for lost government support for health and welfare services. The United Way suggests that the baby boomlet, a continued increase in immigrants, and the aging of the population will all contribute to the growing demand for charitable services. However, few educational courses for undergraduate public relations students are available to help them make contributions decisions. A career interest in philanthrophy must be fostered by including charitable giving in college curricula. Academicians, corporate officers, foundations, and nonprofit groups should meet to develop curricula guidelines for such courses. —Delfin, Stephen M.; *Public Relations Jrnl,* Sep 1985, 41(9): pp. 7-10. Avail. ABI 85-30000

Public relations, Social responsibility, Donations, Charities

A Primer on Corporate Philanthropy (332)

In 1980, for the first time in history, charitable giving by US corporations exceeded total grants by private foundations. A corporation can address its social responsibility by charitable giving. The way corporations distribute their funds is substantially different from the way individuals or foundations distribute. The areas to which corporations give, in order of amounts received, are: 1. education, 2. health and welfare, 3. civic activities, 4. culture and art, and 5. other causes. The correct approach to corporate giving involves the definition of objectives, deciding how much to contribute, who to support, and getting employees involved. A corporation needs to inform many groups about their philanthropic activities: 1. company shareholders, 2. organizations seeking corporate support, 3. community leaders, government officials, and the media, and 4. all others interested in the interaction of business and society. Mismanagement can discourage donors and cripple a nonprofit organizations' program. Profit-making organizations are helping nonprofit organizations become better organized by loaning executives, participating in management workshops, and providing counsel and assistance in necessary areas. –Koch, Frank; *Business & Society Review,* Summer 1981, (38): pp. 48-52. Avail. ABI 81-23073

Corporate responsibility, Social responsibility, Donations, Contributions

Recruiting Newspeople as Volunteers Can Raise (333) Conflict-of-Interest Issues

Charitable organizations regularly recruit media editors, reporters, publishers, and managers under the impression that the influence of these newspeople will secure favorable coverage of their charities. Newspeople express concern that their involvement in such organizations may constitute a conflict of interest. A recent survey conducted by Suburban Communications Corp. sought data from 207 suburban newspapers. Of the nearly 50% that responded, 62% suggested that involvement with charitable institutions creates problems in maintaining objectivity and avoiding the perception of favoritism. John Reddy, Suburban Communications Corp. vice-president, says organizations must develop greater awareness of and sensitivity to the positions of newspeople. In any event, says Reddy, media involvement is usually not very significant in getting positive publicity for a cause. –Delfin, Stephen; *Public Relations Jrnl,* Aug 1984, 40(8): pp. 6-7. Avail. ABI 84-32212

Nonprofit organizations, Editors, Reporters, Community action, Social responsibility, Publishing industry

Responsible Corporate Giving from the Donor's (334) Viewpoint

In recognition that giving is an art, Pennzoil tries to approach philanthropy in a rational and scientific way, using the same approach as that employed in business - concentrating resources to get the maximum benefit from each dollar spent. The company supports tried and true institutions, as well as a limited number of new ones, choosing the ones for which contributions will really count. Gifts are considered investments in the future made on the behalf of corporate shareholders, and they are not given to gain public or governmental favor. Furthermore, emphasis is on helping humanitarian organizations that will, in turn, help employees. Pennzoil has given to such efforts as the fight against cancer and the Interferon Foundation, the endowment of museums, theaters, and symphonies and it has donated a research facility to Louisiana State University (Shreveport). It acknowledges that enlightened giving requires corporations and private citizens to coordinate their efforts to find and support the most deserving projects. – Kerr, Baine P.; *Fund Raising Mgmt*, Sep 1983, 14(7): pp. 62-65. Avail. ABI 83-24417

  Corporate responsibility, Donations, Pennzoil-Houston, Case studies, Oil companies

Service to Humanity ... The Best Work of Life   (335)

Maurice Blond, a general agent for The Travelers Insurance Co. (New York), helped develop the concept of charitable giving through life insurance. In addition, he is an internationally recognized authority on underwriting insurance for the physically and mentally handicapped. Blond feels lucky to have been born poor on the lower East Side of Manhattan and is most grateful for the settlement houses, which provided opportunities for the slum-dwellers. Blond feels that insurance people should give of themselves and their talents, thereby gaining satisfaction of knowing they made a difference. Another charitable avenue to explore is the establishment of an organizational plan, and there are 2 types of Charitable Reminder Trusts - the UNI Trust and Annuity Trust - both requiring a contribution to a qualified charity of a principal sum, while retaining an annual income flow to a noncharitable beneficiary. –Blond, Maurice; *National Underwriter (Life/Health)*, Nov 5, 1984, 88(44A): pp. 24-25,32-33. Avail. ABI 84-37224

  Life insurance, Donations, Fund raising, Social responsibility

"Shape Up" or Lose Corporate Backing   (336)

As government support has decreased, numerous volunteer agencies have turned to corporations for financial aid. The private sector has responded by producing a wide variety of corporate support programs. However, due to the vast number of soliciting agencies, corporations have become selective about the agencies they support. Corporations also tend to expect more from the nonprofits they fund and require from them: 1. more earned income, 2. better management, 3. cooperation among groups, and 4. consistent quality. For agencies to meet corporate expectations in return for financial support, a trend is emerging of corporate willingness to underwrite projects aimed at making these improvements. The Chemical Bank, for example, has developed a basic grant program that provides nonprofits with the ability to project revenues, among other helpful methods of operation. The Chemical Bank's volunteer center and public education office also aid nonprofits in developing management skills. Corporate efforts to augment contribution monies with services illustrate a growing trend that is becoming a sub-profession within corporate philanthropy. –Stern, Marian; *Fund Raising Mgmt*, Apr 1983, 14(2): pp. 46-47,51. Avail. ABI 83-11183

  Nonprofit organizations, Charitable foundations, Corporate, Donations, Social responsibility, Arts, Volunteers, Fund raising

Shareholders Get to Vote on Charity (337)

Large corporations frequently deprive shareholders of the opportunity to vote on charities to which the company gives money. Warren E. Buffett, chairman of Berkshire Hathaway Inc. (Omaha, Nebraska), felt such a policy was inequitable. Thus, he has supervised the mailing of ballots to shareholders. The ballots give shareholders the chance to distribute about $2 million to the charities of their choice. With nearly one million shares outstanding, each share gives its owner the right to allocate $2 to charity. The plan has tax advantages, since corporate charitable contributions are treated as business expenses and are not taxed. Buffett estimates that as many as 85% of shareholders will respond. Several corporate executives have described Buffett's plan as imaginative, but expressed reservations. It remains to be seen whether the plan will be widely imitated. —Smith, Lee; *Fortune,* Nov 30, 1981, 104(11): pp. 169-170. Avail. ABI 81-27344

Case studies, Donations, Stockholders, Voting, Corporate responsibility

Social Action by the Industry (338)

American and Canadian insurance companies in the period since 1972 gave over $240 million in contributions to communities and invested an average of $1 billion per year in social programs and community projects, according to Stanley G. Karson, director of the Clearinghouse on Corporate Social Responsibility in Washington, DC. The establishment of the Clearinghouse resulted from the identification of critical social issues such as health and housing. Insurance companies needed programs to deal with these social issues. Insurance companies respond to social problems with outright contributions and with investments such as energy programs. Many insurance companies lend management personnel to assist in community projects. The Clearinghouse initiated 4 programs which would only be effective on an industry-wide basis. One program provides experts in areas such as housing to local member companies. The other programs are: 1. a council on health education, 2. assistance to black colleges, and 3. scholarships for medical researchers. —Anonymous; *Life Association News,* Sep 1980, 75(9): pp. 143-150. Avail. ABI 80-17997

Insurance companies, Social responsibility, Contributions, Community, Projects, Insurance industry

The Sound of Music Reverberating in the Boardroom (339)

Businesses spend 5 times as much to sponsor sports events as to sponsor all arts. Persons in the arts circles speak of educating businessmen to accept their responsibilities to sponsor arts, but these businessmen are dealing with difficult economic problems. The best arguments for business sponsorship of the arts are: 1. the social side, and 2. the opportunity to show the business to customers and prospective clients in a favorable way. Sponsorships must be ones the senior management feel comfortable supporting. Companies need not be industrial giants to sponsor arts programs.Each corporate sponsor for the Royal Philharmonic Orchestra receives a number of benefits such as full page ads in the program. Sponsorhip payments are not automatically eligible for tax relief, but the Revenue takes a sympathetic view when the amounts are a relatively small portion of the advertising budget. Donations to recipients registered as charities can be made with full tax relief under a deed of covenant, but it is a rarer form of sponsorship and requires a long period of commitment. It may be better for the arts organization to have several small sponsors than a single large sponsor. – Spooner, Peter; *Chief Executive Monthly (UK)*, Feb 1980, pp. 36-40. Avail. ABI 80-07734

Performing arts, Fine arts, Corporate responsibility, Social responsibility, Fund raising, Donations, Business, Sponsors

Sponsorship: A Growing Attraction (340)

Sponsorship has proliferated beyond anyone's wildest expectations. Companies' contributions to the worlds of art, sport, and other areas are growing by leaps and bounds. Furthermore, companies are finding that sponsorship of smaller, local affairs can produce the same kind of public relations benefits associated with backing major occurrences. Today's sponsorship is becoming a business transaction, frequently negotiated under competitive conditions. The practice has evolved into subtle marketing, and the criteria of where to place the company's money have hardened. This ties in with the concept of stressing the company image. Often, professional assistance is required to match a particular company's image with the proper event. Sponsorship can also produce beneficial tax considerations. Additionally, some events, particularly sporting ones, can attract enormous media coverage. Sponsorship schemes may also be used as a tool of management development. –Underwood, Lynn; *Chief Executive (UK)*, Feb 1982, pp. 26,27. Avail. ABI 82-08757

Corporate responsibility, Social responsibility, Performing arts, UK, Sports, Tax benefits

Sports Sponsorship Requires Marketing Expertise, (341)
Realistic Expectations, and Social Responsibility

In an interview, Lois Lazarus, sports marketing consultant and president of Lazarus & Associates Inc., expressed her views on the expectations and evaluation of sports sponsorship and the responsibilities that it entails. The sports sponsorship programs of many companies reveal unrealistic expectations and a lack of professional sports marketing expertise, which is essential in evaluating a sport for possible sponsorship. To select a sport for sponsorship, marketers must analyze: 1. the sport's image, 2. the advantages sponsorship would provide over the competition, 3. impact on sales and brand awareness, 4. growth potential, and 5. the promoters' reputation. Lazarus stresses that sport sponsors must not ignore the social and moral responsibilities that sponsorship involves. She advocates legislation requiring medical standards for children participating in sports to protect them from long-term injury. –Anonymous; *Marketing News,* Apr 13, 1984, 18(8): pp. 14. Avail. ABI 84-14570

Sports, Marketing, Sponsors, Corporate objectives, Image, Market research, Market strategy

Tea and Sympathy (342)

Entrepreneur Ron Schultz has created 2 tea companies: Delphin Corp. with sales of about $250,000 annually, and Medicine for Children Inc., which sells Christmas Spice Tea and donates all of its profits to charity. Schultz formed the Delphin spiced tea firm about 8 years ago. Four years ago, in the process of donating part of the company's profits from $1 million in sales to charity, he began to investigate the charities more carefully, subjecting them to the same scrutiny he gave his own operations. As a result, he decided to create a company designed solely to give money to one carefully selected charity. One such charity, the Lalmba Association, provides medical aid to people in Sudan. The organization accepted only $20,000 of Schultz's $40,000 offer, so Schultz cut back sales projections for Christmas Spice Tea to keep production in line with donations. Schultz is careful to differentiate between his product and his philosophy. He urges customers to buy his tea because of its quality, not because profits go to charities. So far, Schultz has avoided conflict with the Internal Revenue Service. —Buchsbaum, Susan; *Inc.*, Jun 1984, 6(6): pp. 97-100. Avail. ABI 84-19674

Corporate responsibility, Social responsibility, Donations, Food products, Food industry, Entrepreneurs, Personal, Profiles, Case studies

The Unsentimental Corporate Giver (343)

While cutting the budget, the Reagan Administration has suggested that corporations rescue at least some of the programs that the federal government will no longer be able to support. However, corporate philanthropy could not begin to fill those expectations. If corporations gave the maximum that the Internal Revenue Service allows them to deduct, which is 5% of taxable income, their contributions would only come to about $12 billion, which is only a third of the reduction in planned federal spending for fiscal 1982. Generally, corporations give because it serves their own interests or appears to. Companies may give for a variety of reasons, because giving builds good will or because they may need the services of a facility to which they contribute. Just how much corporations give is impossible to determine precisely. Dollars given can be accounted for, but it is difficult to keep track of donations of company employees' time or use of company facilities. Companies have a wide variety of approaches as to how they decide which organization gets their contributions. Charts. Graphs. —Smith, Lee; *Fortune*, Sep 21, 1981, 104(6): pp. 121-140. Avail. ABI 81-21542

Corporate responsibility, Social responsibility, Donations, Manycompanies, Gifts

The Untapped Resource: Corporate Matching Gifts (344)

Employees working for one of the 939 known corporations in the US that have matching gift programs are eligible to apply for a match from their companies for an organization to which they contribute. Health or social welfare organizations, civic service agencies, educational institutions or any cultural organizations are eligible to receive corporate matching gifts. A company's matching gift is often worth much more than a contributor's gift alone, because the company may double or triple the amount of the gift. Cultural and secondary education sectors have seen the greatest changes in the numbers of companies matching gifts other than for higher education. Matching gifts to hospitals and health-related organizations are the areas with the greatest growth potential. Corporations may be interested in instituting a program or expanding existing policies for matching gifts: 1. as an incentive for employee support of charity, 2. as recognition of employee volunteer time, 3. due to employee interest in company social responsibility, or 4. because of pressure from recipient organizations. Three areas in an annual fund raising program which should tap available matching gifts dollars include individual gifts, deferred gifts, and corporate gifts. Tables. Graph. —Davis, Margaret Bergan; *Fund Raising Mgmt,* May 1983, 14(3): pp. 20-24. Avail. ABI 83-14594

Fund raising, Nonprofit organizations, Corporate, Contributions, Education, Donations

The Uses of Philanthropy (345)

To understand the relationship between the private and the public sectors, the sources and beneficiaries of philanthropical donations must be considered. A recent Urban Institute monograph reports that nonprofit organizations are the chief nongovernmental providers of public goods. The monograph also notes that budget cuts are undermining the financial health of private nonprofit organizations. Both the government and the private sector have certain roles and responsibilities. In setting public priorities, the government must consider the public good. The private sector can focus on narrow issues without having any formal obligation to serve everyone equally. Private philanthropy, especially that of foundations and voluntary agencies, has traditionally focused on identifying problems and testing various methods. Corporate philanthropy has represented a somewhat different set of values and objectives, and is now more closely linked to overall corporate objectives. —Paley, Martin A.; *Cornell Executive,* Spring 1983, 9(2): pp. 42-44. Avail. ABI 83-28409

Private sector, Donations, Social services, Corporate responsibility, Social responsibility, Public sector, Economic aid, Social policy

Vast Wasteland Revisited (346)

It is apparent that step-by-step visual instruction in antisocial behavior is sweeping through television. The question thus arises as to whose responsibility it is to do something about this deplorable and socially damaging trend. Government censorship is undesirable, and the public, for the most part, does not seem repelled by the antisocial television program. It follows that the job of diminishing or wholly eliminating the amount of offensive programming falls to the advertiser who can eliminate the violence by withholding the dollar commitment to such programming. Although advertisers may assert that the responsibility lies with the advertising agency, it is clearly one that must be made by the advertiser. Furthermore, the decision must come straight from the boardroom. This should not be taken to mean that companies should act as censors. Management must decide whether the bottom line is the only thing that counts or if it is willing to pay the price of business' responsibility to society. The challenge of responding to a decision by business to avoid sponsorship of the objectionable programs rests with the networks. Surely they can find rewarding and enriching shows which are exciting, informative, and inspiring to all audiences. —Kelmenson, Leo-Arthur; *Harvard Business Review,* Nov/Dec 1980, 58(6): pp. 28-29. Avail. ABI 80-22225

Television, Programs, Violence, Ratings, Advertisers, Corporate responsibility

What Corporations Get by Giving (347)

In 1982, while corporate profits decreased 23%, corporate donations to the arts and charity rose 13%. In 1983, corporate philanthropy increased another 7%. Corporate donations are becoming less a function of charity and more an established part of conducting business. When the Conference Board (New York) began tracking corporate donations in 1943, it found 55 companies that were significant contributors. Today, 450-500 companies employ someone who spends 75% of work time on contributions. For 1983, corporations donated a total of $3 billion, which represents a 30% increase over 1980 donations. Corporations seek to enhance their images through corporate advertising, and some companies discuss their social works as a part of image building. While developing corporate philanthropy as a marketing tool is an appealing idea, most companies are still only experimenting with the idea. Graphs. —Maher, Philip; *Business Marketing,* Dec 1984, 69(12): pp. 80-89. Avail. ABI 85-02168

Donations, Corporate responsibility, Corporate image, Market strategy

Whatever Happened to Corporate Social Responsibility? (348)

Among top companies, there are currently programs dealing with the interests of various groups within the corporation. Other corporations, however, have seemed to let social responsibility languish. The phenomenon changes every few years, with pre-1967 efforts largely focused on philanthropy. Then came an era of trying to solve problems the government couldn't, and finally, in the late 1970s, companies began zeroing in on the social and human impact of business decisions. The Reagan era, as seen by some, may put attention back on philanthropy. Generally, the more consumer-oriented the company, the greater its showing of corporate responsibility. Chemical, steel, and oil industries have relatively poor records, with the exceptions of Dow Chemical, Monsanto, and Atlantic-Richfield. Society's increased affluence has meant it is less willing to take risks in the workplace, and corporations have responded to that. Utilities are notable exceptions, and the record for department stores is mixed. Some see the Reagan philosophy as consistent with the corporate de-unionization movement, but others predict a backlash against this. Some experts believe that by handling the corporations responsibility for social programs, Reagan is transferring to them blame for whatever goes wrong. Others think that by unshackling private industry, Reagan has given it a chance to become more responsible. —Thomas, Clarke; *Managing,* 1982, (1): pp. 10-15,33. Avail. ABI 82-12404

Corporate responsibility, Social responsibility, Changes, Concepts, Manycompanies

When Business and the Community 'Cooperate' (349)

There are a number of benefits to corporations that engage in philanthropy or social responsibility. Aside from tax benefits, corporate participation helps to create a prosperous community with more dollars to buy goods and services. A recent survey by the Conference Board has determined that corporate contributions increased by 22% in 1978 to $2.07 billion, representing 1% of pretax net income. Corporate contributions are usually handled through: 1. a company foundation, 2. a decision at the community location, or 3. a request from branch-office personnel to headquarters. Three basic ratios are used by the majority of firms in determining the size of their basic contributions: 1. designated percent of pretax net income, 2. designated percent of assets, and 3. a specific amount for every employee. The major portions go to health and welfare and to education (37% to each). Interviews with executives of 3 firms offer insight toward their philosophies of corporate social and community responsibility. Graph. –Lippin, Paula; *Administrative Mgmt,* Feb 1981, 42(2): pp. 34-35,66-72. Avail. ABI 81-05902

Corporate, Community relations, Social responsibility, Donations, Contributions, Corporate responsibility, Community, Manycompanies

Why 'Good Works' Are Good for Business (350)

UK companies acknowledge that they cannot operate in isolation from the communities in which they are located and that they must behave as responsible citizens as well as commercial enterprises. Companies can do this by making donations to appropriate good causes, but giving should also include donations of advice, manpower, ideas, and equipment. Some firms are providing management time, allowing managers or specialists to sit on advisory boards or councils. Legal and General Group makes its primary contribution to the community in the form of management time, allowing its executives to assist in planning of specific community projects and giving advice where required. The firm is also playing its part in training programs for the youthful unemployed. By engaging in community projects that are considered worthwhile and that have desirable objectives, companies hope to gain the respect of their peers in industry and commerce, as well as make a genuine contribution to their communities. –Skae, John; *Personnel Mgmt (UK),* Sep 1983, 15(9): pp. 5. Avail. ABI 83-29255

Corporate responsibility, Donations, UK, Contributions, Small business, Social responsibility

3

Product Responsibility

The Anatomy of Corporate Social Response: The Rely, (351)
Firestone 500, and Pinto Cases
While corporations have increasingly recognized the importance of social issues, they have not always taken meaningful social action. In the case of Rely tampons, Procter & Gamble (P & G) went through 3 stages that resulted in a positive social action: 1. P & G began laboratory testing and assembled a panel of experts. 2. P & G questioned the data linking their product to toxic shock syndrome. 3. P & G worked out a consent decree with the Food and Drug Administration and bought back all unused Rely tampons. The Firestone and Ford Companies did not have the same response to their products. Firestone contended that there was nothing defective in the design of its tire and blamed the problems on the customer. It made use of several delaying tactics, including questioning the authority of the Traffic Safety Administration. The Ford Motor Company lobbied for 8 years against a law that would force the redesign of the Pinto because such a redesign would not be profitable. In the meantime, there were 400,000 auto fires annually, and 42% of the collision-ruptured fuel-tank cases involved Ford products, although Ford only produces 24% of the cars on US roads. Figures. References. –Gatewood, Elizabeth and Carroll, Archie B.; *Business Horizons,* Sep/Oct 1981, 24(5): pp. 9-16. Avail. ABI 81-21341

Corporate responsibility, Social responsibility, Strategy, Product safety, Procter & Gamble-Cincinnati, Firestone Tire & Rubber-Akron Ohio, Ford Motor-Dearborn Mich, Product, Failure, Public relations

An Anniversary Review and Critique: The Tylenol (352)
Crisis/Reply
The Tylenol crisis in the US in the fall of 1982 demonstrated the need to recognize public relations (PR) as a top-management, independent function. The crisis points out how public relations relates to marketing and sales-promotion practices. Examination of Johnson & Johnson's (J&J) handling of the Tylenol crisis suggests that the company's PR effort was lacking. Despite problems in the PR area, the firm's marketing apparatus functioned very well. The basic problems of J&J's public-relations department were related to the fact that it had no emergency plans for handling a crisis situation and that it lacked an operational plan which interpreted and

detailed a working procedure based on the company's philosophy. In response, J&J feels that no plan could have been written to meet a crisis of Tylenol's magnitude. The company does have written plans covering other types of emergencies. References. –Snyder, Leonard and Foster, Lawrence G.; *Public Relations Review,* Fall 1983, 9(3): pp. 24-34. Avail. ABI 83-30927

Johnson & Johnson-New Brunswick NJ, Public relations, Drugs, Market research, Public opinion surveys, Promotions (ADV), Management of crises, Marketing management, Social responsibility, Case studies

Corporate Responsibility in a Changing Legal Environment   (353)

In the last decade, the rapid expansion of tort law and regulatory law has substantially altered the legal environment of business. Existing models of corporate social responsibility, as illustrated by Gatewood and Carroll's (1981) treatment of Procter & Gamble's (P&G) decision to demarket Rely brand tampons in the aftermath of the toxic shock syndrome controversy, do not accurately describe the present legal environment for business. These models contain 4 major misconceptions: 1. The law is merely a set of rules to be obeyed. 2. There is a clear distinction between law and choice. 3. The most important feature of law is content, not process. 4. Law and business are engaged in a zero-sum game, where the losses exactly equal the winnings. The P&G decision is examined more closely to refute these misconceptions. The general notion that law always exerts a negative force on corporations must be discarded. References. –Foote, Susan Bartlett; *California Mgmt Review,* Spring 1984, 26(3): pp. 217-228. Avail. ABI 84-23214

Corporate responsibility, Social responsibility, Product safety, Law

Demarketing Strategies: Assessment and Implementation   (354)

Demarketing strategies are reviewed, along with the possible problems and benefits associated with their use. Passive demarketing discourages use of a product by consumers while maintaining product availability for those who cannot be discouraged from use. Passive demarketing may be undertaken to improve a firm's image of social responsibility, by educating consumers about the possible negative impacts of a product. However, for passive strategies to be effective, they must be fully supported within the firm and be capable of actually altering consumer behavior. Active demarketing focuses on reducing sales of a product for which resources are scarce and for which demand exceeds supply. Active demarketing may be more successful when directed to particular market segments. With complete demarketing, a firm attempts to eliminate demand for a product which has been withdrawn from the market because of its potentially harmful effects. While complete demarketing is costly in the face of lost sales, it carried the benefits of enhancing a firm's image as being concerned with the welfare of customers. Chart. References. –Lepisto, Lawrence R.; *Mid-Atlantic Jrnl of Business,* Winter 1983/1984, 22(1): pp. 31-41. Avail. ABI 84-09124

Market strategy, Implementations, Market planning, Studies

Design Management and New Product Development (355)

If one analyzes why one company succeeds or fails in comparison to another, it is usually found that it is because it has a comparative strength in one or more of these 3 directions: innovation, communication, and control. As it relates to innovation, the best route to improved control is generally through the better management of design. Improved management of design is often thwarted by some important obstacles. First is a lack of awareness that design has a quite new significance for UK industry now. The attributes which should define the ideal product for a British manufacturing exporter are high added value, high technology, high quality, high social responsibility, and high value for money. Another obstacle is the fear that too much variety in industry defies generalization. An additional obstacle is the failure to perceive product innovation as one specific area of management. There are a number of actions that can be taken to correct such problems. —Smith, Brian; *European Jrnl of Marketing (UK)*, 1981, 15(5): pp. 51-60. Avail. MCB 82-08681

Product development, Design, Management, Innovations, Problems

Fighting a Boycott (356)

After losing an estimated $40 million because of a US boycott against its products that started in 1977, Nestle SA, the Swiss multinational, began to fight back. In the last 3 years, after dismissing 2 of the largest public relations firms in the US and reestablishing its reputation, Nestle is now recognized by some as a leader in implementing a humane marketing code for infant formula. Nestle's efforts may help firms in the US that increasingly face such social responsibility issues from both domestic and overseas groups. One of Nestle's initial steps was to endorse the World Health Organization (WHO) Code of Marketing for Breast Milk Substitutes. Nestle then sought an ethical group with whom it could work in developing compliance with the code, choosing the Methodist Task Force on Infant Formula. Nestle also changed its media policy to an "open-door, candid approach" and established a 10-member advisory panel to monitor its compliance with the WHO Code and to examine complaints against its marketing practices. —Nelson-Horchler, Joani; *Industry Week*, Jan 23, 1984, 220(2): pp. 54-55. Avail. ABI 84-06737

Nestle-Switzerland, Social responsibility, Corporate image, Case studies, Boycotts, Marketing management, Multinational corporations

Growth Depends on Ethics (357)

Societal limitations rather than technological ones are most likely to inhibit the phenomenal growth of the information processing industry. The industry has responsibilities to its customers, society at large, and itself. Reliable products and systems are the first thing customers have a right to expect. The real payoff - in both software and hardware - is prevention, which could translate into savings of billions of dollars and, more important, continued public trust. The industry must condemn dishonesty to obtain the public's respect and to reduce the amount of legislation needed. The industry must be more concerned with the image it projects to media - that of cutthroat competition. One of the industry's key obligations to society is education. Computer crime presents a direct challenge to the industry to improve its self-protection and provide more education in security. Leading-edge ethics are just as vital as leading-edge technology. —Akers, John F.; *Canadian Datasystems (Canada),* Oct 1984, 16(10): pp. 41. Avail. ABI 85-03748

Computer industry, Corporate responsibility, Crime, Competition

A. H. Robins Hauls a Judge into Court   (358)

Drug company A. H. Robins Co. (Richmond, Virginia) is taking US District Judge Miles W. Lord to court on charges of bias in cases against the company's intrauterine contraceptive, the Dalkon Shield. Robins charges that Lord took sides against the company when he handled cases against Robins in February 1984. Robins' lawyer is former US Attorney General Griffin B. Bell; Lord is to be defended by Ramsey Clark, also a former US Attorney General. The case centers around an incident in which Lord demanded that Robins' chief executive, chief counsel, and research director appear before Lord to settle 2 of the cases. Once there, Lord insisted that they read a lengthy speech on corporate ethics, and then he delivered a stinging 14-page criticism of Robins' tactics in the cases. He accused Robins of deliberate delay, obfuscation, and intimidation of witnesses. The outcome of the case against Lord could have important effects on the independence of the judiciary. —Anonymous; *Business Week,* Jul 16, 1984, (2851): pp. 27-28. Avail. ABI 84-23065

Robins-Richmond Va, Case studies, Litigation, Social responsibility, Product safety

How to Manage Liability   (359)

Eventually, every company will make or sell a defective product. The ensuing statements and recalls can ruin a corporate image overnight. Even the premature release of information about the chances of product failure can cause tremendous difficulties. Liability is getting even stricter as a result of the UK Parliament's new laws, the growing power of a consumer lobby, and the European Economic Community (EEC) directive on product liability. Reasons for product recalls include: 1. design or formulation defect, 2. manufacturer error, or 3. failure to warn consumers. To reduce exposure to product liability, management should establish a product safety program that includes a product recall plan and ways to deal with product extortion or sabotage. Because people make products unsafe, management also should arrange an individually tailored risk financing package. Some firms are preparing for potential product liability by: 1. conducting product safety audits, 2. conducting workshops with senior management on the safety risk involved in seemingly simple tasks, and 3. having catalogs audited and amended to reduce exposure. —Abbott, Howard; *Management Today (UK),* Jul 1983, pp. 50-53. Avail. ABI 83-23734

Product safety, Corporate responsibility, Product recalls, UK, Products liability, Consumer protection, Corporate image

New Directions in Product-Safety Regulation   (360)

Ten regulatory trends that will affect the product safety regulatory environment are described. The trends, which will demand an intensified role for a company's directors, are: 1. increasing concern for product safety among corporate executives, 2. increasing cooperation among consumers, producers, and regulators in achieving product safety goals, 3. growing voluntary compliance with safety regulations to avoid the involvement of lawyers and the expenses of litigation, 4. more cooperative sharing of product hazard/consumer complaint information between producers and regulators, 5. continued advances in product safety under the initiative of food and drug manufacturers, 6. enhanced consumer education initiatives by both regulators and manufacturers, 7. growing emphasis on product safety attributes in marketing efforts, 8. increasing retailer participation in product safety efforts, 9. enhanced international cooperation in the promotion of product safety, and 10. greater manufacturer and consumer involvement in setting product safety priorities and regulations. —Steorts, Nancy Harvey; *Directors & Boards,* Summer 1984, 8(4): pp. 28-32. Avail. ABI 84-35453

Product safety, Regulation, Trends, Consumer protection, Consumer education, Corporate responsibility, Boards of directors

Pledged to Help (361)

British Telecom is strongly committed to providing telecommunications service to its disabled and elderly customers. It has established British Telecom Action in the Interest of the Disabled (BTAID) to help maintain and improve service to this particular group of customers. British Telecom has developed amplifying handsets with adjustable volume control, lamp signaling devices, and extension bells of varying tone for customers who are hard of hearing. It has also designed a community alarm system known as Monita for the elderly and those at risk in their homes. Customers can summon help through a central monitoring station by setting off a trigger in the home. To safeguard and encourage these developments, BTAID must ensure that maximum help is given to disabled customers. It must establish priorities in order to get the most out of its limited resources, and also must seek out and improve relations with all relevant organizations. —Wood, John; *British Telecom Jrnl (UK),* Autumn 1984, 5(3): pp. 32-34. Avail. ABI 85-04714

British Telecom-UK, Telephone service, Older people, Handicapped, Case studies, Corporate responsibility

Product Safety and Liability Prevention (362)

Product safety can be achieved with the same types of management programs that are used for employee safety, quality control, and production control. Top management support is needed, along with documented product safety objectives. A procedures manual should be developed that describes the responsibilities of each phase of production from original design concept to product installation and ultimate disposal. This manual is for safety as well as for efficient quality production. A product design safety review should be established. The review is a formal, documented, systematic examination of a design by experts not directly associated with its development. A review should be conducted on all new designs, all design changes, and all old designs that have not been reviewed. The need to place warning labels on the product must be considered. Some of the problems of a product safety program that could lead to liability claims include: 1. lack of knowledge of standards and regulations, 2. absence of labeling, and 3.

relaxation of quality control. **References.** —Dodge, David A.; *Professional Safety,* Mar 1985, 30(3): pp. 25-30. Avail. ABI 85-22206

Product safety, Products liability, Negligence, Warranties, Documentation, Design, Quality control, Labeling, Social responsibility

Product 'Watchdogs' on a Long Leash (363)

The concept of using product responsibility is not a new one. Allied Corp., then Allied Chemical, introduced its Anso IV carpet fibers in early 1980 as a result of application of product responsibility. Use of this concept allowed Allied to identify and effectively use a safe chemical to repel dirt in its carpet fibers. The concept of product responsibility has been enhanced during the 1970s by government regulations and laws spurred by the rise in product-liability lawsuits. Having a "product-watchdog" function helps corporations improve their credibility with the public. According to E. E. Merrill of Dow Chemical's quality-assurance department, the public has a right to know about the possible hazards of a product; thus a company is concerned about what can go wrong with a product after it is sold. Product responsibility entails much up front study prior to investing in a new product line, as known risks must be balanced with known benefits. Product responsibility could cause the abandonment of potentially lucrative markets. Gillette experienced such a situation when a new antiperspirant failed inhalation tests. Large or small, product responsibility staffs deal with product safety for their employees and users alike. —Johnson, Greg; *Industry Week,* Jun 28, 1982, 213(7): pp. 65-68. Avail. ABI 82-17902

Allied Chemical-Morristown NJ, Case studies, Product safety, Product, Quality, Gillette-Boston, Product testing, Hazardous substances, Corporate responsibility

Putting Products to the Test (364)

Factors that have put more emphasis on the need for thorough pre-marketing tests include: 1. the growth of social responsibility, 2. increased consumer legislation, 3. proliferating national and international standards on product safety and performance, and 4. the widespread threat of product liability law cases. Companies use a variety of techniques in testing their products. Car companies are leading the way in the development of highly sophisticated testing methods. Ford Motor Co., for example, has a transatlantic computer link that permits European subsidiaries to run complex computer models simulating stress and crash testing on a massive US computer during nonoffice hours in the US. Fisher-Price Toys, a division of Quaker Oats Co. in the US, has developed a world-wide reputation for producing safe, resilient, and durable toys. Most companies attempt to make their tests as realistic as possible. For example, at UK-headquartered packaging firm Metal Box Ltd., it was apparent that the only way to realistically test its "child-proof" container tops was to see whether children could actually open them. —Bickerstaffe, George; *International Mgmt (UK),* Dec 1981, 36(12): pp. 10-11,13-14. Avail. ABI 82-02733

Product testing, Product safety, Toy industry, Motor vehicle industry, Manycompanies

Vaccines and Product Liability: A Case of Contagious Litigation (365)

Virtually all medical authorities agree that the public health balance hangs overwhelmingly in favor of vaccination, yet the existence of product liability law threatens to make both existing and potential new vaccines sporadically or entirely unavailable to the public and the medical community. The first court decision to focus on the problem was Reyes versus Wyeth Laboratories (1974), which assumed that a warning of possible side effects might make a difference as to whether someone would accept the vaccine. Other prominent cases have involved the Sabin oral polio and the pertussis vaccines. The most astonishing aspect of these cases was the award for punitive damages to the family of a child who took the Sabin vaccine and contracted polio. In response to such decisions, numerous companies have ceased production of vaccines. However, efforts to obtain reform legislation and to deal with the compensation issue have been initiated by such groups as the American Academy of Pediatrics. References. —Kitch, Edmund W.; *Regulation,* May/Jun 1985, 9(3): pp. 11-18. Avail. ABI 85-27370

Products liability, Pharmaceutical industry, Vaccines, Litigation, Federal court decisions-US, Social responsibility

4

Social And Political Issues

Affirmative Action - Making It Effective in the Public   **(366)**
Sector
Public administrators and their private sector counterparts have responded to social responsibility pressures in recent years with affirmative action. Many agencies view affirmative action in terms of quotas and often oversell managerial jobs. This raises recruits' expectations, distorting the view of the available job and resulting in high turnover. The process known as Realistic Job Preview (RJP) concentrates on the recruits' point of view, focusing on: 1. recruits' needs rather than their abilities, 2. participation rather than performance, and 3. satisfaction rather than suitability. RJPs benefit the individual through: 1. negating false expectations, 2. increasing job satisfaction, and 3. providing better ability to cope with problematic job incidents. RJPs are the first step for successful recruitment and retention of target groups necessary for the contribution to future community needs and the well-being of an organization. References. —Templer, Andrew J. and Tolliver, James M.; *Public Personnel Mgmt,* Summer 1983, 12(2): pp. 211-217. Avail. ABI 83-20392

    Public administration, Personnel management, Affirmative action, Effectiveness, Recruitment, Job descriptions, Techniques

After the Burning, How Can Business Help?   **(367)**
After the 1981 riots in Brixton, Marks & Spencer, Citibank, Business in the Community, and the London Enterprise Agency have been working to prevent inner city decay. These organizations, known as Brixton United, have encouraged the creation of new small firms, job training, and the provision of workshops and small shops. Citibank's main concern in the rehabilitation program has been housing, especially in places like Railton Road, the front line of the 1981 riots. In mid-Sussex, Schering Chemicals supports the welfare of the elderly, and this year contributed towards equipment for a toddlers' play park. At Citibank in the UK, 1% of pretax earnings is earmarked for external use. Its support for OUTSET, a charity that helps disabled people get jobs, involves management help, training, free office space, and an interest-free loan to help with cash flow problems.

Citibank's need for a healthy, prosperous community in which to do business 20 years from now has prompted the company's actions. In many projects, money is secondary to expertise offered to the project through the loan of high-calibre staff, or secondees. —Young, Peter; *Chief Executive (UK)*, Nov 1984, pp. 35,38. Avail. ABI 85-05579

Urban renewal, UK, Community development, Social responsibility

Animals in Testing: How the CPI Is Handling a Hot Issue   (368)

Animal rights activists have become more effective in challenging such animal testing practices as the lethal dose 50% (LD50) test through demonstrations, write-in campaigns, and newspaper advertisements. Established animal welfare organizations have become more militant, and some animal rights groups, particularly in Europe, have turned to violence. In the US, however, efforts spearheaded by animal rights activist Henry Spira have attempted to achieve more cooperation between cosmetic, pharmaceutical, and chemical companies that use animal tests and the animal rights groups. For example, in 1980, Spira targeted Revlon's use of the Draize test on rabbits in a full-page ad campaign in New York City newspapers only after Revlon hedged on providing funds for research into alternatives. Thereafter, Revlon provided a $750,000 grant, and Avon and Estee Lauder soon followed suit. In Europe, the Council of Europe has taken the lead on regulation of animal testing. However, Swiss antivivisectionists are applying pressure to prohibit all animal experiments. —Anonymous; *Chemical Week*, Dec 5, 1984, 135(23): pp. 36-40. Avail. ABI 85-25111

Activists, Social issues, Animals, Testing, Social responsibility, Policy, R&D, Manycompanies, Chemical industry, Cosmetics industry, Pharmaceutical industry

Assessing Social Impacts of New Products: An Attempt to Operationalize the Macromarketing Concept   (369)

The introduction of new products is one area where the consideration of social impacts and the corporate publics' reactions to them would be helpful. There are a number of marketing failures or controversies that point to the danger to firms and to society of not considering all relevant publics in marketing decisions. A methodology or decision rule for decision making on new products or ventures is presented. The proposed 2-stage decision rule for new product introductions explicitly and systematically considers the impacts on relevant corporate publics. Consequently, it provides an approach to operationalizing the macromarketing concept. One strength of the multistage rule is its recognition of the need for satisfaction of the basic, initial requirement for the financial feasibility of a new venture. Tables. Charts. References. —Upah, Gregory D. and Wokutch, Richard E.; *Jrnl of Public Policy & Marketing*, 1985, 4): pp. 166-178. Avail. ABI 85-26788

Product introduction, Social impact, Studies, Marketing, Concepts, Social responsibility, Decision making

A Business Approach to Criminal Violence   (370)

Business can and should become involved in social problems, but it cannot replace the federal government. Addressing such social problems as criminal violence can be profitable for business, however. In the late 1950s and early 1960s, the civil rights movement was not taken seriously by many businesses. Nevertheless, Giant Foods (Washington, DC) became concerned and contacted the city's youth rehabilitation program offering help. A full-time coordinator worked with street organizations, and the company was sensitive to community problems. When violence erupted in the wake of Martin Luther King's assassination, Giant Foods lost only 1 window while surrounding neighborhoods were destroyed. Drug Fair, a drug store chain in the mid-Atlantic states, solved a competition problem and labor difficulties by initiating a drug abuse information program. Under the banner of the National Institute on Drug Abuse, Drug Fair began an advertising campaign, organized parent groups, sponsored neighborhood parent workshops on drug abuse, and trained pharmacists as drug abuse information sources. Its Straight Talk on Drug Abuse radio, newspaper, and television campaign was a huge success, causing Drug Fair's name to stand out over the competition's and establishing it as a professional pharmacy, hence solving its labor problem. As these examples show, business alone cannot solve society's problems, but it can play a far greater role in those solutions. —Forbes, Paul S.; *Public Relations Review,* Spring 1982, 8(1): pp. 59-64. Avail. ABI 82-09964

Crime, Violence, Prevention, Drug abuse, Programs, Case studies, Corporate responsibility

The Corporate Response to YTS - Part I: Investment or (371) Social Responsibility?

One of the most serious problems of the early 1980s is youth unemployment. The UK government recently has made efforts to provide training alternatives to employment, such as the Youth Training Scheme (YTS). This approach is laissez-faire, even though the scale of intervention is enormous. YTS has acquired an ambiguous image, being variously portrayed as an essential manpower strategy to improve economic performance, a social program designed to alleviate a social problem, and a political trick to disguise the full extent of unemployment. The policy selected by the government, which emphasizes a low inflation rate, is such that the behavior of employers will be the dominant factor and will ultimately determine which image of YTS comes closest to reality. Government pressure to limit public expenditure leads to a level of financial incentives to firms that produces a low or negative rate of return for simply providing YTS places. Involvement in YTS should be associated with firms that have: 1. apprenticeship training schemes, 2. in-house training, 3. specific types of corporate cost strategy, and 4. socially oriented policies. References. —Joyce, Paul; Woods, Adrian; and Hayes, Mike; *Jrnl of European Industrial Training (UK),* 1985, 9(3): pp. 13-16. Avail. MCB 85-32462

UK, Youth, Unemployment, Younger workers, Training, Policy, Social responsibility

Corporate Responsibility in Cases of Sexual (372) Harassment

Harassment of women in the form of unwanted verbal and physical sexual advances is now a recognized problem of such magnitude that managers and personnel directors must undertake measures to protect both their employees and themselves from legal and other consequences. Over the past few years, an increasing number of cases have been brought under Title VII of the Civil Rights Act of 1964 which prohibits unfair employment discrimination on the basis of race, sex, religion, national origin, or color. In order to file a suit under Title VII, the plaintiff must be able to show several facts: 1. The sexual harassment is gender-specific. 2. She was treated unfavorably in a subsequent personnel decision because of refusal to submit to her supervisor's sexual advances. 3. The sexual harassment must have occurred with either the explicit or tacit approval of the employer. The number of sexual harassment cases that have reached the federal courts coupled with the success of the plaintiffs points to the importance of developing and implementing preventive policies. References. —Leap, Terry L. and Gray, Edmund R.; *Business Horizons,* Oct 1980, 23(5): pp. 58-65. Avail. ABI 80-20605

Sexual, Harassment, Sex discrimination, EEOC, Affirmative action, Court decisions, Liability, Costs

How Corporations Balance Economic and Social Concerns (373)

In attempting to fulfill social responsibilities, General Motors (GM) has encountered instances where commercial interests and important social interests conflict. In 1970, GM established a Public Policy Committee to recommend policies that promote the interests of the corporation and the community. Areas of tension between GM's basic mission and social concerns include: 1. highway safety, 2. hazardous wastes, 3. employment effects of global markets, and 4. the special responsibilities of multinational corporations in certain host countries. GM has held seminars and consulted a theologian and professor of ethics in examining the issue of highway safety. A GM director, Reverend Leon H. Sullivan, proposed a set of principles to which GM and many other US companies subscribe in their relations with South Africa. GM hopes that its programs and interactions with church leaders will make management more sensitive to the social responsibility concerns of GM's constituencies. —Johnson, Elmer W.; *Business & Society Review,* Summer 1985, (54): pp. 10-14. Avail. ABI 85-33831

Corporate responsibility, Social responsibility, Case studies, Automobile industry, General Motors-Detroit, Social issues, Policies

Philippe Villers, the Social Conscience of Route 128 (374)

French computer expert Philippe Villers is the force behind Computervision Corp. and Automatix Inc., and recently started Cognition Corp. in Massachusetts. The 49-year-old Villers is equally active politically in organizations that include Amnesty International and the Villers Foundation to help the elderly. He seems to attract controversy in business and politics; he left Computervision to found Automatix after Computervision executives overruled his proposal to expand the firm into robotics. Although Computervision sued Villers for allegedly stealing confidential material, Villers won the case. Automatix has not yet made a profit and is being investigated by the Securities & Exchange Commission. However, Villers says he is leaving Automatix to start Cognition because Automatix was not challenging enough. Cognition will specialize in computer-aided engineering systems, and Villers expects it to gross $100 million in 5 years. Villers has been a pioneer in several emerging technologies. —Buell, Barbara and Frons, Marc; *Business Week,* Feb 25, 1985, (2882)(Industrial/Technology Edition): pp. 65. Avail. ABI 85-09721

Chief executive officer, Personal, Profiles, Social responsibility, Human rights, Manycompanies, Electronics industry

Plant Closing Legislation - A Congressional Dialogue (375)

HR 2847, a bill requiring advance notice to the community prior to plant closings, received considerable congressional attention in 1983. While the US government traditionally has allowed businesses maximum freedom of mobility, Representative William Clay of Missouri feels that HR 2847 is in the national interest. However, Representative Marge Roukema of New Jersey feels the bill is not in the national interest because it would limit a company's ability to relocate. Clay says that, since companies often know 5 years in advance that they are going to close a plant, the people who will be directly affected deserve at least a year's advance notice. Roukema contends that, while a plant may be in trouble, it often has some chance of survival. However, advance notification of closing could cause people to lose confidence in the company. In such a case, all chance for survival would be eliminated. The 2 answered a variety of related questions in a joint interview. —Sparks, Robert M.; *Economic Development Review,* Summer 1984, 2(2): pp. 29-31. Avail. ABI 84-28534

Legislation, Shutdowns, Industrial development, Industrial, Policy, Social issues, Corporate responsibility, Social responsibility

The Politicizing of the Chief Executive (376)

The last 2 decades have brought about the increasing involvement of industry in the political process and the emergence of the Chief Executive Officer (CEO) as a spokesman and political activist. Studies show that CEOs spend as much as 50% of their time on external affairs, such as social responsibility programs, government relations and regulatory matters. Today's CEOs spend time tracking down and identifying issues before legislation is proposed. They also formulate corporate policies and communicate these policies to modify or forestall restrictive legislation. Many companies have formal programs to deal with public-policy issues as the interest in interceding in public-policy issues is growing rapidly. In effect, CEOs have become politicized. —Fox, James F.; *Public Relations Jrnl,* Aug 1982, 38(8): pp. 20-24. Avail. ABI 82-22365

Chief executive officer, Public relations, Strategy, Public policy, Industry

The Tyranny of Small Decisions, Temporal Conflict, (377)
and the Necessity for Politicization of the Market Place

Even though the needs of consumers are expected to be met through effective competition, there is an inherent defect in the market system that can be corrected only by means of political action. This inherent defect has as its basis what has been termed "the tyranny of small decisions". It is related to both the temporal perspective of consumers and firms and to their social orientation. The problem may be the underlying cause of much consumer discontent with the functioning of the market economy. The politicization of the market place can be expressed through 2 social forces: 1. the formation of consumer groups, and 2. the movement to develop a more socially responsible corporate community. There is little doubt that the socially undesirable outcomes of the tyranny of small decisions will be made in the traditional political-legislative way. If this method fails to correct what the market place is unable to correct, then politicization will likely move into the open market place. Chart. References. –Bliss, Perry and McCullough, Jim; *Business & Society,* Winter 1980, 19(2) /v20n1: pp. 48-55. Avail. ABI 80-13729

Market economies, Consumer behavior, Self interest, Public interest, Corporate responsibility, Social responsibility

When Business Closes Down: Social Responsibilities   (378)
and Management Actions
Plant closings may have resulted in the loss of as many as 38 million jobs during the 1970s. Because of the magnitude of the problem, both the federal and state governments have proposed legislation to require employers who plan to close or relocate plants to provide sufficient notice and benefits to affected employees. Businesses must investigate alternatives to closedown, actively seeking new owners for the business, and providing sufficient lead time to explore employee ownership options. Once the closedown decision has been made, businesses must conduct a community impact analysis to allow modification of plans to minimize negative effects. They must give advance notice to employees and the community, providing employees with transfer, relocation, and displacement assistance, and helping communities attract replacement industry. References. –Carroll, Archie B.; *California Mgmt Review,* Winter 1984, 26(2): pp. 125-140. Avail. ABI 84-11841

Business failures, Shutdowns, Social responsibility, Relocation of industry, Social issues, Corporate responsibility, Outplacement

URBAN DEVELOPMENT

Big Brothers and the Business Connection: Partnership   (379)
or Paternalism?
The Business Connection is a unique partnership between several major corporations and businesses and the Big Brothers and Sisters of America. It promotes volunteerism and in-service contributions from area industries to benefit youth in the community. The Business Connection works with Big Brothers to bring youth into direct contact with successfully employed adults. The program has been tried in 8 cities. The San Diego, California, program is discussed. The success of this kind of program depends upon a sensitive, aware professional staff and an enlightened, committed policy board. The board members in the San Diego program generated a sense of responsibility and sponsorship of immeasurable value to its early success. The Business Connection program could be especially helpful as a "networking" strategy

between black youth and the corporate community. References. —Ellis, Arthur L.; *Adherent,* Winter 1982, 9(3): pp. 56-66. Avail. ABI 83-06991

Social issues, Unemployment, Community relations, Social responsibility, Social impact, Blacks

Business and the Cities: New Directions for the Eighties (380)

The large amounts of time and money that have been spent on the problems of social deterioration and economic decline in US cities have produced minimal results. Two major factors explain the failure of these programs: 1. suburbanization, a pattern followed by metropolitan growth in the past 2 decades, and 2. a "culture of poverty" existing among the urban poor that urban renewal programs did not address. Suburbanization occurred because of a fundamental social change that could not be reversed by programs to make the cities more attractive. Also, the failure of planners to appreciate the culture of poverty and its different values meant that programs and policies aimed at the urban poor were based on erroneous assumptions and could only fail. Planners must realize that the US is now entering a post-industrial era. The President's Commission for a National Agenda for the Eighties put forward certain considerations: 1. There are no "national urban problems," only local ones. 2. Policies to aid people directly need priority. 3. The private sector and the federal government need to develop joint strategies. References. —Buchholz, Rogene A.; *Business Horizons,* Jan/Feb 1983, 26(1): pp. 79-84. Avail. ABI 83-03944

Urban renewal, Urban development, Corporate responsibility, Social responsibility, Government, Programs, Economic aid

How the Community Touch Can Help You Grow (381)

In 1979, the enterprise agency movement began with the aim of bringing together interested parties to look into ways of easing inner-city problems. The interested parties included companies, local authorities unions, and the voluntary sector. A working party was later formed to look into community involvement in the enterprise concept. Twelve organizations agreed to set up an enterprise organization, Business in the Community (BIC). The Executive Unit of the BIC was formed in June 1981 with 2 staff seconded from the Department of the Environment (DoE) and Shell. The BIC hoped to encourage industry and commerce to be more involved in identifying and meeting the economic, social, and environmental needs of local communities and to support and encourage existing initiatives and organizations. The necessary ingredients for an effective agency are: 1. leadership by the business community, 2. support and collaboration from the local authority, and 3. the appointment of an effective manager/director. —Bagust, Warren; *Accountancy (UK),* Nov 1983, 94(1083): pp. 132. Avail. ABI 84-03547

Corporate responsibility, Social responsibility, Community relations, UK, Programs

Innovative Joint Ventures: The Role of Residential (382) Development Agencies

Through the creation of independent nonprofit corporations, business leaders have been developing innovative partnerships with public agencies for almost 10 years. Most of the early efforts were aimed at stimulating the recovery of depressed central business districts. The major benefit of the nonprofit form has been its flexibility, which has been most apparent in the housing field. Nonprofit Residential Development Agencies (RDA) can carry out a variety of functions in the roles of: 1. development catalyst, 2. program operator, and 3. developer. The RDA's function as a development catalyst is to create an environment conducive to the improvement and expansion of the housing stock. Functioning as a developer, the RDA can bridge the gap between the public and the private sectors that has prevented the building of affordable housing. As a program operator, the RDA can enter into contracts with the municipality, other public agencies, and private developers to operate programs directly. —Nolon, John R.; *Jrnl of Housing,* Jan/Feb 1983, 40(1): pp. 13-15,18-19. Avail. ABI 83-06799

Development, Agencies, Public housing, Corporate responsibility, Donations, Nonprofit organizations, Joint ventures

The Minneapolis Story: A Primer On Social Concern (383)

The Minneapolis business community has illustrated its social responsibility in many ways. Minneapolis was a pioneer of the Five Percent Club movement. In order to join the club, a firm must donate 5% of its pretax profits to charitable causes. In addition to donations for the arts and other charitable causes, some companies in Minneapolis have sponsored projects to renovate rundown neighborhoods. David K. Roe, president of the Minnesota AFL-CIO, thinks that the Minneapolis business community has been ahead of other cities in trying to solve community problems. However, the executive director of the Minneapolis Urban League, Gleason Glover, criticizes the business community for not being responsive to high unemployment among blacks and the poor living conditions of the city's minority groups. —Moskal, Brian S.; *Industry Week,* Aug 10, 1981, 210(3): pp. 59-61. Avail. ABI 81-20097

Minnesota, Cities, Social responsibility, Corporate responsibility, Manycompanies

Mortgage Lending, Social Responsibility, and Public (384) Policy: Some Perspectives on HMDA and CRA

Congressional concern for the vitality of urban neighborhoods and feelings that discriminatory mortgage lending ("redlining") was responsible for neighborhood decay led to passage of the Home Mortgage Disclosure Act of 1975 (HMDA) and the Community Reinvestment Act of 1977 (CRA). The HMDA requires depository institutions to prepare annual summaries of mortgage loans, while the CRA requires that regulatory agencies look at the institution's record when considering requests for new branches or mergers. A study has been made of lending practices based on a model of the neighborhood housing market, using evidence presented at the HMDA and CRA Hearings. It appears that the HMDA will achieve its goal of revealing where a depository mortgage lender has made its mortgages. However, it cannot show why no loans were made in a specified area. The CRA is more difficult to evaluate because it has a nebulous goal and uncertain requirements. There are many apparent problems, such as determining the credit needs of a community, but no apparent remedies. References. —King,

A. Thomas; *AREUEA Jrnl (Amer Real Estate & Urban Economics Assn),* Spring 1980, 8(1):
pp. 77-90. Avail. ABI 80-19495

> Public policy, Social responsibility, Redlining, Community Reinvestment Act 1977-US,
> Urban, Housing, FHA (housing), Mortgages, Home financing, Needs, Neighborhoods,
> Studies

Providing Industrial Jobs in the Inner City (385)

In addressing the issue of whether corporate social responsibility and
profitability can coexist, this analysis describes the operation of one private
sector industrial plant that, for over a decade, has provided several hundred
high-quality industrial jobs to some of those 24 million Americans living in
poverty, as defined by the US Census Bureau. The plant is the Selby bindery,
operated by Control Data Corp. in St. Paul, Minnesota's inner city. The plant
has been able to meet the private-market test for profitability, as well as
providing job opportunities, and it has achieved these goals without
substantial public subsidies and with quite limited input from the parent
corporation. While other companies may want to emulate the Selby
operation, some constraints are involved which should be noted: 1. Jobs
provided are not necessarily net additions to total jobs in the economy. 2.
Jobs must not be portrayed as better than they actually are. While the Selby
operation might be successfully copied by other firms, the number of jobs
provided would be few in relation to the needs of inner-city residents. Tables.
References. —Bendick, Marc, Jr. and Egan, Mary Lou; *Business,* Jan-Mar 1982, 32(1): pp.
2-9. Avail. ABI 82-05498

> Urban development, Cities, Inner city, Plant location, Case studies, Control Data-
> Minneapolis

Public Fund Administrators Feel the Heat from Housing (386)

Political pressure is being applied to salvage the housing industry, and fund
investors are concerned that much of the weight will fall heavily on public
fund sponsors, who will be urged to use their huge cash pools to bail out the
industry. They fear such pressures applied legislatively will threaten their
fiduciary responsibility to obtain the highest possible return for the
investment of funds entrusted to them. They further charge lobbying that
spurs permissive laws emanated from savings and loans, and home builders
associations. Ohio has passed a bill illustrative of the trend, which drops the
single A-rating previously required on mortgage investments. Although
lobbyists deny the allegation, it appears the legislatures often back fund
directors into the corner and lean on them to provide subsidized mortgages.
Industry expert Donald Smart believes the trend toward state investment in
home mortgages threatens the image of social investing, but he also affirms
public fund managers may have brought current problems on themselves by
not considering prudent instate investments when economic times were
better than they are now. Nevertheless, fund managers pressured to bolster
economies of their states fear dangerous precedents are being set. —Blanton,
Kimberly; *Pensions & Investment Age,* Feb 15, 1982, 10(4): pp. 11,22. Avail. Pensions 82-06121

> Public, Pension funds, Housing, Social responsibility, Social, Investments, Mortgages

Ralston Purina's Urban Commitment (387)

The Ralston Purina Co., the $5 billion agribusiness giant, has transformed the area surrounding its St. Louis, Missouri headquarters, called Checkerboard Square, from a slum into a well-manicured community with new homes, rehabilitated 100-year-old town houses, apartments for the elderly, low-income housing, churches, and commercial and light industrial facilities. Ralston Purina gave the hard-pressed St. Louis government $1.1 million so it could come up with the matching funds required to qualify for federal urban renewal money. Company executives reasoned that more attractive, safer surroundings would attract the very best employees to the company. Incidentally, the company's real estate in the area increased in value and the company reaped a public relations bonanza. A total of $4.5 million was spent. In order to avoid having speculators invade the area, Ralston Purina required purchasers to begin rehabilitating within 30 days and to complete the work in 18 months. The city bought the buildings that could be saved, and the LaSalle Park Development Corp. found buyers for them. —Adkins, Lynn; *Dun's Business Month,* Jan 1982, 119(1): pp. 98-100. Avail. ABI 82-03439

Ralston Purina-St Louis, Case studies, Corporate responsibility, Social responsibility, Urban renewal, Urban development

The Renaissance of the Inner City (388)

Detroit Renaissance is a commercial venture by 51 Detroit firms that is a prime example of what cooperation between local authorities and private enterprise can achieve in restoring the fortunes of depressed inner cities. Reasons for which companies are becoming involved in such ventures include: 1. acceptance of the fact that they have a social responsibility towards the people who live in depressed urban areas, 2. creating goodwill in the local community, and 3. protecting existing investments in buildings, equipment, and people. Detroit Renaissance was instigated by Henry Ford II, who persuaded 50 companies to join him in the project to create the Renaissance Center, a $350-million complex of offices, shops, and hotel accommodations. General Motors has also been active in rehabilitating decayed neighborhoods in the Detroit area. Honeywell, Continental Bank in Chicago, and Tesco Stores Ltd. are other companies that have been involved in similar projects in their areas. —Clutterbuck, David; *International Mgmt (UK),* Feb 1981, 36(2): pp. 12-16. Avail. ABI 81-06802

Inner city, Restorations, Urban, Rehabilitation, Projects, Manycompanies, Urban renewal

Slow Dancing in the Industrial Heartland (389)

A handful of local communities in the US are developing their economies via a form of public/private cooperation that most economists never imagined was possible. The efforts cannot be described within either the traditional free market nor the national planning models of ideologically oriented economists. One such effort took place in Baltimore, Maryland. The Greater Baltimore Committee, which included heads of the largest firms in the metropolitan area, developed a plan for clearing 22 acres and constructing public and private buildings and other facilities with a self-financing structure. In Jamestown, New York, the Jamestown Area Labor

Management Committee was formed to improve area labor relations, workforce training and development, and productivity via in-plant labor/ management cooperation. It demonstrated a concern for revitalizing declining industries and improving quality of work life while creating a new image for the city. –Hocevar, Susan Page; *New Mgmt,* 1984, 2(2): pp. 55-60. Avail. ABI 84-36268

Shutdowns, Community action, Community development, Corporate responsibility, Community relations, Cooperation, Public relations, Manycompanies

Starved Cities Hunger for Corporate Aid (390)

Because private citizens, businesses, and foundations are becoming increasingly involved in operating and rebuilding US cities, some fundamental changes are taking place in many urban areas. These include: 1. sharing of responsibility for local government, 2. growth in diversity, 3. power shift away from local officials toward those who control private resources, and 4. increased participation by middle-class people in civic affairs. The psychology of operating cities has changed, along with the reality, since the decline in federal resources has forced cities to look for increased local resources. Services once provided by government workers have become increasingly "privatized" by leases or franchises to private companies, and governments are also divesting themselves of buildings, grounds and equipment. Indianapolis, Indiana, got an early start in turning toward the private sector. The Greater Indianapolis Progress Committee (Gipsy), composed of 300 business leaders, attorneys, and elected officials, is often more influential than the city government. Along with the mayor of Indianapolis, Gipsy is pushing a plan that is revitalizing the downtown area with extraordinary speed. –Herbers, John; *Business & Society Review,* Spring 1983, (45): pp. 8-11. Avail. ABI 83-15136

Local government, Private sector, Assistance, Urban development, Support, Corporate, Participation, Public, Services, Social responsibility, Donations

To the Rescue: Corporate Volunteers Aid Cities (391)

More and more corporations are trying to help their cities as local, state, and federal budget cuts inhibit programs and services. Baltimore, Maryland, for example, would have had to pay $12.1 million for the work done last fiscal year by volunteer corporations. While many such volunteer programs existed prior to the Presidential Task Force on Private Sector Initiatives, cities' current budget reductions have resulted in expansion in the old programs and creation of many new ones. Since 1980, Cleveland, Ohio, has enlisted the aid of 89 businesspeople to help with projects, studies, and services the city cannot afford to buy. The J. C. Penney Co., for example, publicizes the need for volunteers and fits volunteers to jobs. Awards are provided to top volunteers. Not all volunteer programs are completely successful, and some have complained about the slow-moving bureaucracy. Overall though, the corporate volunteers have been indispensable to the cities they served. – Anonymous; *Business Week,* Apr 12, 1982, (2734)(Industrial Edition): pp. 126A,126D. Avail. ABI 82-10480

Corporate responsibility, Social responsibility, Volunteers, Cities

When the Chief Executive Gets Involved (392)

The city of Cleveland, Ohio has been the butt of many jokes over the years. Within a month of taking office in 1979, Mayor George Voinovich proposed a program that would have the private sector take a major role in streamlining the operations of the city. The mayor wanted to bring modern management techniques to the outdated municipal operation that employed over 10,000 people and spent $500 million of taxpayers' money each year. Chief executive officers (CEO) from a variety of businesses responded enthusiastically to serving on the Operations Improvement Task Force. Commitments of 90 loaned executives and over $800,000 in funding were obtained in just 3 weeks. A 12-week study phase resulted in a final report with 650 recommendations to improve city operations. Some 88% of these recommendations could be implemented by executive action. Cleveland had the potential of a one-time savings of $37 million and annual savings of $57 million. If CEOs in other troubled cities will get personally involved and call for action instead of studies, there can be very positive results. –de Windt, E. Mandell; *Chief Executive,* Winter 1982/1983, (22): pp. 10-12. Avail. Chief 83-04931

Chief executive officer, Corporate responsibility, Social responsibility, Cities, Ohio, Task forces, Local government, Improvements

EDUCATION

Big Business in the Classroom (393)

A memorandum issued in 1971 by Supreme Court Justice Lewis F. Powell, entitled "Attack on the American Free Enterprise System," recommended that business members: 1. evaluate textbooks, 2. get on school boards, 3. set up speakers' bureaus, 4. produce economic education materials, and 5. establish faculty positions for private enterprise economics at universities. Since the issuance of this memorandum, 16 states have mandated private enterprise economics in their curriculum. A 1977 survey of Fortune's 500 top industries shows that 64% of the companies distribute materials to the schools. Four subject areas are predominant in these "educational" materials: 1. nutrition, 2. energy, 3. the environment, and 4. economics. The classroom materials supplied by business interests are deceptive because they purport to be "educational" while disguising their commercial intent by artistic form. Corporations should satisfy their obligations by producing quality goods at competitive prices, and by providing meaningful employment, fair wages, and safe working conditions rather than by using profits to "infiltrate" the educational system. –Harty, Sheila; *Business & Society Review,* Summer 1981, (38): pp. 36-39. Avail. ABI 81-23070

Big business, Education, Social responsibility, Corporate responsibility, Public, Attitudes, Curricula

Bridging the Gap Between Corporate Public Affairs and (394) Academia — The Long-Term View of Public Affairs

There is a growing gap between the teaching of public affairs, public policy, and social concerns and what is actually happening in the real world of business. This gap is unhealthy for business and may be disastrous in the long run because it reinforces an image of business as being concerned only with the short-term "bottom line." Academics can bridge the gap and help make their teaching more applicable to the real world. Some steps toward this goal include: 1. Teach "global thinking" and emphasize the management of public issues that have serious "bottom-line" ramifications. 2. Get more into the daily flow of business by taking sabbaticals in the business world and becoming involved in long-term business-academic projects. 3. Seek and take roles on corporate committees. 4. Hold frequent "real-world" dialogues with business leaders. 5. Keep current on social issues. 6. Maintain awareness of public policy projects undertaken by business groups and major foundations. —Dennis, Lloyd B.; *Vital Speeches,* Oct 1, 1985, 51(24): pp. 758-761. Avail. ABI 85-33724

Corporate responsibility, Social responsibility, Accountability, Education, Training

Business/Education Partnerships (395)

The 1983 report from the National Commission on Excellence in Education has prompted some corporations to step up their efforts to improve education. Public relations professionals have played a major role in developing sponsorship programs to aid education. Burger King Corp. has developed a social-responsibility program that focuses on education. The program includes scholarships for students and recognition of excellence among educators. Shell Oil Co. started its Century III Leaders project 11 years ago to recognize outstanding student leaders. Century III students develop plans concerning problems the US faces and present their proposals to the President of the US. Corporations are also helping professional educators improve their work by sponsoring projects with universities to teach development programs in science, technology, and other areas. Du Pont has joined with several school districts to send science teachers to National Science Teachers Association meetings, while the Atlantic Richfield Foundation has joined with Franklin Institute of Science to develop an innovative program in which teachers visit the Institute and receive science kits to help in classroom teaching. —Armistead, Lew and Martin, Elizabeth M.; *Public Relations Jrnl,* Sep 1985, 41(9): pp. 16-20. Avail. ABI 85-30001

Public relations, Social responsibility, Sponsors, Education, Schools, Scholarships & fellowships, Manycompanies

Businesses With Class: The Adopt-A-School Effort (396)

Many US companies are now involved in plans to "adopt" public schools and use their corporate resources to improve and encourage education. The largest such program is in Chicago, Illinois. The Chicago program requires participating businesses to stay in the program for at least a year and to contribute personnel as well as material resources. Projects have included: 1. producing student newspapers and television programs, 2. holding seminars, 3. guiding students through employment procedures, and 4. offering internships. Crain Communications Inc. adopted a high school and has tried 3 different approaches. Activities in which students participate were found to be much more successful than those in which Crain employees merely lecture and demonstrate their work. —Halcrow, Allan; *Personnel Jrnl,* Feb 1985, 64(2): pp. 25-26. Avail. ABI 85-09219

Education, Corporate responsibility, Publishing industry, Case studies

Corporate Compact with Boston's Schools (397)

Boston's business community has decided to do something about the poor quality of public school graduates in recent years. Under the Boston Compact, a unique experiment, 135 companies will hire 400 high school graduates this year; the number of firms and graduates will increase each year. The goal is to provide every Boston high school graduate a job by 1988. In return, the schools have pledged that by 1986 every graduate will meet minimum competency standards in reading and writing and that the number of dropouts will be reduced by 5% annually. The schools' problems resulted from: 1. years of neglect, 2. desegregation, which caused many whites to leave the system, and 3. staffing in the schools by recipients of patronage jobs distributed by the Boston School Committee. The Compact has been widely endorsed, although businessmen disagree as to whether they should even be involved. Changes already instituted in the schools include: 1. close scrutiny of attendance records, 2. truant follow-up, 3. the use of outside tutors, 4. the firing of a number of principals, and 5. regular and meaningful teacher evaluations. —Knecht, G. Bruce; *Dun's Business Month,* May 1983, 121(5): pp. 81-82. Avail. ABI 83-14172

High schools, Education, Employment, Desegregation, Busing, Educators, Teaching, Social responsibility

Developing Corporate Classrooms (398)

The most important asset, the critical ingredient for the success of any business, is people. Assembling and nurturing people with talent and skills is the prerequisite to growth for any business and the most challenging task facing any management. Increasingly, business recognizes that the prosperity and competitive vitality of a nation depend more on the acquired skills of its citizens than on natural resources. To continue to develop human resources, it is essential to make a national commitment to excellence in education. This begins with toughening requirements and hiring qualified teachers. The private sector must assume a leading role in the education and training of US workers. Industry must assume the role of the instructor on a broad scale. Growing numbers of workers with obsolete skills are trying to reestablish themselves in decent jobs. Continuing education opportunities are needed in many fields. Industry must organize its resources to match its needs for skilled personnel. —Frey, Donald N.; *Vital Speeches,* Aug 1, 1984, 50(20): pp. 637-640. Avail. ABI 84-26406

Business, Industry, Social responsibility, Commitments, Quality of education, Retraining, Human resources

A Dilemma - Scholarship vs. Entrepreneurship (399)

Industries and universities have established many mutually beneficial cooperative agreements, which may be classified as: 1. personnel exchange, 2. graduate student training, 3. research funding support, and 4. cooperative ventures (long-term programs between a single company and a single university, affiliated industry support for research centers, and university for-profit research corporations). While industry and university scientists differ philosophically, which often leads to unsuccessful relationships, they also have many similar goals, and both expect rewards for their efforts. The potential for conflict in the establishment of industry/university relations can be minimized by following the basic principles of: 1. relevance, to ensure that research efforts are compatible with institutional goals, 2. loyalty of researchers to their institutions, and vice versa, 3. fairness and equity in the distribution of risks and rewards, and 4. mutual trust in the cooperative agreement. References. –Krebs, Robert E.; *Jrnl of the Society of Research Administrators,* Spring 1984, 15(4): pp. 19-28. Avail. ABI 84-21202

Colleges & universities, Business, Cooperation, Industrial research, Conflicts of interest, Subsidies, Corporate responsibility

Do Business and Higher Education Need a Dialogue?   (400)

This review assesses some of the major issues that US business must face during the next decade if the political, social, and economic way of life to which most people in the US are accustomed is to be preserved and advanced. It is hypothesized that business itself must take the primary responsibility for this enhancement. While colleges of business administration can play a pivotal role in making necessary progress possible, academe itself faces challenging issues and problems. It follows that business and colleges of business administration must cooperate closely, for such interaction is important to the future success of business, academe, and the nation. This review illuminates how that dialogue between business and academe should evolve by describing: 1. basic issues ahead for business, 2. the basic function, structure, and process of entrepreneurship and management, and 3. the character, mission, structure, and attributes of colleges of business administration. Tables. References. –Simone, Albert J.; *Enterprise,* Summer 1981, 1(1): pp. 2-10. Avail. ABI 83-05860

Social issues, Social responsibility, Socioeconomic factors, Politics, Economic conditions

Do MBA Students Have Ethics Phobia?   (401)

Many graduate schools of business fail to discuss business ethics with their students. While most students and faculty agree that ethics is important, there remain many fears concerning the issue. The first fear is of the issue itself. Ethics is difficult to teach, and many view it as an abstract area of philosophy that has no application in the "real world" of business. Another major fear is that free competition is hindered by ethical considerations concerning the social responsibility of business. Some view ethical considerations as irrelevant and inefficient. Whistleblowing is one of the most frightening parts of business ethics. Students have to consider how far they are willing to compromise their own ethical principles. This fear of ethics can be broken by changing the public perception of business, and business schools need to integrate ethics into their curricula. –Cuilla, Joanne B.; *Business & Society Review,* Spring 1985, (53): pp. 52-54. Avail. ABI 85-21507

Business schools, Ethics, Curricula, Social responsibility, Corporate responsibility

Exercising Social Responsibility: Bank of Virginia (402) Spearheads Business/Public School Partnerships in Richmond

Educators increasingly are seeking ways to restore the concerned contact between schools, parents, and their communities. Until recently, most banks have not been directly involved in public education, even though few businesses are closer to the community than banking. When Richard C. Hunter became superintendent of the public school system of Richmond, Virginia, in 1976, he faced the challenge of turning school desegregation into integration and involving a broader cross-section of the city in its own education system. He approached the Bank of Virginia with the Adopt-A-School concept, whereby a business shares its own expertise and resources to help fill gaps in the school's curriculum or extracurricular activities. In 1980, Bank of Virginia took the lead by adopting one of Richmond's 3 high schools. Within a year, some 20 other schools were adopted by a variety of businesses or nonprofit organizations. The partnership program, which has included workshops and college scholarships, has been well-received by and beneficial to all in the community. —Nelson, Jane Fant; *United States Banker,* Oct 1984, 95(10): pp. 44-46. Avail. ABI 84-36507

Bank of Virginia Co-Richmond, Banking industry, Case studies, Social responsibility, Corporate responsibility, Schools, Training

Futurize Marketing Courses to Prepare Today's (403) Students for Tomorrow's Careers

If marketing is to remain a popular career choice among students at business schools, educators are going to have to anticipate business' needs, futurize their courses, and pay more attention to student values. It is going to be necessary to look at the long-term, rather than the short-term perspective and prepare managers for a career, not just a job. Computerization, the world economic and political situations, and changing social values will affect business in the upcoming years. The most prominent long-term organizational issues are: 1. planning, 2. management of information, 3. concern about the environment, 4. internationalization, 5. emerging markets, 6. corporate responsibility, and 7. sensitivity to human problems. Changes in the educational scene must take place. Students should participate in the planning of curriculum and be aware of changing technology and its effect on society. Professors need to interact with colleagues, for instance, in team teaching, so material does not overlap. More practical research must also be done. —Kelley, Eugene J. and Huntington, Kate E.; *Marketing News,* Jul 24, 1981, 15(2): pp. 1,16,19. Avail. ABI 81-18661

Marketing, Education, Business schools, Changes

How Business Is Joining the Fight Against Functional (404) Illiteracy

Functional illiteracy has resulted in costs that range from pittances to major financial losses. US management is worrying about employees' level of knowledge and what it means for the economy, today and tomorrow. In response, increasing numbers of companies are directing money and manpower into remedial education. In order to function in today's society, people need a higher level of reading ability and associated math and problem-solving skills. It has been estimated that one adult in 7 is functionally illiterate, and the problem is growing. Basic social forces serve to perpetuate the problem, which is the heart of chronic unemployment. While companies fighting illiteracy deplore its social effects, their primary motive for change is illiteracy's corporate cost. To fight illiteracy, companies are: 1. giving aid to current programs, 2. training employees, and 3. working with public schools. —Anonymous; *Business Week,* Apr 16, 1984, (2838)(Industrial/Technology Edition): pp. 94,98. Avail. ABI 84-15128

Education, Training, Social issues, Illiteracy, Social responsibility

Meeting Technology and Human Resource Needs — (405) University and Industry Interface

It is possible to meet technology and human resource needs through a university/industry interface. There are compelling reasons for universities and industry to cooperate. Policy must ensure that students seeking careers in business are appropriately trained and educated. No single institution can afford the resources needed to keep up with changes in technology and the development of practical applications for that technology. Business and universities can cooperate despite the problems and challenges they face. There are ways to overcome mutual distrust, exclusive singlemindedness, and the issue of academic freedom. Business and universities can work together on joint-research projects in which universities share the economic benefits of industry-supported research and maintain the freedom to pursue their own objectives. Cooperation between industry and academia is particularly important for predominantly black schools. By working together, business can recognize and utilize students at black colleges as an excellent source of talent. —Johnson, C. W.; *Vital Speeches,* Sep 15, 1985, 51(23): pp. 719-722. Avail. ABI 85-33339

Colleges & universities, Cooperation, Industry, Business, Social responsibility, Relations, Blacks

The Other 338: Why a Majority of Our Schools of (406) Business Administration Do Not Offer a Course in Business Ethics

In a survey of schools of business administration, Hoffman and Moore (1982) found that only 316 of 665 responding colleges and universities offered courses on business ethics and social responsibility. The other 338 schools, the majority, did not teach ethics or social responsibility as part of their business curricula. A series of personal experiences in attempting to establish a business ethics course at a university suggest reasons business administration schools oppose teaching business ethics. A primary reason is that business administration faculty have generally failed to appreciate the complexity of ethical issues facing businesses, perceiving them to be simply dichotomous choice issues for which personal moral standards are sufficient for resolution. In addition, the need for teaching business ethics has been obscured by a dominant theme in economic theory that economic markets function optimally, with profit-maximizing firms efficiency using resources to the benefit of most members of society. Finally, business ethics has been opposed on the grounds that its study is unscientific. References. —Hosmer, LaRue T.; *Jrnl of Business Ethics (Netherlands),* Feb 1985, 4(1): pp. 17-22. Avail. ABI 85-13704

Ethics, Business schools, Education, Colleges & universities, Higher education, Social responsibility, Pareto optimum

A Program of More Than Junior Achievement   (407)

Junior Achievement (JA) was created in 1919 by Horace Moses and Thomas Vail. Their idea was to bring to city youths the types of experiences that 4-H had brought to a generation of rural youths. Currently, more than 80% of the Fortune 500 and more than 90,000 US businesses actively support JA by supplying funds and managerial talent. Among them are Xerox, Allstate, Union Oil, 3M, Motorola, Walgreens, US Steel, United Airlines, and Sears. The funding for a typical JA company is $150, and the participants sell stock, arrange for production of a product, sell their product, keep financial records, pay taxes, and perform all of the functions a large company performs but on a smaller scale. The success rate for JA companies is amazing: about 80% of them break even or show a profit. For the remaining 20%, a special effort is made to teach the students why the company was not profitable. Sometimes the students find jobs with the company that sponsored their JA company after they graduate from college. —Heide, Christen; *Advertising Age,* Jan 24, 1983, 54(4): pp. M-41. Avail. ABI 83-04678

Corporate responsibility, Social responsibility, Youth, Teenagers, Education, Programs

Roots of Research   (408)

The origins of computers, movies, and Einstein's theory of relativity may be traced to the research of various US universities. Much industrial research draws on the vast body of information developed by US colleges and universities. Currently, 60% of all basic research in the US is carried out at university campuses. Nearly two-thirds of the US' 141 Nobel Prize winners in science work or did work at a private university. Although corporate support of university research is rising, US colleges and universities are concerned that the funding is inadequate to continue to draw the finest scientific minds needed to carry on the research. Universities are mainly supported from 4 basic sources: 1. tuition, 2. private endowments, 3. government grants, and 4. corporate contributions. Corporate support of university research is increasingly vital, due to the rising costs of the work and researchers and the growing importance of the US' future as the world's leading industrial nation. —Anonymous; *Research Mgmt,* Sep 1981, 24(5): pp. 7. Avail. ABI 81-23606

Industrial research, Colleges & universities, Corporate responsibility, Funding

Taxation 101   (409)

Changes in the tax code produced by the Economic Recovery Tax Act of 1981 (ERTA) make it much more advantageous for businesses to make donations to universities. The most popular incentive for corporate contributions to date has been a deduction for gifts of scientific equipment. Companies can deduct book value in addition to 50% of the retail profit margin on the equipment. With such lenient requirements, millions of dollars in scientific equipment have poured into universities throughout the US. ERTA also encourages scientific research in that there is a credit for companies that contract out research to universities and other institutions. There is one problem in that the Internal Revenue Service (IRS) has not issued definite guidelines about which types of research will qualify. Since companies do not know whether this credit will be extended beyond 1986, they must start their projects now and hope that the IRS will approve. – Andresky, Jill; *Forbes,* Feb 28, 1983, 131(5): pp. 43,46. Avail. ABI 83-07184

Colleges & universities, Donations, Gifts, Corporate responsibility, Tax credits, Tax deductions

Teaching Social Responsibility (410)

Because there was a rapid erosion of business credibility in the public eye during the 1970s, teaching social responsibility to business students also increased. The teaching of social responsibility promises to continue as a hot issue in academic circles during the 1980s. There are conflicting ideas about what comprises a responsible posture for corporate management in a private enterprise system, given the notion that the marketplace cannot by itself resolve all the unwholesome side effects of business activity. Teaching social responsibility for business in the '80s requires both an historical viewpoint and a systems view of society. Executives who are concerned with social responsibility need to be aware of the following trends: 1. Corporations will increasingly develop public affairs departments. 2. The public relations function will be improved, with possible direct corporate involvement in political action. 3. Managers will need to take a proactive stance toward environmental issues. 4. "Business and society" courses should be required of business students. –Bernthal, Wilmar F.; *Los Angeles Business & Economics,* Winter 1981, 6(1): pp. 11-12. Avail. ABI 81-07285

Corporate responsibility, Social responsibility, Managers, Executives, Business schools, Education, Teaching

Toward a "Social Control in the Advertising Agency" (411)

Professional education should include not only the provision of skills but also a penetrating analysis of the profession in which the students will one day be engaged. This analysis should especially include a thorough investigation of the effects of that activity upon the society at large and upon those engaged in it. Advertising agencies, like other organizations, exercise social control over their members, but virtually nothing about this phenomenon and its consequences can be found in advertising texts, and undergraduates are typically unaware of it. Since the students do not realize they will be molded and shaped by their working experiences, advertising teachers have a moral obligation to discuss this area with their students. A fundamental question to ask about advertising concerns to what extent its nature and functions are compatible with one's values. Given the demands and pressures of the advertising business, one must ask if honesty, sincerity, and a sense of social responsibility are traits that would enable one to thrive, both spiritually and financially, in advertising. Some first-hand observations indicate that the answer is no. Students need to be exposed to the "facts of life" of working in the advertising business. References. —Norris, Vincent P.; *Jrnl of Advertising,* 1983, 12(1): pp. 30-33. Avail. ABI 83-11496

Advertising agencies, Social, Control, Employees, Colleges & universities, Students, Ethics

Two Views of Business Ethics: A Popular Philosophical (412) Approach and a Value Based Interdisciplinary One

The popular philosophical approach to business ethics is based on the assumption that businesspeople are morally conscientious and strive for ethical solutions to moral problems. Therefore, the function of business ethics education is to aid managers in resolving moral problems by teaching them normative ethical principles and developing their skills in applying those principles to concrete situations. A major problem with the philosophical approach to teaching business ethics is that normative ethical theory was not originally developed for applied ethics or the determination of right and wrong in given situations. It is proposed that a value-based interdisciplinary approach to business ethics is needed since business basically has functioned in an amoral - if not immoral - manner. With a value-based approach, business lifestyles can be analyzed for their positive and negative moral consequences, showing the extent to which modern business is characterized by morality, and allowing identification of needed moral changes. References. —Klein, Sherwin; *Jrnl of Business Ethics (Netherlands),* Feb 1985, 4(1): pp. 71-79. Avail. ABI 85-13711

Ethics, Morality, Corporate responsibility

The University as Landlord (413)

Columbia University has more than half of its investments in real estate. Most of the newer acquisitions have been in the campus area which has enabled the university to stabilize a once-crumbling neighborhood. However, recently, Columbia's investment director, Ronald Rayevich, and his colleagues at 5 other leading universities have been exploring the possibility of setting up a commingled real estate fund similar to those in which pension funds invest. The fund, which would be a real estate investment trust with trustees from each participant, woudl expand to $100 million in assets by investing in industrial properties, warehouses, shopping centers, and suburban office buildings. Rayevich sees this plan as the only way universities like Columbia can achieve national diversification in a competitive real estate market.Rayevich is proud of the fact that Columbia's assets are almost exclusively self-run. He is also unafraid to tackle the question of the social responsibility of the university's investments. While the school strives to invest in socially responsible companies, it also must present no risk to the university assets. —VerMeulen, Michael; *Institutional Investor,* May 1980, 14(5): pp. 119-122. Avail. Institutional 80-11098

Colleges & universities, Real estate, Investments, REITs, Internal, Management, Social responsibility

The University-Academic Connection in Research: (414) Corporate Purposes and Social Responsibilities

The US, the world leader in the development of scientific knowledge, has fallen behind other countries in the use of knowledge to support economic growth. Industry/university research collaboration has been hampered by differences in culture and objectives. Industry is concerned with output and ownership of research results, while academe is concerned with the creation of knowledge for the public good, rather than for commercial exploitation. Universities must recognize that the primary goal of industry is to provide goods and services to meet public needs; they must accept their social responsibility to deliver technology for commercial application. Research agreements can be established on a mutual cost/benefit basis. To circumvent the commercial exploitation controversy, collaborative research agreements should initially focus on support for fundamental research. References. – David, Edward E., Jr.; *Jrnl of the Society of Research Administrators,* Fall 1982, 14(2): pp. 5-12. Avail. ABI 83-00365

Colleges & universities, Research, Commercial, Applications, Funds, Grants, Agreements

University-Industry Relationships: A University's (415) Perspective

Industry/university research collaboration has resulted in the rapid application of basic science to products and production processes. This collaboration gives industry a pool of skilled professionals, while universities benefit by increased research opportunities for faculty and students. However, there are many potential hazards in these relationships. Universities have a social responsibility to promote free inquiry and independent thought; in research collaboration, the profit motive must be prevented from influencing research work and the free flow of information. A conflict of interest exists if research relationships result in biased research, neglect of university responsibilities, exploitation of students, or strictures on the free publication of research results. A possible safeguard is to require faculty members involved in industrial research to file a disclosure of financial interest in the private sector for which the research is being conducted. However, this represents only a small potential solution for a complex problem. –Kendrick, J. B., Jr.; *Jrnl of the Society of Research Administrators,* Fall 1982, 14(2): pp. 13-17. Avail. ABI 83-00366

Colleges & universities, Research, Industrial, Cooperation

We'd Better Do Something about Science Education (416)

The future of US companies depends on science. Without science, there is no research, and without research, the US' ability to compete with other nations will be seriously impaired. Recent studies have indicated a lack of pre-college science training in the US and a lack of science teachers. Furthermore, this problem is receiving little attention from the national government. Federal aid to science education has been reduced. Fewer science courses, lack of qualified teachers, dwindling supplies, and unresponsive federal government combine to present 2 dangers: 1. The decline in the number of students exposed to science will mean fewer people who are science-literate. 2. This decline in science education will have a dramatic impact on the number of scientists and quality of scientific research. Because of a lack of concern and support at the federal level, local communities will have to take responsibility for science education. Business people can help directly by closing the gap in supplies and equipment and by participating in co-op programs. They can recognize the achievements of science teachers and work to draw the federal government's attention to the need for adequate science education. —Sturzenegger, Otto; *Industry Week,* Jul 26, 1982, 214(2): pp. 13. Avail. ABI 82-20127

Science, Education, Corporate responsibility

HEALTH AND SAFETY

AIDS, Hepatitis, and the National Blood Policy (417)

Despite development of a blood test to check for acquired immune deficiency syndrome (AIDS), the safety of the nation's blood supply is not guaranteed. The AIDS test entails a 4% error rate; also there is no way to test for the presence of some forms of hepatitis. Economist Ross Eckert argues that the federal policy of suppressing innovative competition among blood banks and discouraging paid blood donations has needlessly impaired the safety of the blood supply. Others defend federal policy in a debate that started long before the current AIDS crisis began. Eckert says the key risks in blood collection are how donors are screened and where centers are located - and not whether the blood is bought. In 1973, federal policy was announced to move toward an all-volunteer blood donation system and to eliminate commercialism. That policy has worked until now, but with the AIDS crisis, commercial plasma suppliers have gained the advantage by targeting low-risk donors. The AIDS crisis has also called into question the ethic of "community responsibility;" those involved in the debate seem more concerned about the ethical climate than about improving public health. — Anonymous; *Regulation,* Jul/Aug 1985, 9(4): pp. 5-7. Avail. ABI 85-32314

Blood, Testing, Donations, Regulation, FDA, Companies, Diseases, Social responsibility

Alcohol Industry Campaigns Against Alcohol Abuse (418)

The Licensed Beverage Information Council (LBIC) was formed by the alcoholic beverage industry in response to a 1978 study indicating that public education was needed to increase women's awareness of the dangers of drinking during pregnancy. The LBIC faced a complex challenge in dealing with fetal alcohol syndrome. Its objective was to motivate and inform. The LBIC adopted a platform statement as a guide to all groups interested in the campaign. An education program was developed to inform public and private education leaders about the dangers of alcohol beverage misuse during pregnancy. The LBIC offered an outreach network through its local councils and other health institution members to reach alcoholic women and their families. The message on fetal alcohol syndrome was printed in 2 leading books on prenatal and infant care. Messages were also conveyed via poster, radio, and television. The LBIC has developed a 2nd phase of its program to educate the public and expand its activities regarding other aspects of alcohol abuse. The LBIC believes that an effective, responsible public education program is a most important way to meet its social responsibility. —Gavaghan, Paul F.; *Public Relations Qtrly,* Summer 1983, 28(2): pp. 11-16. Avail. ABI 83-22868

Public relations, Advertising campaigns, Alcoholism, Liquor industry, Women, Strategy, Programs, Media

Alcohol Problems at Work - Some Medical and Legal (419) Considerations

One of the earliest indications of problem drinking is a detrimental change in attitude, performance, and efficiency at work, which may be detected by an alert supervisor. The absence of appropriate training and of an alcohol policy frequently results in negative and collusionist attitudes from employers and colleagues until a crisis takes place that results in dismissal. A properly implemented alcohol policy will allow the employee to obtain help at an early stage in the illness. Such a policy is cost-effective for the employer and very relevant to an employer's legal obligations with regard to fair dismissal. An alcohol policy should be clearly communicated, applied to all employees, and geared to the employee's willingness to use it to obtain help. The policy should also include: 1. appropriate education and training, 2. a precise method of referral for treatment, and 3. follow-up. Chart. References. —Knox, Jean and Fenley, Anthony; *Personnel Review (UK),* 1985, 14(1): pp. 32-35. Avail. ABI 85-27864

Employee problems, Alcoholism, Personnel policies, Social responsibility, Guidelines, UK

Analysis Techniques Help IEs Evaluate Ethical (420) Dimensions of On-the-Job Decisions

Industrial engineers (IE) often have to make decisions concerning the benefits and risks involved in producing products that have the potential to harm large numbers of unsuspecting people. Several approaches can be employed to help optimize the decision-making process involving these issues. Even with the current high level of corporate concern about possible accidents and adverse effects of their products, accidents still occur and ethical decisions still must be made by management, often on the basis of subjectively determined probability analysis. Two useful forms of analysis for these types of decisions are decision trees and fault trees. IEs can use these operations research techniques to aid in making a prudent decision about a product's benefits and risks. IEs can greatly reduce their employers' and their own potential product liability risks by maintaining a strong social awareness of the ethical dimensions of their decisions and by using the available analytical tools. Table. Charts. References. —Stewart, W. T. and Paustenbach, Dennis J.; *Industrial Engineering,* Apr 1984, 16(4): pp. 68-76. Avail. ABI 84-14405

Industrial engineering, Ethics, Social issues, Safety management, Social responsibility, Environmental accounting

Caring (421)

Caring is the major product line of a health care institution; consumers both expect and demand caring. In organizations where caring is viewed as the essence of the product, this added dimension sets the care team apart from the competition. However, the drama behind care giving often fails to influence the administrators. These executives have not learned that to achieve excellent management results and patient outcomes, management must communicate its caring to the care givers. The care team begins with the chief executive officer, who serves as a role model in establishing the culture of caring. These executives balance authority and caring so that when it is applied to the daily management of care givers, an attitude of advocacy is visible. Management must realize that how it thinks about its care givers, its mission, and its role in product delivery influences the product quality. Caring about the patient and about the care givers is management at its best. —Settlemyre, Jean T.; *Hospital Forum,* May/Jun 1984, 27(3): pp. 48-53. Avail. ABI 84-19363

Health care delivery, Hospitals, Executives, Social responsibility

Corporate Culpability in Work-Place Fatalities — A Growing Trend?   (422)

Criminal charges brought against employers for workplace fatalities are part of a trend which began in 1908. The Federal Employers' Liability Act of 1908 disposed of 3 employer defenses: 1. assumption of risk, 2. contributory negligence, and 3. the fellow-servant doctrine. In the 1970s, the Occupational Safety and Health Act instituted fines for employers with safety violations. Although some state courts have been slow to hold corporations criminally liable, others have considered corporations to be "persons" under their legislatures' definition and have imposed fines. The new trend in common law likely will not affect corporate executives because of: 1. traditional legal theories that do not support the concept of "respondeat superior," 2. influential sectors of society that would be reluctant to convict corporate officials, and 3. the need for executive knowledge of the crime. However, if criminal culpability is shown, criminal prosecution is possible. Criminal culpability includes: 1. negligence, 2. recklessness, and 3. intentional behavior. —Castagnera, James O.; *Personnel,* Sep 1985, 62(9): pp. 8-12. Avail. ABI 85-34538

Occupational safety, Death, Corporate responsibility, Liability, Trends, Court decisions, Professional liability

Corporate Executives: Reclaim Health Care Role   (423)

A Business Week conference which centered on the topic "Cost-Effective Strategies for Corporate Healthcare" was attended by more than 150 corporate executives. They reviewed new insights and perspectives in reclaiming the corporate and individual role in health care. As payor, provider, and consumer, corporations must learn to assess the approaches taken to administer their health care programs. Health-related programs are measured against 3 kinds of objectives: 1. economic effect in cost/benefit terms, 2. human relations implications, and 3. business considerations, which mesh the first two. An adequate data base for projecting and modeling decisions pertaining to operations, marketing, and financial control already has been developed by health care planners. Cost-effectiveness, consideration of health as an aspect of corporate planning, and collection of information about health status and health programs are goals for future employee health programming. —Anonymous; *Employee Benefit Plan Review,* Jan 1981, 35(7): pp. 28,30. Avail. ABI 81-03755

Health care, Executives, Roles, HMOs, Planning, Corporate responsibility

Credit Market Conditions Affecting Healthcare (424) Institutions in 1985

Economic forecasters generally agree that economic growth will slow during 1985 temporarily, with a return to more rapid growth during the 4th quarter. Both households and business are expected to demand significantly more capital, with projections calling for requirements of $485 billion, or 63% of all funds. Hospitals raise the vast majority of their debt capital in the tax-exempt bond market. The availability of those funds in 1985 will be affected by: 1. an expected strong supply of funds from individuals and bond funds, 2. the possibility of increased buying from casualty insurers, and 3. negative effects on bank purchases because of provisions in the 1984 tax law. Hospital demands for capital are projected to be strong in 1985, and its uses and the ability to attract capital will be based on: 1. organizational and marketing shifts in health care delivery, 2. efficiency improvements, and 3. the industry's political skill and social responsibility. If interest rates drop as expected at the end of 1985, the long-term bond market should be receptive to strong capital demands by hospitals. Tables. Graph. References. – Mansdorf, Bruce D.; *Healthcare Financial Mgmt*, Feb 1985, 39(2): pp. 48-58. Avail. ABI 85-08418

Health facilities, Capital markets, Health care industry, Economic growth, Municipal bonds, Bond markets, Predictions, Financing, Interest rates, Statistical data

Employers' Perceptions of Benefits Accrued from (425) Physical Fitness Programs

About 50,000 companies in the US have programs promoting exercise to keep their employees physically fit. These programs are justified by the organizations' belief that the individual is personally helped and productivity is improved. A model is available that reflects the basis of current thought by leaders in business and industry-sponsored fitness programs. Initially management feels that exercise will lead to increased fitness. Once physical fitness levels increase, increases in wellness, cohesiveness, and satisfaction follow. The increased wellness causes a decrease in health care claims, which ultimately benefits the organization. Some benefits of a fitness program include decreases in absenteeism, turnover, sick days, and health care claims. Physical fitness programs may afford an indirect gain for the company in terms of company visibility in the community and/or industry and meeting social responsibility by positively contributing to employee well being. Chart. –Driver, Russell W. and Ratliff, Ronald A.; *Personnel Administrator*, Aug 1982, 27(8): pp. 21-26. Avail. ABI 82-21247

Employee benefits, Physical fitness, Programs, Exercise, Personnel management, Perceptions, Models, Job satisfaction

Ergonomics, part 1: How Can An IE Justify a Human (426) Factors Activities Program to Management?

Industrial engineers (IEs) can use one of 3 basic approaches to justify ergonomics activities in production facilities to management. The easiest approach is to argue that ergonomics can improve productivity. This approach should be used when the firm: 1. does not have engineered work standards, 2. is relatively new or has recently introduced a new product line, 3. has recently introduced technological change, or 4. has devoted limited time and resources to classical engineering activities. Justification can also be made on the basis that ergonomics can reduce non-productive time and overhead expenses. This approach should be used when the firm: 1. is experiencing an unusually high accident rate, 2. has a high percentage of highly skilled labor, 3. is experiencing high rates of absenteeism, turnover, or trips to the doctor, or 4. has employees who take a disproportionately large number of breaks. Finally, the case for ergonomics can be made on the basis of social or legal responsibilities. This approach is most appropriate when the firm: 1. employs non-union labor, 2. is in a tight labor market or tight product market, or 3. produces a product with a high liability potential. A case study is included. Charts. References. –Smith, Leo A. and Smith, James L.; *Industrial Engineering*, Feb 1982, 14(2): pp. 38-43. Avail. ABI 82-05959

Ergonomics, Industrial engineering, Projects, Productivity, Improvements, Social responsibility, Quality of work

Managing Without Disaster: Doing Away with Visiting Firemen   (427)

Compliance with fire regulations is only one part of management's fire-reduction responsibilities. Management's concern to prevent or reduce fire losses goes beyond regulations, which are geared chiefly to protecting human life and health. Larger warehouses, more complex storage systems, and the presence of highly combustible products, such as liquified petroleum gas (LPG), should make fire prevention a priority concern for business managers. Fire losses may be of greater magnitude than is realized by corporate executives. In the UK, fire losses to businesses between 1979 and 1980 increased by 32%, more than twice the increase in the inflation rate. Some 43% of British businesses hit by fire never trade again. Fire losses can be prevented or reduced by following 4 recommendations of the Fire Protection Association (FPA): 1. identifying risk, 2. determining precautions required, 3. establishing a fire precaution system, and 4. maintaining the system on a day-to-day basis. Fire spread can be limited by use of sprinkler systems and strategically located fire walls. Corporate responsibility for fire prevention belongs with top management; responsibilities should be clearly placed on line managers also. –Peek, Edward; *Management Today (UK)*, Dec 1981, pp. 70-74. Avail. ABI 82-03696

UK, Fires, Prevention, Risk management, Fire protection

Winning with a Short-Subject Film   (428)

"Ridin the Edge" is a short-subject film sponsored by Allstate Insurance Co. It is a good public relations film in that it helps change attitudes and correct biases and misconceptions. Since 1971, Allstate has campaigned for air-bags as standard equipment in new cars. In 1976, Allstate participated in a crash scene in a feature film called "Moving Violation" by supplying 2 cars equipped with air cushions from their test fleet. A camera was concealed in one of the cars and it recorded, in ultra-slow motion, the only existing color film footage of a live driver crashing into a concrete wall at more than 30 miles per hour. Allstate reviewed the footage and found that it was a powerful illustration of the lifesaving capabilities of an air cushion. By the end of 1980, the film had been seen by some 46 million people. It has earned several awards. —Costa, Don; *Public Relations Jrnl,* Sep 1982, 38(9): pp. 24-26. Avail. ABI 82-23511

Public relations, Social responsibility, Corporate, Motion pictures, Automobiles, Safety, Documentary films

ENVIRONMENT

Accounting for Hazardous Waste (429)

Many manufacturers routinely use or produce materials that are increasingly considered hazardous to the environment. Accounting for costs relating to hazardous wastes has not been significantly addressed in the authoritative and other relevant literatures. There are at least 4 types of waste costs: 1. current operations waste disposal, 2. future closure and monitoring of waste sites, 3. previously produced wastes, and 4. "orphaned" waste sites. Determination that a liability exists is vital to subsequent accounting. Perhaps the easiest expenditures to account for are current waste disposal expenditures in current operations. In accounting for future monitoring costs of waste sites, it must be realized that legal obligations arise even though current expenditures are not made. Costs relating to previously produced waste should be expensed as incurred unless the obligation meets the criteria for accrual of loss contingencies. The accounting question for costs related to orphaned sites focuses on when to record social responsibility expenditures. Table. Chart. —Ross, Allan John; *Jrnl of Accountancy,* Mar 1985, 159(3): pp. 72-82. Avail. ABI 85-13538

Waste disposal, Accounting procedures, Hazardous substances, Costs, FASB statements, Taxes

Advance Planning Needed to Cope with Crises (430)

Crisis management experts warn that failure to anticipate and prepare for crises can no longer be tolerated given the current frequency of corporate crises. Union Carbide's handling of the methyl isocyanate leak at Bhopal, India, should be analyzed to determine what lessons can be learned. According to Gerald Meyers of Carnegie-Mellon University (Pittsburgh, Pennsylvania), it is clear that Carbide did not do any crisis planning and did not anticipate what might happen despite ongoing quality problems at the plant. Nevertheless, some benefits ultimately may be gleaned from such a crisis, e.g., acceleration of needed change and development of early warning systems. Effective communication with the outside world is an important part of effective crisis management. Meyers advises every firm to have a crisis team in place to handle eventualities effectively. According to Stephen Greyser of Harvard, the fundamentals of crisis management begin with having the facts at hand. —Higgins, Kevin; *Marketing News,* Apr 26, 1985, 19(9): pp. 14-15. Avail. ABI 85-17783

Management of crises, Communication, Public relations, Case studies, Union Carbide-Danbury Conn, India, Social responsibility, Chemical industry

The Best of Thieves - Restoring Trust in Business (431)

Businesspeople are largely to blame for negative public attitudes toward them. Public mistrust stems mainly from fears brought by ignorance, and these fears prevent rational evaluation of cost/benefit considerations. The public needs to understand that costs can become too high. Marginal improvements may cost a great deal in lost jobs and other areas, as well as money. While favoring environmental cleanups, we must make the public aware of the costs. An informed public can make a difference, as Monsanto found after the chemical plant accident in Bhopal, India. Monsanto reevaluated safety programs and informed the communities. Monsanto will continue to stress safety and communication and take part in activities in support of the environment. Some of its activities have included: 1. supporting reauthorization of the Superfund, 2. working to protect wetlands, and 3. joining forces to accelerate the cleanup of toxic dumps. Monsanto's success serves as an example to other business people to listen to the public and seek to cooperate with them. –Corbett, Harold J.; *Vital Speeches,* Mar 15, 1985, 51(11): pp. 349-352. Avail. ABI 85-13353

Chemical industry, Public relations, Community relations, Communication, Education, Corporate responsibility, Social responsibility, Monsanto-St Louis

Bhopal: Legislative Fallout in the U.S./Bhopal: A Less (432) Frenzied Legislative Pace Abroad

The December 3, 1984, accident at the Union Carbide India Ltd. plant in Bhopal, India, where methyl isocyanate was released into the air, has generated considerable legislative activity in the US. The Environmental Protection Agency and the chemical industry believe new legislation concerning Bhopal issues will not be effective. However, several proposals for stricter guidelines for chemical users and producers have been introduced. These include a package by Representative James J. Florio, efforts to adopt a strict corporate responsibility law, and plans to amend the Clean Air Act to cover the release of chemicals. In addition, the Organization for Economic Cooperation & Development is trying to develop international environmental standards. Attempts at legislative reform have been much slower outside the US. No new environmental regulation has been passed in India. Brazil, however, is becoming more aware of the effects of development on the environment, and a bill has been proposed in Mexico to restrict land use around hydrocarbon installations. –Rich, Laurie A.; Dwyer, Paula; and Block, Paula M.; *Chemical Week,* Feb 6, 1985, 136(6): pp. 26-30. Avail. ABI 85-08356

Chemical industry, Proposed, Legislation, Multinational corporations, EPA, Hazardous substances, Industrial accidents, Waste disposal

The Business of Business Is Not Solely Business (433)

Western companies are increasingly awakening to their social responsibilities, and some have taken steps to make public their fulfillment of these responsibilities. There is no denying the possibly adverse social implications of many of the business activities of firms in developing countries like Malaysia. It remains to be seen if they will embrace the concept of social responsibility as their Western counterparts have already done.

Malaysian companies are becoming more aware of the adverse effects of some of their activities. These effects include a polluted environment, ecological problems, and depletion of scarce resources. The primary mission of a business is to make profits, but a business must also become active in matters of social concern in the environment in which it operates. The practice of reporting social performance of companies in Malaysia is practically non-existent, even though awareness may be on the increase. Bertelsmann Co. and Deutsche Shell have both embraced a social reporting/goal accounting concept with the support of top management. This should be considered a model for Malaysian companies. —Yap, Teoh Hai and Sin, Gregory Thong Tin; *ASEAN Business Qtrly (Singapore)*, Second Quarter 1981, 5(2): pp. 20-22. Avail. Asia 81-18602

Social responsibility, Corporate responsibility, Malaysia, Regulation, Social goals

Ecologically & Socially Concerned Consumers Profiled (434)

Marketing research by Michael A. Belch of San Diego State University indicates that ecologically and socially concerned Americans, who comprise an important segment of the population, have distinct lifestyles and consumption patterns, as well as distinct attitudes and interests. Belch believes that psychographic variables are better predictors than demographics or personality characteristics. He presented his findings at the AMA-sponsored Second Quadrennial Conference on Ecological Marketing.A profile of the typical ecologically and socially concerned consumer includes some of the following traits: 1. young male or female of the higher strata in respect to income, education, and general socioeconomic standing, 2. persons tending to be open-minded, liberal, and secure, 3. persons who are rational and conservative in respect to their consuming behaviors. This segment has strong conservationist attitudes regarding gasoline, and it appears to be antiautomobile. Moreover, pollution is another primary concern of these individuals who would pay more income tax for a program of federal pollution control. These individuals are also typified by the following: 1. They opt for health foods, exercise, and fresh air. 2. They endorse the idea of participatory democracy, and the luxuries of life lack importance to them. —Anonymous; *Marketing News*, Feb 8, 1980, 13(16): pp. 8. Avail. ABI 80-05038

Market segments, Social responsibility, Environmentalists, Consumer behavior, Customer buying behavior, Studies

An Evaluation of Environmental Disclosures Made in (435) Corporate Annual Reports

The demands of society for a cleaner environment reflected in extensive environmental legislation have forced US corporations to undertake and actively participate in extensive pollution control programs. The involvement of US corporations in environmentally related activities has initiated the need and demand for a measurement and reporting system to account for corporate environmental performance. The current state of environmental reporting by corporations remains principally voluntary because no system has been uniformly adopted. A study was conducted to examine the quality of voluntary environmental disclosures made by corporations in their annual reports. An overview of the corporate environmental reporting issue is provided. The companies sampled included 26 of the largest steel, oil, and pulp and paper industries. Results indicate that the voluntary environmental disclosures of the companies were incomplete and inadequate. It was demonstrated that no relationship existed between the measured contents of the firms' environmental disclosures and the firms' environmental performance. Tables. References. Appendices. —Wiseman, Joanne; *Accounting, Organizations & Society (UK)*, 1982, 7(1): pp. 53-63. Avail. ABI 82-11680

Annual reports, Disclosure, Information, Environmental accounting, Performance, Reporting, Studies, Social responsibility

Federal Rescue for the Nuclear Establishment (436)

The lack of a safe, permanent storage site for the abundance of radioactive wastes has challenged the nuclear industry for years. Nuclear energy is considered to be more cost effective than coal, but recent rises in security systems cost, the need for more public relations, and more legal expenses arising from damage suits, must all be reassessed for the nuclear industry. The nuclear industry receives direct subsidies from the government through: 1. cost-plus contracts at the Department of Energy (DOE) weapons facilities, 2. DOE facilities providing enrichment of uranium, research priorities, and 3. resources in nuclear weapons facilities which can be applied to nuclear energy techniques. The Federal government has also promised responsibility for the wastes. DOE is the Federal agency responsible for research and development of energy alternatives, but it has devoted a disproportionate amount of its budget (25%) to nuclear energy programs. DOE develops nuclear weapons techniques that can be directly taken to the private sector of nuclear energy. DOE's bias is the main vehicle for nuclear development and applications today. —Solo, Pam and Jendrzejczyk, Mike; *Business & Society Review*, Spring 1980, (33): pp. 4-8. Avail. ABI 80-13343

Nuclear energy, Nuclear waste, Waste disposal, Costs, Energy Dept-US, Social responsibility

Industry and the Environment: A Communication Gap (437)

The Bureau of the Census has estimated that, from 1973 to 1980, industry spent over $100 billion for pollution control equipment and operation costs. Even with this substantial investment in maintaining and improving environmental quality, industry is seen as doing only the minimum required by law. This lingering negative perception has been fostered by industry's failure to communicate its efforts to reduce pollution and to ensure safe use of air, water, and land. Even dramatic reversals of pollution-ridden natural resources have not been publicized, although sophisticated communication channels are available to industry. Business must communicate the message that it has committed billions to environmental cleanup. Flexible new approaches to regulation can provide new incentives for more expeditious cleanup, and business has the skills to help formulate regulation based on scientific fact. Moreover, industry must reiterate that it is a willing partner in environmental cleanup. References. –Prout, Gerald R.; *Public Relations Review,* Winter 1983, 9(4): pp. 41-52. Avail. ABI 84-04100

Pollution control, Environmentalists, Public relations, Public opinion, Corporate responsibility, Publicity, Regulation

Investor Reaction to a Corporate Social Accounting   (438)

The long-term response of investors to corporate performance with regard to social responsibility is analyzed by examining the effect of pollution control expenditures on profitability, systematic risk, and the cash position in 6 US industries. All financial data on the 67 companies were obtained from the COMPUSTAT annual tape. The measure of profitability used is the average market return on common stock for each company during the 1967-1978 period. Pollution control expenditures do not necessarily lead to lower profitability or affect the cash position. Such expenditures do, however, appear to affect systematic risk in a manner consistent with the "rational economic investor" concept rather than the "ethical investor" concept. Investors view pollution control expenditures as a drain on resources that could have been invested profitably, and do not reward the companies for socially responsible behavior. Tables. Equations. Appendix. References. – Mahapatra, Sitikantha; *Jrnl of Business Finance & Accounting (UK),* Spring 1984, 11(1): pp. 29-40. Avail. ABI 84-13922

Social responsibility, Corporate responsibility, Accountability, Investors, Impacts, Pollution control, Expenditures, Economic impact, Studies, Statistical analysis, Manyindustries, Risk, Profitability

Market Response to Environmental Information   (439)
Produced Outside the Firm

There have been numerous proposals over the last 10 years for accountants to develop methods to measure and report on corporate social performance. In the same time span, large corporations have significantly increased their voluntary disclosures of socially oriented information in annual reports. A number of external organizations, such as the Council on Economic Priorities (CEP), have also been active in producing information bearing on firms' social performances, particularly with respect to pollution control. The question of whether security price movements were associated with the release of external information, is investigated. Security price movements associated with the release of 8 major studies conducted by the CEP of firms' environmental performances in different industries are specifically investigated. The externally produced information about companies' performances in the pollution-control area has attributes of consistency and comparability not typically found in voluntarily reported, socially oriented data. It was observed that price movements were consistent with changes in investors' perceptions of the probability distributions of future cash flows of the sample firms at the times of the release of CEP studies. The results of the study are also consistent with investors using the information released by the CEP to discriminate between companies with different pollution-control

performance records. Equations. Tables. Appendix. References. —Shane, Philip
B. and Spicer, Barry H.; *Accounting Review,* Jul 1983, 58(3): pp. 521-538. Avail. ABI 83-19818
  Social responsibility, Pollution control, Voluntary, Disclosure, Annual reports, Effects, Stock
  prices, Investments, Decision making, Studies, Rates of return, Statistical analysis, Social
  accounting

New Mexico's Environmental Peacemaker (440)

Thanks to President Jerry D. Geist, Public Service Co. of New Mexico
(PNM) has earned the respect of environmental leaders. When Geist took
over the presidency of PNM in 1976, he decided that cooperation with
environmental groups was easier than fighting. PNM spends heavily for
pollution control, and even allows the Sierra Club to review specifications
and technical data for pollution control equipment. This cooperative spirit
was responsible for installing pollution-control equipment before it was
required - equipment that exceeds Clean Air Act requirements. In return,
PNM has gotten support from environmentalists in seeking rate increases,
partly due to the cost of their environmental sensitivity. They have also been
assured by the environmentalists that they would not delay certain
construction plans through litigation. This will make it easier for PNM to
borrow the necessary funds for construction projects. This type of
relationship could not have begun if it were not for Geist, and it will be
certain to continue because of him. —Miller, William H.; *Industry Week,* May 31, 1982,
213(5): pp. 49-50,53. Avail. ABI 82-16259
  New Mexico, Public utilities, Environment, Environmentalists, Corporate responsibility,
  Costs, Revenue

Offering Business a Peace Pipe: Conservationists Are (441)
Taking a More Conciliatory Stance in Settling Disputes

The National Wildlife Federation will begin a 3-year experiment in
"corporate detente" with a meeting among executives from 12 major US
corporations and environmentalists. They will begin hammering out
strategies to blend the goals of economic growth and environmental
protection. The meeting represents a dramatic shift to a spirit of cooperation.
Conservationists are stressing that corporate contributions can be mutually
profitable as well as environmentally sound. The tax benefits of donating
large tracts of land to private conservation groups or state governments have
made such gifts staples of corporate image-polishing campaigns. Still,
environmentalists say corporate support is a small percentage of their
revenue. In some cases, donations are little more than bribes. Conservation
groups hope that setting up a dialogue with business will attract more
corporate dollars. —Anonymous; *Business Week,* Feb 21, 1983, (2778)(Industrial Edition):
pp. 98H. Avail. ABI 83-06272
  Conservation, Environmentalists, Donations, Corporate responsibility

Preserving Wildlife and Land: 'It's Good Business' (442)

The benefits to the corporation of conservation activities include: 1. tax
savings, 2. a positive corporate image, and 3. employee participation in
company-sponsored conservation efforts. Sometimes charitable donations of
property produce better aftertax returns than if property is sold on the open

market. In addition, if a firm wishes to donate land without any ecological value for preservation, the conservancy can resell the property and invest the proceeds in appropriate lands. In the last 3 years, 70% to 80% of donated trade lands have come from chemical businesses. Other ways of assisting conservation efforts are exemplified by Tenneco's artificial reef project and DuPont's donations of $50,000 in each of 2 years to the Fish and Wildlife Service's captive bald eagle breeding program. An agreement between 12 companies, including Conoco, Dow, Monsanto, North Carolina Phosphate, Exxon, and Kimberly-Clark, with the National Wildlife Federation developed a corporate wetlands policy. This policy is the first tangible product of the 2-year-old Corporate Conservation Council. —Anonymous; *Chemical Week,* Oct 24, 1984, 135(17): pp. 30-32,34. Avail. ABI 84-36307

Chemical industry, Conservation, Land reclamation, Donations, Corporate responsibility

Profiling Environmentally Responsible Consumer- (443) Citizens

As environmental quality becomes a more important social issue, marketing research interest in the consumption-behavior dimensions of environmental issues is increasing, particularly the establishment of profiles of environmentally concerned individuals. This study examines differences between proven environmentally responsible individuals and the general public on 6 variables: 1. internal-external control of reinforcements, 2. social responsibility, 3. social class, 4. age, 5. income, and 6. environmental responsibility. An experimental choice situation of environmentally responsible decisions (selection of soft drinks in cans vs. returnable bottles and selection of high-phosphate vs. low-phosphate laundry detergents) was combined with self-report measures. The generalized social responsibility correlates of internal-external control and social class were revealed to be significant univariate and well as multivariate predictors of environmental responsibility. For marketers, the most significant implication is that environmentally responsible target markets may be substantial enough to warrant the use of marketing programs that are environmentally oriented. Tables. References. —Tucker, Lewis R., Jr.; Dolich, Ira J.; and Wilson, David T.; *Jrnl of the Academy of Marketing Science,* Fall 1981, 9(4): pp. 454-477. Avail. ABI 82-05586

Environmentalists, Social responsibility, Consumer, Profiles, Social issues, Environment, Market segments, Market research

The Relationship Between Pollution Control Records (444) and Financial Indicators Revisited and Further Comment

In a recent study, Spicer concluded that there is evidence substantiating existence of a moderate to strong association between the investment value of a company's common shares and its social performance record. Further analyzing the data used by Spicer indicates that the moderate-to-strong associations between a company's pollution control record and financial indicators are spurious due to at least one common background variable, size. An investor's primary concern is return on his investment, and a concern for pollution control is relevant to the extent that failure to have adequate pollution control endangers earnings of the firm.Spicer believes that Chen and Metcalf fundamentally misinterpreted his study. He also feels that Chen and Metcalf hold a rather extreme view of what constitutes research and explains this point at length. Tables. Charts. References. —Chen, Kung H.; Metcalf, Richard W.; and Spicer, Barry H.; *Accounting Review,* Jan 1980, 55(1): pp. 168-185. Avail. ABI 80-04001

   Correlation analysis, Causality, Pollution control, Corporate responsibility, Social responsibility, Profitability, Price earnings ratio, Size of enterprise, Studies, Paper industry

Using Private Market Incentives for Air Cleanup   (445)

Utility management continues to face the challenge of accepting its corporate responsibility for reducing air pollution emissions, while seeking to keep its capital operating and carrying costs to a minimum. It appears that electric-power-generating operators, using the regulatory reform movement, can bring about: 1. additional fuel savings, 2. public financing of boiler conversion costs, 3. improvements in service forecasting, 4. improvements in local economic conditions, and 5. innovative justifications for rate increase requests. Opportunities to take advantage of the regulatory reform movement exist in many forms, developed from the use of 3 mechanisms: 1. bubble, 2. offset, or 3. banking. An emission reduction credit could be used as an incentive or a deterrence to a cogeneration project. Risks, however, stem from the uncertainty of regulatory treatment and market conditions. There are also tax risks and rate-making risks. All of the risks are resolvable through experience and the dedicated involvement of financial advisors in the environmental process. Exhibits. —Stathos, Dan T. and Treitman, Michael S.; *Public Utilities Fortnightly,* Jul 30, 1981, 108(3): pp. 13-21. Avail. Public 81-18511

   Air pollution, Pollution control, Incentives, Electric utilities, EPA, Regulatory reform, Public utilities

5

Financial Management And Social Investing

Accountability and the Corporate Board (446)

The answer to the accountability of the corporate power question can be found in the corporate boardroom. Traditionally, 2 answers have served to alleviate concern over the issue of whether economic power is accountable to the public good. The first response has been that the discipline of the marketplace checks, and ultimately destroys, those who are irrational in the exercise of corporate power. The second answer most often used to challenge the need for mechanisms of corporate accountability rests on the theory that the board of directors, as the shareholders' surrogate, acts as a watchdog of management power. However, the facts do not substantiate this theory since the record of board performance shows that directors seldom turn out ineffective management and react exceedingly slowly to corporate deterioration. A strong and effective board is a valuable corporate asset, and both management and directors must collaborate to develop a board that can bring to management the best, most informed and most objective advice, support, and guidance. Reference. —Williams, Harold M.; *Jrnl of Accountancy,* Nov 1980, 150(5): pp. 80-85. Avail. ABI 80-23182

Corporate, Power, Accountability, Boards of directors, Effectiveness, Corporate responsibility, Social accounting

Accountants Assess the Social Audit (447)

The social audit refers to a technique which attempts to document the activities of a firm in regard to such issues as the hiring and promotion of women and minorities, corporate donations, etc. This concept has gained in popularity during the past decade because corporations have become more aware of their responsibility to society, and the social audit serves as the documentation of this social responsibility. The idea is somewhat controversial, as some corporate managers believe it is impossible to quantify social activities. A study was conducted to examine the views of members of 3 professional accounting organizations on various aspects of the social audit. A random sample of 200 members was selected from the 3 professional accounting associations, and participants completed a questionnaire. The results indicated that: 1. There is not strong support in the accounting community for the use of social-accounting techniques at this time. 2. An audit that begins with a managerial assessment of social responsibility activities and then measures the actions of a firm relative to its social goals is most popular. 3. The managerially oriented social audit should be conducted every year or 2 and used for internal and external purposes. Tables. Charts. References. –Murphy, Patrick E. and Burton, E. James; *Business,* Sep/Oct 1980, 30(5): pp. 33-40. Avail. ABI 80-19201

> Social audit, Social accounting, Corporate responsibility, Opinions, Accountants, Surveys, Attitude surveys

Accounting and Corporate Accountability   **(448)**

The idea of organizational legitimacy is an important basis for the concept of corporate accountability. Equity or fairness is another root of the corporate accountability concept. It is derived from the assumption that corporations are managed in ways that damage people who are unable to protect themselves. There are four types of limitations on managerial discretion to act other than in the interests of shareholders: 1. the market of goods and services, 2. the market for finance and for corporate control, 3. the market for managerial services, and 4. internal and external monitoring systems. The corporation should be responsible to employees, customers, creditors, and the general public as well as to the shareholders. Public and internal reports characterize corporate social accounting. The numbers would be integrated into the company's annual financial statements for public consumption and they would be included in internal management reports for internal consumption. An analysis has concluded that shareholders are likely to be well served by the accounting procedures voluntarily adopted by corporate managers and directors. The imposition of negative externalities on the general public is one area that is not likely to be self-regulating. References. –Benston, George J.; *Accounting, Organizations & Society (UK),* May 1982, 7(2): pp. 87-105. Avail. ABI 82-19681

> Corporate responsibility, Social responsibility, Accounting, Accountability

Accounting Standard Setting: From Plato to Robin Hood?   **(449)**

Accounting is being touted as a social choice mechanism, which is defined here as a means by which welfare, sometimes equated with wealth, is transferred from one group of people in a society to another. Accounting information has value; there are economic consequences associated with changes in accounting rules. By selecting one standard over another, a standard-setting body automatically chooses which group in society will gain and which will lose - except in the rate case where everyone is made equally well off. Both the Securities and Exchange Commission (SEC) and the Financial Accounting Standards Board (FASB) have commissioned studies of the economic consequences of their pronouncements. Accounting standards may force some private information to be disclosed to the market which previously was not incorporated into the share prices. Due to this disclosure, some companies' share prices will drop, and other companies' share prices will rise, depending on how the market perceives the new information. The choice of standards with fair economic repercussions is in no way easy or unambiguous. References. —Boritz, J. Efrim; *CA Magazine (Canada)*, Jun 1982, 115(6): pp. 30-36. Avail. ABI 82-19219

Accounting standards, Accounting policies, Information, Economic impact, Social impact, Accountants, Social responsibility, Roles

Another Look at Corporate Social Responsibility and (450) Reporting: An Empirical Study in a Developing Country

Corporate social responsibility accounting and reporting are considered from the perspective of a developing country. The study is based on a personal interview questionnaire survey conducted mainly with chief executive officers in 100 companies operating in Malaysia. Various aspects of corporate social performance, including social reporting, are examined. Findings reveal that social reporting lags behind corporate social involvement and that the majority of corporate attention is devoted to activities relating to employees and products/services. In addition, corporate size and national origin of corporate ownership are relevant to the extent of social commitments made by companies. Little evidence is found of any attempt by all respondent companies to report social performance on a systematic and formal basis. Thus, it seems that any further progress by companies in undertaking greater social responsibilities and reporting should come from larger, foreign-owned companies. Tables. References. —Teoh, Hai-Yap and Thong, Gregory; *Accounting, Organizations & Society (UK)*, 1984, 9(2): pp. 189-206. Avail. ABI 84-10707

Corporate responsibility, Social responsibility, Responsibility accounting, Reporting, Disclosure, Chief executive officer, Surveys, Malaysia, Studies, Statistical data

An Attitude Survey Approach to the Social Audit: The (451) Southam Press Experience

Based on the audit experience of the Southam Press Limited, a large conglomerate with 1978 revenues exceeding C$384 million, a social attitude survey can definitely enrich the social audit process by increasing the level of broadly based input for analysis, at reasonable cost. Since 1974, the Investment Committee of the United Church of Canada has been auditing the social performance of 6 of its larger investee corporations, and found that traditional social audit approaches were insufficiently comparable, predictive, and insightful. Advantages of the internal social attitude survey approach include: 1. The ability to compare employees' social attitudes horizontally, vertically, or functionally within an organization, between companies or even industries. 2. An increased awareness among employees which has been shown to lower absenteeism and turnover, and raise the importance of both corporate social performance and profit in the eyes of company employees. Tables. Bibliography. Appendix. Exhibits. —Brooks, L. J., Jr.; *Accounting, Organizations & Society (UK)*, 1980, 5(3): pp. 341-355. Avail. ABI 80-22704

Social audit, Techniques, Attitude surveys, Social responsibility, Attitudes, Case studies

Auditing SRA Systems: New Uses for Old Standards (452)

Users of social responsibility accounting (SRA) system statements and reports need assurance that the reports are factual, and this is where the auditor comes in. By devising a series of system checks, it is possible to determine whether corporate social aims are being met. The internal auditor will be involved in this task. The internal auditor must determine whether corporate departments and divisions are following social responsibility policies that have been set at the top. However, there is also growing pressure for external social audits. The role of the external independent auditor in such an audit will be much like his role in a financial audit. It will not be necessary to devise a whole new set of procedures for external independent social audits as many of the present procedures for financial audits can be adapted. Although the SRA audit will be a challenge for the external auditor, it also offers an opportunity to help develop generally accepted social auditing standards. —Anderson, Robert H.; *CA Magazine (Canada)*, May 1981, 114(5): pp. 47-51. Avail. ABI 81-14982

Canada, Accountants, Social responsibility, Responsibility accounting, Corporate, Performance, Measurement, Reporting, Professional responsibilities, Roles, Boards of directors, Public interest, Audit committees, Internal, Auditors, Auditing standards

The Business Manager's Dilemma-IV. Evaluating Corporate Social Performance (453)

The major problem in the development of a meaningful social audit is the lack of universally recognized measurement standards. The cost of a social program does not convey its effectiveness in terms of actual benefits to society. Benefits are difficult if not impossible, to quantify. Existing social audits fail to account for the social costs of a company's operations. Another variable which compounds the difficulty of measuring the social impact of an individual firm arises when more than one company creates the same social benefit or social cost. Managers may have to continue evaluating their company's social performance without a fixed formula in standardized numerical terms. Under present definitions, the goal of corporate social evaluation probably cannot be achieved. Nonetheless, it would be unfortunate if social reporting were to be discontinued because of a failure to solve the measurement problem. References. —Strier, Franklin; *Jrnl of Enterprise Mgmt*, 1980, 2(2): pp. 127-129. Avail. ABI 81-00444

Social responsibility, Corporate responsibility, Social audit, Social costs

Content Analysis of Annual Reports for Corporate Strategy and Risk (454)

Corporate annual reports can be a valuable source of data on industries as well as individual firms. Content analysis of annual reports involves coding words, phrases, and sentences against particular schema of interest. The food processing, computer peripherals, and container industries are studied. The validity of the content analysis of annual reports was checked by a matched sample of companies and line-by-line coding of their social responsibility activities and international activity. Content analysis can also deal with growth rates in an industry and strategic risk issues. The analysis of annual reports can provide clues to competitors' strategy and can increase understanding of corporate strategy. For instance, annual report content analysis can measure a company's attitude toward risk by measuring: 1. the use of the word "new" in the president's letter, 2. litigation, 3. percentage of research and development, and 4. long-term debt divided by equity. Tables. Chart. References. —Bowman, Edward H.; *Interfaces,* Jan/Feb 1984, 14(1): pp. 61-71. Avail. ABI 84-19077

Annual reports, Financial, Analysis, Studies, Manycompanies, Corporate, Strategy, Risk, Food processing industry, Container industry, Computer peripherals, Electronics industry, Rates of return

Corporate Audit Committees and the Foreign Corrupt Practices Act (455)

The appearance of the corporate audit committee and the expansion of its role has been one of the most irrepressible occurrences in the history of corporate governance. Audit committees have been able to satisfy various needs, ranging from heightened public awareness of corporate responsibility to management's desire for self-regulation. Such a committee may be a company's best defense against government regulation in general and the Foreign Corrupt Practices Act in particular. The Act regulates foreign corrupt practices of business, but it is not limited to companies doing business abroad, and is not restricted to corrupt payments. The second part of the Act covers internal control and record keeping and may have a greater impact. This Act could be the forerunner of more intrusive government regulation. It enables the Securities and Exchange Commission (SEC) to influence the substantive conduct of management and to specify its disclosure responsibilities. At this time, a company needs an alert, capable, and dedicated audit committee. —Neumann, Frederick L.; *Business Horizons,* Jun 1980, 23(3): pp. 62-71. Avail. ABI 80-13396

Foreign Corrupt Practices Act 1977-US, Corporate, Audit committees, Corporate responsibility, Internal controls, Economic impact

Corporate Financial Reporting in New Zealand: An Analysis of User Preferences, Corporate Characteristics and Disclosure Practices for Discretionary Information (456)

The corporate financial information preferences of financial editors and stockbrokers in New Zealand were studied, and the extent of corporate disclosure of discretionary information by manufacturing corporations listed on the New Zealand Stock exchange was examined. Financial editors and stockbrokers considered the most important sources of financial information to be profit and dividend forecasts, data on capital expenditures and earnings per share, and historical data on corporate operations and finances. Data on personnel, advertising, and social responsibility were ranked as least important. In general, corporate financial disclosures failed to provide the information most needed by financial editors and stockbrokers. Firm size was positively associated with the extent to which discretionary information was disclosed. However, no association was found between the size and prestige of a corporation's auditing firm and the extent of the corporation's financial disclosures. Tables. References. Appendices. —McNally, Graeme M.; Eng, Lee Hock; and Hasseldine, C. Roy; *Accounting & Business Research (UK),* Winter 1982, 13(49): pp. 11-20. Avail. ABI 83-13039

New Zealand, Financial reporting, Disclosure, Surveys, Accounting standards, Stock brokers, Auditors, Statistical analysis

Corporate Governance: Its Impact on the Profession (457)

The issue of corporate governance is much discussed in corporate circles. There has been considerable activity by the Securities & Exchange Commission (SEC) and other government agencies in the area of corporate accountability. The Foreign Corrupt Practices Act of 1977 (FCPA) requires that corporations reporting to the SEC maintain accurate books and records and internal controls designed to satisfy specified objectives. However, the SEC has indicated that it is not totally satisfied with the efforts by the accounting profession to improve independence and establish tighter controls over auditing adequacy. The SEC has also said that it intends to exercise a more vigorous and active oversight over the auditing profession. The consumer movement has also had a severe impact on corporations and has caused firms to be more sensitized to their social responsibilities than in the past. —Sommer, A. A., Jr.; *Jrnl of Accountancy,* Jul 1980, 150(1): pp. 52-60. Avail. ABI 80-14579

Corporate, Accountability, Corporate responsibility, Social responsibility, Federal legislation, Consumerism, SEC, Foreign Corrupt Practices Act 1977-US, Boards of directors, Auditing

Corporate Responsibility: Part I-In the Public Eye: (458) Reporting Social Performance

More than ever, companies are under pressure by shareholders, consumer groups, and government agencies to engage in socially responsible activities. An evaluation of current social performance reporting shows that the content and reporting of information varies from company to company and from year to year. A reporting system should present useful information in a manner to assist the reader in evaluating the company's progress in fulfilling its role as a corporate citizen. According to the results of an Ernst & Whinney survey, developing a social performance reporting system is an evolutionary process involving 3 stages: 1. establishing a foundation, 2. improving reporting quality, and 3. refining the system. Throughout the 3 stages, the company must consider the best medium for disclosing information, and a separate section should be devoted to social responsibility activities in order to present the interrelationship of the company's resources and personnel commitments in the most meaningful and effective manner. A reporting system reinforces corporate social consciousness and exemplifies the balance between the primary corporate objective of profitability and the company's obligation to society. —Cowen, Scott S. and Segal, Mitchell G.; *Financial Executive,* Jan 1981, 49(1): pp. 10-16. Avail. ABI 81-03093

Corporate responsibility, Social responsibility, Reporting, Disclosure, Implementations

Corporate Social Responsibility: Is No News Good (459) News?-Part 2

The literature on the subject of social responsibility accounting notes that the 2 ways to identify socially significant actions of corporations are: 1. to attempt to measure all corporate activities having any social impact, and 2. to focus on actions directly affecting a large number of people. After identification comes quantification of the actions, usually in monetarist terms, but also by units of measure indigenous to the impact. These methods may be combined by expressing results in nonmonetary terms and translating them, via a conversion table, into monetary values. There is no definitive method for implementing an effective and socially accepted system of social accounting due to company reluctance, for a variety of reasons, to disclose voluntarily their degree of social involvement. Although relatively few annual reports disclose, on an objective basis, the degree of a company's involvement in social responsibility, some are noteworthily different. General Foods, Canadian Industries Ltd., Imperial Oil, Fina, John Labatt Ltd., Imasco, Gaz Metropolitan, and Bombardier have all taken positive steps in the field of social responsibility. References. Table. Chart. –Demers, Louis and Wayland, Donald; *CA Magazine (Canada),* Feb 1982, 115(2): pp. 56-60. Avail. ABI 82-09565

Corporate responsibility, Social responsibility, Manycompanies, Canada, Accountability

Corporate Social Responsibility and Public Accountability   (460)

The topic of the development of legislation determining corporate behavior offers insight into the societal problems of corporate enterprise as they are related to accounting, administration, and external reporting. Some specific implications for accounting are considered. A crucial element in the functioning of social accountability is whether accountants want to get involved in social audits and whether they are the most suitable people to conduct them. The question of whether corporate social performance measurement and reporting should become obligatory and to what extent is discussed. A general framework for the implementation of corporate social accounting systems is presented and guidelines for its auditing are recommended. A tentative set of social auditing standards is then outlined along with its methodological accompaniments. References. Appendix. – Filios, Vassilios P.; *Jrnl of Business Ethics (Netherlands),* Nov 1984, 3(4): pp. 305-314. Avail. ABI 85-09456

Corporate responsibility, Accountability, Social responsibility, Social accounting, Environmental accounting, Social audit, Level

The Development of Social Accounting Models: A Comparative Analysis   (461)

Business social accounting models have been developed that emphasize varying degrees of comprehensiveness and complexity. At one extreme, narrative disclosures are advocated in the description of business' social responsiveness. More complexity is found in models that support monetary and nonmonetary quantifications of business efforts to alleviate particular social problems.The demand for business social responsibility is very much a reality. Many recognize the need for assessing the social manifestations of business activity. There are several frameworks that have been developed for communicating information with respect to business' social responsibility. However, the pragmatic application of these models has been sparse. There are 2 major weaknesses in current social accounting models that preclude their applicability: 1. the fact that objects utilized in developing those models are assumed, and 2. the lack of detail concerning how business actions of social importance are to be measured. Table. References. —Ratcliffe, Thomas A. and Munter, Paul; *Business & Society,* Winter 1980, 19(2) /v20n1: pp. 56-66. Avail. ABI 80-13730

Social accounting, Models, Manypeople, Comparative analysis

The Disclosure of Social Accounting Information   (462)

One measure of how business firms have responded to the concern about the performance of their social responsibility can be obtained through an analysis of social measurement disclosures (SMDs) in annual reports. An assessment of the SMDs contained in the annual reports of the largest corporations in North America showed that the SMDs ranged from no more than one or 2 lines in a president's letter to ones that provided a reasonably comprehensive profile of the activities reported upon. A study in the US indicated that the corporate social responsibility areas receiving greatest attention are those in which legislation is pushing corporations toward prescribed performance such as in equal opportunity hiring and promotion, pollution control/environmental impact, and employee safety. Many firms that did not provide any social measurement disclosure claimed that they had in existence, or were initiating, programs along these lines for internal planning and control purposes. Tables. References. —Burke, Richard C.; *Cost & Mgmt (Canada),* May/Jun 1980, 54(3): pp. 21-24. Avail. ABI 80-16724

Social accounting, Information, Disclosure, Studies, Statistical analysis, Measurement, Annual reports, Canada

Efficient Markets and the Social Role of Accounting   (463)

Two related phenomena highlight the problems of the efficient market hypothesis (EMH): functional fixation on earnings and the assumption of symmetric market rationality. The observation that the market reacts to an announcement of an unexpected level of earnings does not necessarily mean that the information is valuable; it only means that the market believes it to be so. The average expected return on the stock market is partly determined by accounting information. If this information is biased in some way, there is no evidence that, even though they supposedly do so for individual securities, investors will make the "right" adjustment for the whole market. There are different social perceptions of the need for change in accounting principles. Another supported theory indicates that authoritatively enforced decisions have a faster adoption rate than collective ones, but a poorer long-term acceptance record. References. —Robinson, Chris; *CA Magazine (Canada),* Mar 1980, 113(3): pp. 67-72. Avail. ABI 80-07603

Efficient markets (FIN), Hypotheses, Accounting, Accounting standards, Financial reporting, Disclosure, Social responsibility

Enforced Self-Regulation: A New Strategy for   (464) Corporate Crime Control

The criminal justice system's failure to control corporations has been so great that only radical approaches at reform are capable of remedying this failure. One approach would involve government-enforced self-regulation of illegal corporate conduct. Under the proposed system, each company would devise a set of rules which would then be ratified by the government; a violation of the rules would be an offense. An internal compliance group within each company would monitor compliance and recommend any disciplinary action required. The regulatory agency would be responsible for seeing that: 1. the company rules met guidelines established by government policy, 2. the compliance group was independent within the corporate organization, 3. the compliance group performed its role in detecting violations, and 4. prosecutions were launched, particularly against companies that subverted their compliance groups. Any proposal to reform the corporate criminal justice system must attempt to find an optimal mix of self-regulation and governmental regulation so that the gaps left by one approach are counterbalanced by the strengths of another approach. References. – Braithwaite, John; *Michigan Law Review,* Jun 1982, 80(7): pp. 1466-1507. Avail. Michigan 82-28431

Corporate, Crime, Self regulation, Internal, Compliance, Groups, Law enforcement, White collar crime, Corporate responsibility

"Ethical" Investing: An Empirical Study of Policies and (465) Practices of Catholic Religious Institutions

A questionnaire was sent to 780 "major superiors" of the approximately 1,200 US institutions of Roman Catholic priests, brothers, and sisters to gather empirical data on their ethical investment policies. There was an effective response rate of 21%, and the results showed that: 1. forty-six percent of the respondents had an explicit ethical investment policy, 2. for 74%, investment activities were influenced in some way or another by ethical or corporate social responsibility considerations, 3. ethical investment activities included avoidance of investment/disinvestment, purposeful investment, direct communications, and shareholder resolutions, and 4. the sophisticated investors participated in all categories of ethical investing at a greater rate than the rest of the sample. Tables. Equations. References. –Wokutch, Richard E.; *Akron Business & Economic Review,* Winter 1984, 15(4): pp. 17-24. Avail. ABI 85-05079

Institutional investments, Ethics, Religious organizations, Investment policy, Surveys, Models, Social responsibility

Good Returns with Good Conscience (466)

The United Church of Christ (UCC) has $350 million in a retirement fund that has turned in an exceptional performance record. The fund is run entirely in-house with a small staff and an impressive voluntary counsel made up of experienced professionals. The pension plan permits the participants to allocate their own retirement dollars between a fixed-benefit bond fund and a variable-benefit stock fund. The performance of the variable-benefit fund has been outstanding and is attracting many younger members to the plan. Internal management results in low overhead. John Ordway, pension officer, does not believe in buying or selling to achieve social ends. His first criterion is to make a sound investment. He does not feel the fund is big enough to exert a large influence in the marketplace. The UCC fund will sponsor resolutions directed at the companies whose stocks it owns, but it prefers to approach the managements of companies directly to persuade them that socially sensitive policies benefit everyone. Determining a clear path of social responsibility is very difficult in the present corporate environment. The fund has found persistent persuasion more effective than radical approaches. —Brauer, Molly; *Institutional Investor*, Sep 1981, 15(9): pp. 111-114. Avail. Institutional 81-23836

   Religious organizations, Pension funds, Social, Investment, Social responsibility, Case studies

Have Pension Investment Managers Over-Emphasized   (467) the Needs of Retirees?-Comment

Schotland's analysis maintains the traditional goal of pension investment management is to maximize returns and maintain a certain risk level to assure retirement income security. Advocates of "social investing" would divert pension assets from this goal and seek other socially desirable objectives. The main issue of divergent investment is whether there should be any investment "concession" or hidden subsidy to pursue other goals. Advocates of social investing hold that pension assets offer a promising bridge between society's current problems and the limited resources available to them. Besides higher taxes for governmental employers and a profit squeeze for private employers, divergent investing would interfere with pension funds' maximizing investment returns and threaten retirement security. Thus, divergent investing would be unproductive both in investing and social action. Robinson comments the case against divergent investing is strengthened by the fact that retirement security is a desired objective. Further, the pension incomes accumulated as a by-product act as an additional social purpose, as they increase and facilitate an efficient flow of savings through financial markets. References. —Schotland, Roy A. and Robinson, Thomas R.; *Jrnl of Labor Research*, Fall 1981, 2(2): pp. 265-287. Avail. ABI 81-24010

   Pension funds, Social, Investment, Objectives, Social responsibility, Return on investment, Problems

Henry Parker Fights Apartheid with Investment Clout   (468)

Henry E. Parker, treasurer of the State of Connecticut, administers a $3-billion pension fund that has averaged 10.9% performance for the past 5 years. At the same time, he invests only in programs that are socially beneficial. Connecticut pension and profit-sharing money is invested in, among other things: 1. guaranteed investment contracts, 2. the Yankee Mac Fund, a mortgage finance program, and 3. commercial real estate. Connecticut was the first state to pass a law dealing with a South African investment policy. Rather than prohibiting companies in the portfolio from doing business in South Africa, the law encourages those companies to adhere to certain principles, such as: 1. permitting black workers to join unions and to strike without reprisals, and 2. not selling strategic products to the South African government. Ten of the 25 firms that originally were not in compliance with the law are now in compliance and so are eligible to be put back on the state's investment list. Parker believes that the role of state treasurers is undergoing great change, and that they must be involved in managing that change. —Derven, Ronald; *Pension World*, Aug 1985, 21(8): pp. 37-39. Avail. ABI 85-28646

   Connecticut, State employees, Pension funds, Portfolio management, Diversification, Social responsibility, South Africa

How Desirable Is Social Accounting? (469)

Even though the 1977 government Green Paper supported social accounting, British accountants appear only passively to accept it. A variety of UK industrialists, politicians, trade unionists, and academics support social accounting, and it has been implemented to varying degrees in other western countries, particularly France and the US. Social accounting involves the publication by a company of information to enable interested parties to assess its performance in social terms, rather than just in terms of profitability. The reports include information on the company's effects on the local community and the environment, customer satisfaction, and employee welfare. Professional accounting bodies have failed to exert a major influence on the development of social accounting, partly because there is no agreement that such development should be supported. Support for social accounting may be based on 3 propositions: 1. that companies have social responsibilities, 2. that companies should produce social reports, and 3. that social reports should be produced by accountants in accounting format. It is believed that there is a need for companies to discharge their extended social responsibility through the production of social reports and that accountants should be involved and prepared for this new role. The social report should be based on the extent to which the company has complied with current statutes and official recommendations. –Gray, Rob and Perks, Bob; *Accountancy (UK),* Apr 1982, 93(1064): pp. 101-102. Avail. ABI 82-14348

UK, Social accounting, Social responsibility, Corporate responsibility, Reports

Information Packages for Directors (470)

Corporate boards of directors are becoming actively involved in management direction. Boards are: 1. establishing corporate policies, 2. planning strategic objectives, 3. overseeing management development and succession, and ensuring corporate social responsibility. Boards need a broad range of information to fulfill their new, more demanding roles. A model information package for corporate boards is outlined. The information package should contain a permanent section of schedules, plans, and documents that will remain current throughout the business year. This package should include meeting dates, corporate bylaws, organization charts, and director/executive job descriptions. A current section, providing summarized and segmented financial information, stock reports, and reports on competitors and the firm's competitive status must also be included. Finally, the information package should contain a future section that comprises the agenda, economic and operating forecasts, and proposed changes in policy and operations. Table. Graph. References. –Waldo, Charles N.; *Business Horizons,* Nov/Dec 1984, 27(6): pp. 77-81. Avail. ABI 85-02968

Boards of directors, Information, Needs, Information management, Financial ratios

Insurance Firms Offer New Investment Products (471)

Inflation, the recession, and an unpredictable stock market are causing insurance companies to look for new products for pension customers. Out of 8 companies surveyed only one, CNA of Chicago, indicated that it is satisfied. Connecticut General is considering a real estate separate fund, and a pension-plan-funding-and-design type of product. Aetna is looking into the futures market, and a social responsibility fund. American General is evaluating the use of futures and an options fund. Travelers Investment Management Company, an affiliate of Travelers, is forming a pooled fund to make use of puts rather than call options, and a pooled fund to risk manage for individuals, and in addition, a $120 million real estate fund is being separated into debt and equity investments. John Hancock may add some pooled funds using quantitative techniques. Ohio National's new areas will probably be: 1. real estate, 2. private placements, 3. foreign currencies, and 4. money market funds. Pacific Investment Management, subsidiary of Pacific Mutual, is using or considering: 1. real estate, 2. futures, 3. private placements, 4. mortgage loans, and 5. call features for mortgages. —Conrad, Alix; *Pension World,* Oct 1980, 16(10): pp. 21-24. Avail. ABI 80-21488

Insurance companies, Manycompanies, Pension funds, Investments, Strategy, Investment advisors, Portfolio management

Investment Do-Gooders-A Look at a Dogged Trio of Socially Conscious Mutual Funds (472)

Three mutual funds which aim at purity of investment are Eaton & Howard's Foursquare, Dreyfus Third Century, and the independent Pax World. Pax World invests in firms producing life-supportive services in fields such as health care, education, food and leisure. It shuns liquor, tobacco, and gambling firms, along with companies doing business with the Pentagon. Third Century only invests in firms that pay attention to the environment, natural resources, occupational health and safety, consumer protection, product purity, and equal employment. Foursquare merely avoids investments in liquor, tobacco, and drug stocks. Pax World and Foursquare have demonstrated above average, if less than spectacular, performances, while Dreyfus Third Century, with total assets of $68.4 million, ranks #50 in the Lipper ratings. However, Dreyfus Third Century has failed to attract institutions, and the other 2 funds, which were initially sponsored by church groups, have not had striking success with those groups. Still, the funds have not compromised their principals. The funds are not wanting for investment possibilities, although firms are thoroughly investigated before investments are made. —Pacey, Margaret D.; *Barron's,* Jul 21, 1980, 60(29): pp. 9,20. Avail. ABI 80-14768

Mutual funds, Social responsibility, Social goals, Performance, Stock prices

Investments Reflect Church Policy (473)

In early 1983, Morgan Guaranty Trust Co. of New York told the United Presbyterian Church Pension Board it could not avoid buying General Electric Corp. (GE) stock, because GE was crucial to Morgan's sector-rotation strategy. However, a church list barred investing in GE and 19 other military contractors. Morgan bought the stock after the pension board's finance committee, which oversees the $900 million fund's investments, agreed. The 27-member pension board, as the benefits arm of the major Presbyterian denomination in the US, implements the will of the body's General Assembly. Additionally, the 9-member finance committee is charged with setting out investment guidelines and retaining managers. At the end of 1983, the fund had 30% of its assets in fixed-income products and 61% in equity. In June 1982, the church's General Assembly adopted guidelines for its list of 20 prohibited stocks. —Chernoff, Joel; *Pensions & Investment Age,* Jun 25, 1984, 12(13): pp. 9. Avail. ABI 84-24565

Religious organizations, Pension funds, Investments, Corporate responsibility, Social responsibility, Case studies, Manycompanies

Investor Relations: 'Mr. Chairman, Why . . .'?   (474)

Shareholders are asking a lot of questions concerning the finances of corporations in which they own stock. The 2 types of questions asked most during shareholder meetings in 1984 concern the health of the company and outside issues that could have an impact upon the company. For instance, Xerox Corp. (Stamford, Connecticut) suffered a slip in its profit margins over the period 1971-1983. This prompted stockholders to ask what is being done to increase profits and why the office automation industry is not thought of more highly by stock analysts. This year, shareholders often asked industry-specific questions on such topics as the fierce competition in the home computer field. In general, despite some concern about bank lending practices and Third World debt, the popularity of social-responsibility questions has waned in recent years. Experts attribute this decline to improved economic conditions, as well as the fact that corporations have done quite a bit of internal housekeeping. Despite some tumultuous sessions, observers say most managers handle themselves quite well under shareholder grilling. Indeed, the way the stockholder meeting is managed often reflects the way the company is managed. —Goldstein, Mark L.; *Industry Week,* Jul 23, 1984, 222(2): pp. 34-35. Avail. ABI 84-26885

Shareholder relations, Shareholder meetings, Investors

Mutual Funds with Social Conscience   (475)

Some mavericks in the financial community advocate investments geared not only to profits, but also to social implications. For example, they advise against buying stock in firms dealing with South Africa. The Calvert Social Investment Fund is among the small group of mutual funds with socially responsible investment criteria, others including the Dreyfus Third Century Fund, the Pax World Fund, and the Working Assets Money Fund. Although they do not share exactly the same investment social criteria, they are all profitable. The Dreyfus Fund, for example, is the largest and makes its investment choices according to corporations' records in equal opportunity, occupational health and safety, product quality, and pollution. The Pax World Fund does not purchase stocks of such firms as defense contractors, tobacco producers, and gambling companies. The Corporate Examiner, published by the Interfaith Center for Corporate Responsibility, offers investment advice to socially conscious investors. —Gupta, Udayan; *Black Enterprise,* Nov 1983, 14(4): pp. 35. Avail. ABI 83-28694

Social responsibility, Mutual funds, Portfolio investments

Objectives-Focussed Management and Internal Auditing   (476)

Internal auditors need to focus on strategic internal audit objectives in their audits. Their audits should help in formulating corporate strategy by: 1.

assessing the corporation's current situation, 2. designing forward-looking programs, anticipating problems, 3. developing the annual business plan, and 4. coping with change. A systems approach has been adopted which focuses on the organization's input, activities, and outputs. It emphasizes the definition of objectives before the release of resources and relating performance to objectives. A case study of the internal audit function of a national company reveals that morale was low until management by objectives was applied to its internal audit function so that the department knew what was wanted. Objectives were set with respect to computer audit, forecasting accuracy, profitability, human resource accounting, and social responsibility audits. They were divided into: 1. regular measurable goals, 2. special problem areas needing examination, and 3. innovative and creative areas. Charts. References. —Ordiorne, George S.; *Internal Auditor,* Jun 1980, 37(3): pp. 58-65. Avail. ABI 80-10964

Internal auditing, Management by objectives, Corporate, Strategy, Strategic, Planning, Data processing, Objectives

Paying the Piper and Calling the Tune: Accountability in the Human Services (477)

The issue of accountability is considered from the perspective of administrative implications for both voluntary and governmental human service organizations. Financial and nonfinancial measures of organizational activity are explored. Also, a series of political and pragmatic considerations are examined from the standpoint of human service organization managers. The implications of accountability expectations are reviewed within the areas of: 1. planning and budgeting, 2. raising funds, 3. allocating resources, 4. record keeping, 5. monitoring and evaluating, 6. reporting, and 7. auditing. Service providers are advised to keep in mind that accountability is an integral part of the relationship between their organizations and resource providers. Also, it is suggested that service providers remain well-informed on alternative ways to meet accountability requirements. It is concluded that voluntary service providers face a period of major readjustment of their roles in society. Charts. References. —Elkin, Robert; *Administration in Social Work,* Summer 1985, 9(2): pp. 1-13. Avail. Haworth 85-35310

Social services, Nonprofit organizations, Funding, Subsidies, Accountability, Financial reporting, Social responsibility

Pension Funds and Socially Acceptable Investing: Can Mortgage Bankers Fit In? (478)

Pension funds and investment managers are increasingly being challenged about the proper use of their investments, thus causing a re-examination of the "prudent man" rule. The mortgage industry and mortgage bankers can benefit from current concerns and pressures surrounding the pension fund industry. The mortgage finance industry has created a plethora of investments that can combine social considerations with solid financial results which should be of great interest to pension fund investors. These investors can develop programs to take advantage of these options, singly or in a group. The pressure on pension funds to invest according to sound investment criteria will probably assure that a larger portion of their cash flows will be placed in investments that are mortgage-related than has been true in the past. Mortgage bankers must maintain an awareness of the needs of the pension fund market, for with the growth of the secondary market and Government National Mortgage Association certificates, the mortgage finance industry has become a part of the national capital marketplace. References. —Hague, Donald R.; *Mortgage Banker,* Oct 1980, 41(1): pp. 49-53. Avail. ABI 80-20539

Social responsibility, Pension funds, Investments, Mortgages, Financing, Mortgage banks, Social, Criteria

Pension Funds Solid, Two New Surveys Reveal　　　(479)

The vital signs of the nation's private pension system indicate the plans are in good health. The vital signs are: 1. adequate funding and 2. the ability to help retirees keep pace with inflation. From recent research, it was concluded that, on the average, net assets of the funds exceed accumulated vested benefits. Of the companies surveyed, 93% have increased pensions more than once due to the awareness of growing inflation and a sense of social responsibility. The Financial Accounting Standards Board Statement No. 36 requires figures that do not take into consideration future salary increases. Therefore, the figures tend to understate the benefits that an ongoing pension plan will have to pay and suggest that prior disclosure of unfunded past service liabilities gave a more realistic look at the funded status of pension plans. Since companies are not arranging the funding of their pension plans on the basis of the new ruling, it will not have an immediate negative effect. —Katz, David M.; *National Underwriter (Life/Health),* Jan 2, 1982, 86(1): pp. 3,10. Avail. ABI 82-02711

Pension funds, Funded pension plans, Surveys, Pensions, Increases, Pension costs, Statistical data

Performance Is the Bottom Line: TUCS Representatives　　(480) Speak Out

The Trust Universe Comparison Service (TUCS) is a consortium of 41 banks, insurance companies, and other institutions that evaluates pension plan performance. In a panel discussion, 6 TUCS representatives expressed their views on issues affecting plan sponsors today, including investment performance, asset allocation, and social responsibility. According to Ralph L. Knisley of Irving Trust Co., poor performance by managers has led to interest in using indexed funds, but plan sponsors should be encouraged to take a long-term perspective and judge managers only against others using the same style. Brenda Krueger Teel of Bank of America adds that pension funds tend to change their asset allocation structure and money managers at the wrong times, and index funds currently marketed as passive, reactive investment vehicles are actually more like actively managed portfolios. Wilson H. Ellis of the Citizens and Southern National Bank claims that there is a general industry pattern toward the reduction of cash flows in defined benefit plans and an increase in cash flows in defined contribution plans.

Teel asserts that the issue of social responsibility is being seen more often. —Anonymous; *Pension World,* Sep 1985, 21(9): pp. 40-45,88. Avail. ABI 85-32529

Pension funds, Portfolio investments, Evaluation, Performance, Indexes, Portfolio management, Manypeople

The Political Significance of Corporate Social (481) Reporting in the United States of America

The new significance of corporate social reporting in the US results from: 1. the realization that public expectations of business have changed and that business must react to these changes, and 2. the understanding that public support for enforced reform will depend on the business community's commitment to being socially responsible on its own. Current public expectations of business and reports on interest in regulatory reform are summarized. Particular consideration is given to various disclosure experiments undertaken by some major US enterprises. It is reasonable to expect continuing improvement in the quality of social reporting by US business, especially since the US Department of Commerce has expressed an intention to encourage such improvements. Rather than requiring mandatory reporting and increasing the burdens of bureaucracy and of paperwork, the Department hopes to encourage voluntary efforts. These efforts would help to improve corporate social performance, would enhance public understanding and acceptance of the contribution of business to society, and would reduce the need for additional regulation in the future. Table. References. —Heard, James E. and Bolce, William J.; *Accounting, Organizations & Society (UK),* 1981, 6(3): pp. 247-254. Avail. ABI 81-23039

Corporate, Social, Reporting, Social audit, Social responsibility, Regulatory reform, Eastern Gas & Fuel Associates-Boston, ARCO, Norton-Worcester Mass, Bank of America

Pressure Also Felt by Private Funds (482)

In moves to preserve their independence from takeovers, Grumman Corp. (Bethpage, New York) and the Great Atlantic & Pacific Tea Co. (Montvale, New Jersey) both have used pension fund money to buy large amounts of company stock. The firms believe the adage "charity begins at home", and they believe the action was in the best interests of stockholders. Some construe these actions as a form of in-house social investing of pension fund assets, and some equate social investing of this sort as "social subsidizing", counter to Employee Retirement Income Security Act (ERISA) guidelines. Most firms have not undertaken any formal social investing policy, although firms like Lockheed, Control Data Corp., and United Technologies are seriously reviewing social investing issues. An increasing number of groups are viewing rich pension funds as "the fatted calf in a lean economy", and fund managers find themselves in the bind of not wanting to be labeled as socially irresponsible and yet not wanting "hungry hands" tearing at their portfolios for the funds stored there. According to Bill Marshall, of GTE Investment Management, expert decision-making can be deemed the highest form of social investing, and most funds are already practicing it. —Sahgal, Pavan; *Pensions & Investment Age,* Feb 15, 1982, 10(4): pp. 11,23. Avail. Pensions 82-06122

Social responsibility, Social, Investments, Private, Pension funds, Manycompanies

Pure-Play Investments: Socially Sensitive Portfolios Are (483) Gaining in Popularity

"Socially sensitive" investment accounts are targeted at wealthy liberal individuals and assorted institutional investors, such as churches, foundations, universities, and union-controlled pension funds. Among those firms offering this type of account are: 1. the Calvert group, 2. US Trust of Boston, 3. Shearson/American Express, and 4. Chemical Bank. Figures from US Trust show impressive performances by socially sensitive accounts. Since 1980, the annual compound growth rate for total return on social investment has been 16.9%. These portfolios can be custom-tailored to individual concerns. Principal companies avoided are those involved with: 1. South Africa, 2. military contracting, and 3. nuclear power. Steve Moody of US Trust says he sees no significant difference between performance of these and other accounts, although theoretically inferior performance should result since choice is limited. The chief effect of "purity" tests is to shift investment into smaller companies. These companies tend to outperform the larger-capitalization stocks but are also more volatile. Some questions have been raised about how a "sensitized" fund manager's politics can affect investment judgments. –Brody, Michael; *Barron's,* Jan 24, 1983, 63(4): pp. 13,20,22. Avail. ABI 83-04803

Social accounting, Investments, Social responsibility, Portfolio management, Portfolio performance

Reporting Economic-Not Accounting-Profit (484)

Any discussion of corporate profit is clouded by: 1. a lack of information, 2. considerable misinformation, and 3. conflicts between data offered by industry and those published by politicians, consumer advocates, and the media. The concept of profit used most generally by the media is that reported by the accounting profession. This concept does not take into consideration compensation to the suppliers of equity capital as an expense of doing business. The result is that accounting profit will be considerably greater than economic profit. Accounting profit reflects only historical financial transactions that occur within a prescribed time period. Investors and economists realize that interim profit is an illusion since part of it will be needed to pay the higher price of replacing assets simply to remain in business. These are costs to be deducted from revenue before profits are recognized. In order to make financial statements more meaningful to the public, 2 changes are suggested: 1. an addendum to the traditional income statement reconciling accounting and economic profit, and 2. an adaptation of the "Statement of Changes in Financial Position" to reflect both changes in cash (current liquidity) and changes in replacement cost of assets (future liquidity). It is also recommended that discretionary uses of cash be further refined to show expenditures for social responsibility. Charts. References. – Arthur, William J.; *Business Horizons,* Mar/Apr 1981, 24(2): pp. 50-55. Avail. ABI 81-07962

Economic, Profits, Financial reporting, Financial statements, Income statements, Social responsibility, Funds statements

Research on Corporate Social Reporting: Directions for Development (485)

Research on corporate social reporting should move from a phase of observation and description to one of improvement of techniques and practices. Improvement will result from the development of information systems that will be useful to management in monitoring and altering corporate social performance. A case illustrating the feasibility and the value of innovative research and reporting is provided by the experience of Graphic Controls Corp. (Buffalo, New York) and its systematic survey of employee attitudes about wages and benefits. The quality-of-work-life data discovered by this survey show the usefulness of such research to management now and how that research will have continuing usefulness over time. Two trends in future research are indicated: 1. Better techniques of data collection and analysis must be developed. 2. Managerial use of social performance information and the organizational changes resulting from it must be analyzed. Such research will lead to improvements both in the discipline itself and in the management of large organizations worldwide. Illustrations. References. −Preston, Lee E.; *Accounting, Organizations & Society (UK)*, 1981, 6(3): pp. 255-262. Avail. ABI 81-23040

Corporate, Social, Reporting, Social accounting, Research, Social responsibility, Employees

The Risk Involved in Socially Beneficial Investing-The Wisconsin Case Study (486)

The most important element in a study of socially beneficial investing is the risk inherent in any proposed alteration of present investment policies. Risk is complex and multidimensional in nature. Risk is examined from 2 perspectives: 1. investment risk-risk as it applies to a single investment and investments within a portfolio, and 2. benefit risk-risk as it applies to the assets of pension fund participants. A multidimensional model was created. Primary issues examined in developing the model were: 1. the nature of the risk, 2. the degree of benefit risk, 3. the factors that affect benefit risk, and 4. the way in which the factors affect benefit risk. Factors which influence the risk that beneficiaries will have reduced benefits include: 1. the degree of severity of economic hardship that could occur within Wisconsin, 2. the length of time over which a beneficiary must depend on the fund and the retirement system sponsor to provide benefits, 3. the future of financial markets, 4. the funded status of vested benefits, 5. the size of any concessions granted in the fund, and 6. the extent to which investments of funds become concentrated in the state. Only nominal benefit risk is realized if investment concession is eliminated. Graphs. −Smart, Donald A.; *Employee Benefits Jrnl*, Fall 1980, 5(4): pp. 12-17,41. Avail. ABI 80-22829

Social responsibility, Investments, Risk, Case studies, Liquidity, Portfolio management, Portfolio investments, Models

A Role for Small Businesses in the Social Accounting Area (487)

Corporate social accountability refers to the right of various constituencies to information about corporate activities that may affect their own interests.

Arguments for such accountability are based on the economic and social consequences of business action, and not on the size of the business, so they apply to small businesses as well as large ones. Most business activities result in the creation of social data. These data can be separated into social benefits and social costs. The argument for public reporting of social data has as its basis the empirical evidence that certain segments of society use social data, particularly the business segment. Charts. References. —Roth, Harold P.; *Jrnl of Small Business Mgmt*, Jan 1982, 20(1): pp. 27-31. Avail. ABI 82-07156

Small business, Accountability, Corporate responsibility, Social responsibility

Should Pension Funds Be Used to Achieve "Social" Goals? (488)

The "social" label on the investment of pension funds is over-broad, as everyone agrees that investing for retirement security is a socially responsible goal. "Alternative" or "divergent" investing would be more appropriate labels since the proposal is to use pension assets for goals other than retirement security. Divergent investing goes back as far as 1931 when a state assemblyman proposed to have the state teacher's retirement fund emphasize investment in Wisconsin farm mortgages. Today, the funds most vulnerable to divergent investing are the state and local funds. When divergent investing is tried, only a modest portion of the assets should be used and investment flexibility should not be reduced. An effort to avoid impairment of investment performance is a part of the fiduciary's obligation, and if divergent investing really will not work, and if its advocacy keeps coming up, it should be ignored. This advocacy is being fueled by the fact that traditional pension investing has not done well. However, advocacy of divergent investing would have less force if facts about traditional prudent investing were not used "selectively". Table. Graphs. —Schotland, Roy A.; *Trusts & Estates*, Sep 1980, 119(9): pp. 10-24. Avail. ABI 80-18626

Pension funds, Social, Investments, Strategy, Social responsibility, Portfolio performance, Diversification, Rates of return, Advocacy

Social Accountability in Total Return (489)

There is increasing interest by the labor management community in social/political investing. The approaches to investing can be categoried as: 1. neutral investment policies, 2. socially sensitive investment policies, and 3. socially dictated investment policies. Any program of divergent investing has a formidable task in complying with the Employee Retirement Income Security Act. Effects of social investing include: 1. more private placements and creation of special accounts, 2. more regionalization in allocation of monies, 3. more investing in smaller companies and labor-intensive companies, 4. the favoring of domestic companies and unionized companies, and 5. more cooperation between unions and management. Impact will not be swift, however, because of the slowness of the education process. Investment professionals must find a balance between social/political investing and productive investment programs, allowing constructive use of monies while realizing the pension payments promises. —Burroughs, Eugene; *Pension World,* Oct 1981, 17(10): pp. 29-32. Avail. ABI 81-24836

Social accounting, Investments, Social responsibility, Fringe benefit plans, ERISA, Pension funds

Social Accounting for Beginners (490)

Social accounting includes a wide range of nontraditional forms of reporting, which can be expressed in 3 classes: 1. social responsibility accounting (SRA), 2. total impact accounting (TIA), and 3. socioeconomic accounting (SEA). Measurement is one of the difficulties of social accounting, and 3 possible levels are suggested: 1. Level I, where the activity is identified and described, 2. Level II, where the activity is measured in terms of nonfinancial measures, and 3. Level III, where the measurement is converted into a financial estimate of cost and benefit. SRA involves voluntary disclosures of information in respect of products, employees, energy, the environment, and community involvement. TIA attempts to measure the total cost of production or services by aggregation of public and private costs. SEA refers to attempts at measuring the costs and benefits of government programs. An expansion of this type reporting will occur in the future. References. – Mathews, M. R.; *Australian Accountant (Australia),* Oct 1984, 54(9): pp. 775-777. Avail. ABI 84-37194

Social responsibility, Social accounting, Measurement

Social Criteria Enter Investment Decisions (491)

A study by the Investor Responsibility Research Center (IRRC) in Washington, DC, has found that the growing interest of tax-exempt funds in making investments that are socially responsible has forced money managers to consider social criteria in their investment decision making. Pension fund investment managers are likely to face considerable pressure in the future to use social criteria from such sources as church groups, unions, and public employee pension funds. Lack of satisfaction with government solutions to current social problems like apartheid in South Africa has intensified this sort of pressure. Banks and insurance companies, although skeptical, are using social criteria in screening stocks, and investment advisers are developing social purpose investment programs. The study notes that social purpose investing can foster the development of innovative investment programs. Opponents of the concept complain about the lack of information and about circumventing their primary goal of maximizing return. Insurance companies feel that proxy voting heightens the use of social performance data in investment decisions. —Anonymous; *Pensions & Investment Age,* Oct 25, 1982, 10(22): pp. 28-29. Avail. Pensions 82-28553

Institutional investments, Social, Criteria, Social responsibility, Social issues, Investment policy

Social Goals for Canadian Business (492)

The new challenges for corporate management during the last decade have been reflected in new procedures developed to ensure that challenges are met and responsibilities are carried out. Canadian corporations increasingly must act not only within the law but also ethically in the eyes of its constituent groups. This is a result of the heightened social awareness of executives and continuing pressure from society. Many of the Fortune 500 companies make social performance disclosures in their annual reports. A questionnaire survey of Canada's largest corporations indicated that many were likewise developing statements of corporate social objectives to assist in the management of their social performance. Corporations also are devoting a substantial percentage of disclosure space to company processes for operations, financial management, and human resource management, attempting to justify the underlying credibility of these processes. Tables. References. —Brooks, Leonard James, Jr.; *Cost & Mgmt (Canada),* Mar/Apr 1984, 58(2): pp. 2-8. Avail. ABI 84-16556

Canada, Social responsibility, Social, Objectives, Accountability

Social Investing Debate Rages On   (493)

What began as a discussion of social investing often resulted in a debate of political philosophy at a special conference on retirement income sponsored by the National Journal in Washington, in November, 1980. Randy Barber, co-director of the Peoples Business Commission, indicated that pension fund participants need to play a larger part in the use of those funds than they presently do. Mr. Barber particularly indicated the need for using the better than $500 billion in pension money to aid American industry. Mr. Charles Moran, Chairman and President of Lionel D. Edie and Company Incorporated, asserted that dual purpose investing would not be easy, and he argued that breaking up pension money and watching for social goals, control over investments is weakened. However, Bert Seidman, Director of the Department of Social Security at the American Federation of Labor-Congress of Industrial Organizations (AFL-CIO) argued that as long as those objectives are carefully weighed and followed, a sound pension fund and revitalized American industry could be accomplished. —Cavuto, Neil; *Pensions & Investment Age,* Dec 8, 1980, 8(25): pp. 31. Avail. Pensions 81-00750

Social, Investment, Pension funds, Social goals, Social responsibility, Manypeople

Social Investing Involves Public Funds   (494)

Public pension fund administrators still consider social investing as a possible remedy for their ills. Kansas, Wisconsin, Alabama, New York, Pennsylvania, California, Hawaii, and Massachusetts all have started social investing to some extent. The concept is being discussed in Illinois, Florida, and Minnesota. California Governor Jerry Brown called the idea a key technique of resurrecting declining local economies and exercising more control over finances. Of course, a prevalent question is what constitutes socially desirable investment-the fact that it pays state taxes and aids in supporting the local economy or that it meets other criteria. The Pennsylvania State Employes Retirement System, for example, made a $6 million construction loan to Volkswagen to construct a plant in the state. The Teacher's Fund also contributed to the loan. In addition, Hawaii has a long-standing program of making direct mortgage loans to members of its state system. Finally, some states have started to use social investment criteria, and others are continuing to study the issue. —Epstein, Charles; *Pensions & Investments,* Sep 1, 1980, 8(18): pp. 22,29. Avail. Pensions 80-18389

Social, Investment, Pension funds, Investment, Capital, Public sector, Social responsibility, State government

Social Investing: Doing Good While Doing Well   (495)

Social investment has been around for a while, but it appears now to have come into its own. More people are questioning the wisdom of investing in companies that seek only short-term profit at the expense of long-term social good. In response to changes in Americans' investment concerns, more investment advisers are specializing in making socially aware investments for their clients. The new element in social investing is that groups of individuals with large capital resources are increasingly engaged in the systematic social assessment of the way their resources are invested. Social investors use traditional economic standards for investment decisions, but they also use such additional measures as economic and social return to others. Traditional money managers may not know how to respond to this type of investor. One of the traditional criticisms of social investment is that mixing social philosophy with economic wisdom leads to economic failure. While some companies blatantly ignore social issues, socially responsible corporations are proving that social responsibility and financial responsibility are not contradictory. —Lowry, Ritchie P.; *Futurist,* Apr 1982, 16(2): pp. 22-28. Avail. ABI 82-10909

Social, Investments, Social change, Corporate responsibility, Social responsibility, Industry, Case studies

Social Investment Funds: Fortune or Folly?   (496)

Social investing - the buying and selling of securities according to the "social responsibility" displayed by the offering firm, has been receiving a great deal of attention in the press. In actual practice, though, little social investing goes on. The first problem for the investor who may wish to be socially responsible is to create criteria for separating the good companies from the bad. Several firms publish guides to social investing, including: 1. Shearson/American Express, 2. Moseley, Hallgarten, Estabrook and Weeden, and 3. Working Assets Money Fund. Some of these firms use questionable criteria. For example, some apparently base their recommendations solely on the product manufactured, with no consideration given to how the company may treat its employees. Others do not accept companies associated with weapons manufacture but ignore other concerns. —Moskowitz, Milton; *Business & Society Review,* Spring 1984, (49): pp. 10-14. Avail. ABI 84-18802

Social, Investments, Social responsibility, Investment advisors

Social Responsibility in Investment Policy and the   (497)
Prudent Man Rule

The "prudent man" rule is a constraint on the discretionary investment decisionmaking of trustees and investment managers. The rule has been interpreted as requiring a fiduciary to promote two traditional investment objectives: 1. attainment of an adequate return, and 2. preservation of the trust corpus. However, this conception of the fiduciary's duties has recently

come under attack, and some have urged that trustees be allowed to pursue other, nontraditional objectives in their investment practices. These critics believe that the resources of various institutional funds should be employed to further wholly social goals. At present it is uncertain whether a trustee may pursue, consistently with the prudent man rule, nontraditional investment objectives at the expense of adequate return and corpus safety. Although case law is quite sparse, the standard can be read to permit such a practice.
—Ravikoff, Ronald B. and Curzan, Myron P.; *California Law Review,* May 1980, 68(3): pp. 518-546. Avail. ABI 80-11792

Prudent person rule, ERISA, Fiduciary responsibility, Social responsibility, Social, Investment, Portfolio investments, Standards, Court decisions, Common law

Socially Committed Investments   (498)

The investment policies of colleges, universities, and churches have been at the forefront of the socially responsible investment movement. Nuclear arms, infant formula, commerce with South Africa and retrogressive labor practices are among the concerns of socially responsible investors. The elements of responsible investing include: 1. criteria that define a policy of social responsibility, 2. facts to support the investment, and 3. monitoring of the corporation's performance to assure consistency of policy. Obtaining the facts on social performance is not easy. The Market Conscience Guide, which defines 23 different issues of social concern relevant to investing, can assist investors in setting policies. A computerized data bank of publicly traded companies is another aid. Research institutions such as The Council of Economic Priorities (New York) or the Investor Responsibility Research Center (Washington, DC) can also provide in-depth information to investors. While performance varies among investments, the top performer in 1983 among general purpose money funds was Calvert Social Investment Fund/Money Market Portfolio, which turned in a yield of 9.31%. References. —Moeller, Clark; *Trusts & Estates,* Oct 1984, 123(10): pp. 56-58. Avail. ABI 84-36746

Social responsibility, Investment policy, Trends, Social issues, Information, Sources, Colleges & universities, Pension funds, Institutional investments

South African Trust Director Opposes Sanctions as   (499)
Policy to Speed Reform/Counterpoint Comment: The
Argument for Ethical Investing

In a previous article (1984), Clark Moeller argues that socially responsible investing is effective, as evidenced by the divestment campaign in South Africa. The application of his main principles to South African divestment depends upon 3 requirements: 1. definition and measurement of the relevant social issues, 2. ongoing review of corporate performance, and 3. conformity of investment plans to investors' wishes. These issues are evaluated, revealing certain legal obstacles to socially responsible investing in South Africa. Investors should apply the same criteria to South African investments as they do to US investments, and evaluate each according to its own merits. Moeller counters that a policy of divestment in South Africa helps socially concerned investors avoid investing in companies whose employment practices would be considered unethical in the US. Furthermore, withdrawal by US corporations will not negatively affect black employment in South Africa, as Baigrie suggests. References. —Baigrie, James and Moeller, Clark; *Trusts & Estates,* Oct 1985, 124(10): pp. 18-24. Avail. ABI 85-34621

South Africa, Sanctions, Social responsibility, Investment, Social issues, Sports, Boycotts, Ethics

A Suggested Classification for Social Accounting (500) Research

An attempt is made to alleviate the confusion about what constitutes social accounting. A suggested organization for social accounting research is presented. The philosophical justification for this field of study is set into the context in which it appears most frequently - the consideration of externalities. McDonald (1972) has classified accounting theories as descriptive (theories of accounting) and normative (theories for accounting). This approach indicates that normative frameworks require a clarification of values, a means-ends analysis, and the incorporation of all relevant data. Social accounting encompasses: 1. Social Responsibility Accounting, 2. Total Impact Accounting, 3. Socioeconomic Accounting, and 4. Social Indicators Accounting, which facilitates the identification of ends and consequently of means. The form of organization provided by the structure outlined may be applied to the research and teaching of social accounting. Tables. References. —Mathews, M. R.; *Jrnl of Accounting & Public Policy,* Fall 1984, 3(3): pp. 199-221. Avail. ABI 84-36544

Social accounting, Research, Classification, Accounting theory, Public policy

Toward a More Social Income Statement (501)

There is an increasingly vocal element in the US that criticizes all corporate profits, whether or not the profit represents a fair return on investment. Some of this concern has arisen due to such practices as: 1. illegal political contributions, 2. foreign bribes and other questionable payments, and 3. business fraud. Many businessmen are concerned about how they can explain that fair rates of profit are necessary in a capitalist country. One way may be to de-emphasize profit on the income statement. The traditional income statement could be made more social to show the extent to which the company's affairs are intertwined with the affairs of its employees, creditors, suppliers, and various levels of government.The social income statement first lists total revenues, then shows the allocation of those revenues among the various groups that receive some benefit from the corporation. Percentage figures are also presented to show each group's relative interest in the allocation of the revenue. This method would clearly demonstrate that other parties besides shareholders have a vital stake in the future well-being of the corporation. Charts. —Kreiser, Larry; *Financial Executive,* Jun 1980, 48(6): pp. 24-26. Avail. ABI 80-12275

Corporate profits, Attitudes, Income statements, Social responsibility, Public relations

Trust Departments Grapple with Proxy Voting (502)

According to trust department officials, in voting proxies, social responsibility runs second to fiduciary responsibility. Decisions are driven by making money for clients, not by any effort to change the world. Pension funds managed internally vote their own proxies, but such funds give little or no directions to the banks voting their proxies. All banks interviewed by Investment Age echo the position of Chase Manhattan Bank, which affirms that it ranks investment impact far ahead of social consciousness in the voting of the proxies in its charge. Banks have active proxy committees which track social issues and subscribe to and review corporate responsibility reports. Chase and others will vote on the basis of social issues if they have an impact on earnings per share, and Manufacturers Hanover does not feel being personally or emotionally responsible is necessarily being responsible as a fiduciary. The bank no longer votes proxies for accounts where it is custodian only, and Citibank does not vote for shares held in custody or for investment advisory accounts. Banks are very cognizant of their proxy voting responsibilities and fear conflict-of-interest complications. —Schmerken, Ivy; *Pensions & Investment Age*, Feb 15, 1982, 10(4): pp. 14. Avail. Pensions 82-06123

Trust departments (BNK), Social responsibility, Pension funds, Proxy statements

Two Surveys: Pension System Strong (503)

The 2 vital signs of the nation's private pension system show the plans are in good health. The signs are: 1. adequate funding and 2. the ability to help retirees keep pace with inflation. According to a report by Johnson and Higgins, and Towers, Perrin, Forster & Crosby, a new accounting rule has led to a great deal of confusion about plan funding. The uncertainty could cause securities analysts to undervalue the stock of corporations that are "cutting it close" on their pension funding. A study has shown that 93% of the firms studied have increased pensions more than once. The pension increases have occurred partly because employers are becoming more aware of the impact of inflation and have developed a sense of social responsibility. Much confusion has been created by Financial Accounting Standards Board Statement No. 36 on pension information disclosure, because the figures do not take into consideration future salary increases. The ruling could affect the future value of the stock of companies who are "cutting it close" in terms of unfunded pension liabilities. —Katz, David M.; *National Underwriter (Property/Casualty)*, Jan 8, 1982, (2): pp. 16-17. Avail. ABI 82-03192

Pension funds, Pension plans, Trends, Surveys, FASB statements, Financial reporting

Unanswered Questions Concerning the SEC's Recent (504) Dismissal of Additional Social Disclosure

A federal court of appeals has recently ruled that disclosure in Securities and Exchange Commission (SEC) filings regarding environmental and job-discrimination practices was not within the purview of the SEC's mission. This ruling raises several questions about the position taken by the SEC: 1. Is there any empirical evidence supporting the position that compliance reports would not provide useful information to investors? 2. Has the SEC ignored the existence of investors who are interested in the ethics of a firm? 3. Has the SEC relied too much on an "intrinsic value" definition of investor decision models? 4. Are significant costs involved in disclosing environmental and job-hiring compliance/noncompliance data? The SEC presents no empirical evidence to support a categorical rejection of requiring compliance/noncompliance data, and for some investors, this data might be a major investment decision variable. It is possible that the SEC has summarily dismissed as useless information that may become an important input variable for those investors using a sophisticated portfolio selection mode. References. —Hull, Rita P. and Everett, John O.; *Akron Business & Economic Review,* Fall 1980, 11(3): pp. 48-52. Avail. ABI 80-20049

SEC, Regulations, Disclosure, Environmental impact, Social responsibility, Federal legislation, Court decisions

Unusual Mutual Fund Brings Its Investors Good Early Returns   (505)

The Calvert Social Investment Fund, managed by United States Trust Co. (Boston, Massachusetts), takes into account both social and financial criteria for its investments. It is too early to predict the long-term success of the fund, but so far the money market portfolio has performed much better than a "managed growth" portfolio of stocks and bonds. The opinions of analysts vary as to the wisdom of using a social screen in investments, but Calvert's investment staff has won respect through professionalism and previous success. The fund has invested in several New England companies, including: 1. Stride Rite Corp., 2. BayBanks Inc., 3. Affiliated Publications, 4. Stanadyne Inc., and 5. Citizens Utilities of Stamford, Connecticut. Charts. —van Dam, Laura; *New England Business,* Feb 18, 1985, 7(3): pp. 36-38. Avail. ABI 85-09137

Portfolio investments, Mutual funds, Return on investment, Social responsibility

The Usefulness and Use of Social Reporting Information   (506)

Corporate social accounting and reporting is intended to serve as a basis for the formulation, execution, and control of business social policy by management, and as a database for dialogue with constituencies of the business interested in the performance of the company in the social arena. It is difficult to determine the usefulness and use of corporate social reporting information, as well as to determine if the information is actually changing behavior in a socially responsive direction. The measurement of the usefulness and use of social reporting information is presented as a stepwise process, the steps being: 1. determination of the interest in the concept by the target groups, 2. determination of whether the target groups deem useful the way in which the information is collected, 3. specification of the extent to which the information needs of the target groups are met in the social reports, 4. investigation of whether the report is considered useful, and 5. determination of the information's impact on decision making. Each of these steps is discussed in detail. References. —Dierkes, Meinolf and Antal, Ariane Berthoin; *Accounting, Organizations & Society (UK),* 1985, 10(1): pp. 29-34. Avail. ABI 85-12952

Social responsibility, Corporate responsibility, Social accounting, Reporting, Studies

The Value Added Statement as Part of Corporate Social Reporting   (507)

It is often questioned whether the Value Added Statement (VAS) serves the purpose for which it was intended within the corporate social reporting context. In West Germany, the focal issue of this discussion centers upon whether the VAS should be based on net value added or gross value added. The primary aim of a VAS is to keep interested parties, such as employees, shareholders, creditors, and the government, apprised of the company's success in achieving financial objectives. Thus, the purpose is to disclose the distribution of income in the present period, as well as to indicate trends for future distribution. The VAS must be drawn up according to conventional principles of measuring accounting profit. It is suggested that only a Statement of Net Added Value as part of corporate social reporting indicates the income from the company that has already been attained and may be achieved in the future. References. —Reichmann, Thomas and Lange, Christoph; *Management International Review (Germany)*, 1981, 21(4): pp. 17-22. Avail. ABI 82-02818

Value added, Statements, Financial statements, Corporate responsibility, Social accounting

"You Can't Do That with My Money"-A Search for   (508) Mandatory Social Responsibility in Pension Investments

An important question to consider is whether there are situations involving a legal responsibility to make socially sensitive investments of pension assets. The question can be formulated as follows: Are there situations in which pension participants and beneficiaries, and those responsible for representing their interests, can say to institutional investors and professional money managers or trustees-"You can't do that with my money!'"? The law of pension investments is comprised of 6 elements: 1. the common law prudent person principles, 2. recent court decisions, such as Blankenship v. Boyle and Withers v. Teachers' Retirement System of the City of New York, 3. state statutory "legal lists" of allowable investments and controls on the management of public pensions, 4. The Employee Retirement Income Security Act of 1974, 5. The Internal Revenue Code, and 6. The Taft-Hartley Act, Section 302(c)(5). Undoubtedly, a legal framework does exist for the construction in particular cases of legally enforceable requirements of social prudence. References. —Leibig, Michael T.; *Jrnl of Pension Planning & Compliance*, Sep 1980, 6(5): pp. 358-394. Avail. Panel 80-19306

Social responsibility, Pension funds, Investment, Court decisions, ERISA, Investments, Federal legislation, Pensions

Author Index

Author Index

Rada, S. E. 214
Ratcliffe, Thomas A. 461
Ratliff, Ronald A. 425
Ravikoff, Ronald B. 497
Reagan, Ronald 252
Reddin, W. J. 151
Reichmann, Thomas 507
Reynes, Roberta A. 316
Rich, Laurie A. 432
Richardson, Clara 235
Rivchun, Sylvia 10
Rivlin, Catherine A. 191
Robinson, Chris 463
Robinson, Thomas R. 467
Romano, David J. 112
Ross, Allan John 429
Roth, Harold P. 487
Rozen, Miriam 278

Sahgal, Pavan 482
Samli, A. Coskun 160
Sanders, Doreen 310
Saunders, Frank 290
Scanlon, Walter F. 205
Schaefer, Norbert V. 234
Scheibla, Shirley Hobbs 1
Schmerken, Ivy 502
Schneider, Brenda L. 62
Schofield, Elvin J. 181
Schotland, Roy A. 467, 488
Schram, Rosalyn Weinman 184
Schultz, Ellen 140
Schweiker, Richard S. 208, 248
Scott, Donald C. 313
Sealy, Albert H. 218
Sedlacek, Jerry F. 271
Segal, Mitchell G. 458
Sethi, S. Prakash 18, 43, 166, 201, 221
Settlemyre, Jean T. 421
Shane, Philip B. 439
Shapiro, Irving S. 186
Shuttleworth, Geoffrey 245
Silbey, Joel H. 272
Simone, Albert J. 400
Sin, Gregory Thong Tin 433
Singer, Benjamin D. 31
Sirgy, M. Joseph 160
Skae, John 350
Skinner, Wickham 158
Skousen, Clifford R. 198
Slater, Robert Bruce 42
Smart, Donald A. 486
Smith, Brian 355

Smith, Hayden 308
Smith, James L. 426
Smith, Lee 337, 343
Smith, Leo A. 426
Smith, Timothy H. 36
Snyder, Leonard 352
Solo, Pam 436
Sommer, A. A., Jr. 457
Sonnenfeld, Jeffrey 266
Sparks, Robert M. 375
Spicer, Barry H. 439, 444
Spitzer, Carlton E. 147, 233
Spooner, Peter 89, 339
Stanfield, J. R. 132
Stathos, Dan T. 445
Steorts, Nancy Harvey 360
Stephenson, D. R. 135
Stern, Marian 336
Stevens, George F. 21
Stewart, W. T. 420
Strenski, James B. 206
Strier, Franklin 24, 453
Sturzenegger, Otto 416
Surdam, Robert M. 137
Swann, Peter C. 319

Taylor, Allan R. 20
Templer, Andrew 187
Templer, Andrew J. 366
Teoh, Hai-Yap 450
This, Leslie E. 67
Thomas, Clarke 348
Thomas, Pat Gray 81
Thomas, Raymond E. 238
Thomas, Stephen V. 122
Thong, Gregory 450
Tilson, Donn J. 309
Tolliver, James M. 366
Treitman, Michael S. 445
Trotman, Ken T. 9
Tucker, Lewis R., Jr. 443
Tuthill, Mary 318, 323
Tuzzolino, Frank 171

Ullmann, Arieh A. 70
Ulmer, Melville J. 167
Underwood, Lynn 123, 340
Upah, Gregory D. 369

Valandra, Kent T. 259
van Dam, Andre 168
van Dam, Laura 505
Vance, Donald 309

Subject Index